YACHT JOINERY
AND FITTING

Yacht Joinery
and Fitting

Practical Guidance on the Planning and
Building of Cabin Accommodation
in Sailing and Power Craft

Mike Saunders

Illustrated by
Mike Saunders and Richard F. Reeves

INTERNATIONAL MARINE
PUBLISHING COMPANY
CAMDEN, MAINE 04843

For Liz—as ever.

Published in the United States of America
by International Marine Publishing Company, Camden, Maine 04843

Published simultaneously in Great Britain
by Hollis & Carter, an associate company
of The Bodley Head Ltd, London, England

CONTENTS

Introduction, 7

Colour plate of wood samples, between pages 16 and 17

I Working Wood, 9

  1. What Is Wood? 9

  2. Joining Wood, 19

  3. Laminating, 26

  4. Joining Wood to Other Materials, 29

  5. Fitting Queer Boat Shapes, 31

  6. Tools, 35

  7. Glues and Sealants, 49

  8. Fastenings, 59

II The Shape of Things and Humans, 65

  1. Lying, 66

  2. Sitting, 67

  3. Standing, 69

  4. Worktops, 70

  5. Reaching, Crawling and Climbing, 71

  6. Hands, 73

III Designs and Dimensions, 75

  1. Design Thinking, 75

  2. Designs, 78

IV Finishing, 130

  1. Shape Finishing, 130

  2. Coating, 135

  3. Veneers and Linings, 150

V Other Materials, 155

  1. Plastics, 155

  2. Metals, 160

  3. Ferrocement, 163

Appendices, 168

A Wood Properties and Usage, 168
B Weights of Average Hardwood Ply, 176
C Cleaning Schedules for Gluing, 177
D Adhesives and Sealants, 178
E Comparison of Material Properties, 182
F Wire and Metal Gauges, 184
G Metric Conversion Factors, 185
Index, 187

Introduction

This book has been written to fill a surprisingly large gap in the published informa-tion on boat joinery and it covers mainly, but not exclusively, internal joinery and a range of related subjects like timbers, tools, modern glues and, not least, other materials to which wood is fixed. For it is a fact that most boats are not nowadays built of wood, and yacht joinery has to such an extent become a separate trade that boat builders hardly employ shipwrights so much as 'fitters-out'.

The book is, therefore, intended to supply solid information to 'fitters out', whether they be fledgling tradesmen, home builders or merely handy yachtsmen who would like to sort out some decent shelves and things in the galley, but are not quite certain where to start. As such, the book is entirely practical. I have endeavoured to avoid the vague presentation of good ideas in favour of specific information, and the majority of designs I have either built or used myself. And, as far as possible, I have given pertinent dimensions. But, I make no claim to have covered every, or even most, things. There are a dozen ways of skinning a cat, and there is no reason why my particular design should preclude use of the other eleven.

Dimensions

In Britain we are in a somewhat confused state of transition from Imperial to Metric measurements, while our friends in North America and in Europe adhere respec-tively to the one and the other. In the interests of all, I have, therefore, decided to give both systems. All drawings contain inches, followed by the equivalent in centimetres in brackets, unless otherwise stated. To avoid breaking the word flow unduly, this has not always been done in the text, but the metric figure will generally be found in a drawing.

But do not get out your calculator to check whether the metric figure is exact. It may be, but it is more likely to be an equivalent. To give an example: $\frac{3}{4} \times 1\frac{1}{4}$ in is a common size of wood section. This would usually be translated as around 2×3 cm, or perhaps 2×3.5 cm, if the $1\frac{1}{4}$ inch is on the light side. If dimensions are more critical, (as in the construction of blocks), it would be 1.9×3.2 cm, and if it is intended to equate somehow to standard ply, then it would be given as 1.8×3.2 cm. What it would never be is 1.905×3.175 cm, the exact value.

Acknowledgements

I wish to thank, for technical information, Mr. Collins of Blakes Paints, Mr. Bryant of International Paints, Mr. Orr of Ault & Wiborg, Miss Diane Poole of the Princes Risborough Laboratory of the Building Research Establishment, GKN Wood Screws, the Timber Research and Development Association, Mr. Lines of Howard Bros., and many others without whose help this book would have been a poorer thing. The wood samples reproduced in colour between pp. 16 and 17 have been supplied by courtesy of the Timber Research and Development Association. To the artist, Richard Reeves, my thanks for the accurate and professional interpretation of my drawings. My especial thanks to Denny Desoutter, editor of this book and of *Practical Boat Owner*, whose advice is ever prompt, pertinent and sound. Finally, slightly wondering thanks to my wife, Liz, who not only puts up cheerfully with the hassle and histrionics that even a modest book entails, but finds the time to translate my Urdic-like manuscrawl into typescript.

M.S.

PART I

Working Wood

1. What is Wood?

Wood is a complex material, provided by nature in a tremendous range of weights, strengths and textures, but all woods are composed of a single basic substance built up in different ways. This basic cellulose substance is a very strong material, about $1\frac{1}{2}$ times the density of water, assembled into a sort of tangled hollow fibre structure with lignum. It is rather like a great bundle of reeds held together here and there with sticky stuff, the reeds themselves being built of smaller reeds, and so on down to the cellulose molecule. The molecules and fibres lie roughly parallel, which gives all woods strongly directional properties; i.e., strength and movement along the grain differ from that across the grain. Consequently, when working in wood, whether cutting or screwing, gluing or designing, you are always faced with the directional nature of wood.

Clearly the wood structure must be full of pores; 94 per cent for balsa, nearly 60 per cent for teak, and even a very dense wood like greenheart is one third pores. Density, then, is one of the things that distinguishes woods and influences their properties, mainly strength and reaction to moisture. Another difference is the way the structure is woven—a long straight grain makes for a strong springy wood, while the percentage of cells radiating outwards from the centre of the tree, as opposed to running parallel to the trunk, governs resistance to splitting. Yet other differences spring from the oils and resins in the wood, which affect smell, feel, appearance and resistance to decay.

A   STRENGTH BEHAVIOUR

Given the directional structure of wood, it is hardly surprising that its strength is directional too. Fig. 1 illustrates how nearly all the strength is along the grain, hardly any across it. The ratio of strengths is roughly 15 to 1 for hardwoods, and 30 to 1 for softwoods, so you would never dream, for instance, of building a companion step with the grain running across instead of along. The same goes for nearly everything designed in wood. If strength is required in both directions, then two lots of wood must be used with their grains running perpendicular, examples being the planks and frames of a wooden hull, and, of course, plywood.

The use of screws and nails is another example of directional strength, for if they are driven into the end grain, the fibres merely part to allow them passage and offer

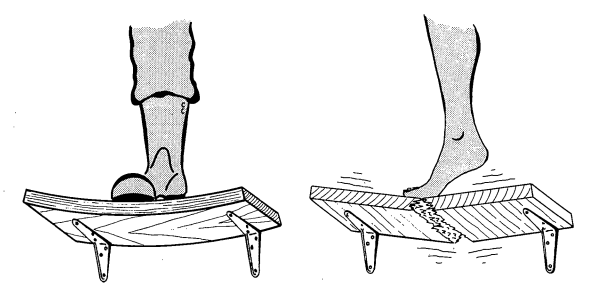

Figure 1. THE STRENGTH OF WOOD IS VASTLY GREATER ALONG THE GRAIN
THAN ACROSS THE GRAIN

little grip. Fastenings must *always* penetrate across the grain, a point we'll come across later in this chapter.

Strengths of woods, together with other properties, are given in Appendix A.

B   MOISTURE AND MOVEMENT

One of the most infuriating properties of wood is its refusal to stay still (Photo 1). Movement occurs because water is absorbed into the pores, where it shoves its way between the molecular fibres, forcing them apart. This happens at the ends of fibres too, but since there are many more fibres side by side than end to end, wood expands and shrinks far more across the grain than along it; roughly ten times more, in fact.

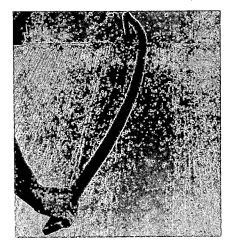

1. The nomadic qualities of iroko. This piece, once straight, now warps (both ways) differently every season.

The absorbed water is not liquid, of course, but is almost chemically bonded, and is in equilibrium with the water vapour of the surrounding air. In other words, the moisture content of wood changes with relative humidity as shown in Fig. 2. At a relative humidity of 100 per cent, wood reaches saturation point, normally in the region of 25 per cent to 30 per cent moisture, at which point it still looks and feels dry;

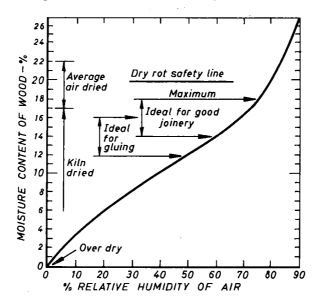

Figure 2. REPRESENTATIVE MOISTURE CURVE OF WOOD
IN EQUILIBRIUM WITH AIR (60°F/15°C)

above this the wood can absorb yet more moisture by becoming water-logged, but the moisture will be present as free moisture in the pores and will not substantially affect the properties of the wood. Properties, therefore, change with the weather. A reduction of moisture from, say, 25 per cent to 15 per cent (winter to summer) can shrink a pine plank a half inch for every ten inches across the grain, increase its stiffness by a third and its compressive strength by two thirds.

Changes are not instantaneous, because the moisture takes time to penetrate; the thicker the wood, the denser the wood and the oilier the wood, the slower the change in moisture. Typically, a heavy hardwood might take nine months or more per inch (25 mm) of board thickness to adjust to the surrounding air, a pine only a quarter as long. Unfortunately the response to moisture change, especially rapid change, is seldom even, so that warping or even splitting occurs. This also happens if you glue together woods of widely differing moisture contents.

All this panting behaviour is most disheartening, but there are a number of things that can be done to minimise the effect of moisture change:

● In every application, bear in mind that wood will move with moisture, and make allowances. With moving parts, such as hatches and doors, for instance, always leave gaps to allow for expansion, roughly a quarter inch for every foot across the grain, and the same for every 10 feet along the grain.

● Take particular care when joining wood to other materials, a subject treated more fully in Section I 4.

● Never use green wood. Use stuff that you know is reasonably dry. Store it flat under a cover with spaces between, for as long as possible, and only glue woods that have been in roughly the same conditions.

● In places where violent moisture fluctuations occur, e.g. hatches and cockpit, use the heavier, oilier woods, ideally teak.

    Alternatively, laminating and joining several pieces together stabilises the work.

● Always use some sort of coating—such as oil, paint or preservative—to slow down the rate of moisture change. This is discussed more fully in Section IV 2.

Seasoning is not merely drying out, but a process of elimination and hardening of the natural juices in green wood, which results in a more stable and rot-resistant timber. It is a long process which can actually take place under seawater, or running water, with often superior results. Normally it is done in air, over a period of two to four years, or in a kiln over a few weeks, but the latter process is too rapid for stability, and artificially seasoned wood should be treated with suspicion.

C   ROT

While timber movement presents many problems, rot is certainly the most dreaded defect of wood. Both 'wet' and 'dry' varieties are species of fungi, which destroy the fibres and turn timber into cheesecake. The main points that affect the practical yachtsman are:

● Both wet and dry rots occur in the presence of moisture; below 20 per cent moisture content, wood is virtually immune (see Fig. 2). Danger spots are unventilated pockets, and great care should be taken either to avoid these, or to fill them with sticky stuff when doing the joinery.

● Fresh water is an arch promoter of rot, and any place where rainwater or condensation can collect is a hazard. Seawater, on the other hand, kills rot, which is why the old work boats were 'pickled', by packing salt into the counter and other inaccessible places. At one point, in the Napoleonic wars, the French were sinking their ships to save them—not from perfidious Albion, but from dry rot!

● Sap is a serious rot hazard, i.e. in sapwood, unseasoned wood, or trees cut in summer when the sap was high. Certain woods are rot-prone; oak, for example, ash, European redwood and mahogany (usually wet rot only). Others, like teak, iroko and red cedar are highly rot-resistant (see Appendix A). Preventatives are, therefore: good wood, no pockets of stale air, fresh-water-free conditions, and various treatments, like Cuprinol, or even diesel oil. A good paint or sealer system is also effective.

There is no magic cure for rot. Once the wood fibres have been damaged, they cannot be resuscitated, and the best procedure is surgery. Cut it out! Hack back well into the sound wood, for the danger is that this too has been penetrated by fungus spores, ready to spring into action the moment your back is turned. Dry rot is especially prone to spread insidiously, and everything in the vicinity should be saturated with preservative before a new piece of timber is graved in.

A shortcut treatment for rot is to apply a thin epoxy resin, the best known being Git Rot, directly on to the affected wood. The resin is intended to soak in and set, thereby replacing the wood structurally and sealing it off from further attack. It is a costly treatment, and the danger is that penetration will not be complete enough to prevent the rot continuing in secret.

D JOINERY WOODS

Wood is classified as either a softwood, which simply means that it comes from a coniferous, evergreen tree, or a hardwood, which hails from a deciduous one. Of the many varieties, we will look here only at those commonly used in boat work. A fuller list of timbers, their properties and uses, is given in Appendix A. And to aid identification, colour photographs of the more important woods are shown in the plate between pp. 16 and 17.

i. Softwoods

Softwoods, pines for the most part, are used less in Europe than in North America, where there is a good selection of fine timber at reasonable prices.

The image of softwoods as having a long straight grain, being light and soft yet strong, and being susceptible to rot, is partially true. But it is only fair to point out that some softwoods are harder, tougher, and more durable than many hardwoods. Each wood must be considered on its individual merits.

Douglas fir (also called Oregon and Columbian pine), a wood on the heavyish side, rates fairly well in terms of strength, cost, and ease of working. It is moderately durable, but the open grain tends to absorb water, thereby exposing the timber to rot, so it should be well treated and painted. It displays a tendency to check, and steel fastenings stain it.

Douglas fir has been used extensively on boats in applications demanding good strength, reasonable weight, and long lengths—deck planking, stringers, rubbing strakes and, frequently, solid masts for large vessels. For the lighter joinery and general work with which we are concerned, I suggest the main use is in hidden joinery work, like battens, supports, and cleats to join plywood. In fact, for this kind of work, a clear Douglas fir would be my first choice.

Western red cedar is similar to, but weaker than, Alaska, Port Orford and white cedars, all of which are widely used in North America. Red cedar is now commonly available in England, and has several advantages for joinery work. It is light, works very easily, and is stable. It is a naturally impregnated wood, highly resistant to decay, with a nice smell and an attractive appearance, that needs only to be wiped down with oil, or lightly sealed. It has a corrosive effect on metals which should be coated when in contact with it. The principal drawback to the timber is its softness, which renders it liable to mark easily. Because of this, and because of its relatively low strength, Western red cedar should be used in thicker sections than, say, the mahogany it has displaced. Western red should not be confused with South American cedar, a lightish red hardwood with rather similar properties and applications.

Pitch pine This sturdy timber, traditionally used for planking, and church pews, is heavy and durable, though not to the extent that is commonly supposed. Availability of the Caribbean pitch pine is limited now, and general use on board is, in any case, restricted to heavy structural work, like sole beams. It exudes resin, which makes it difficult to work and sometimes affects the paint.

Larch Remarks made on Douglas fir apply in large measure to larch, though the latter has a soapy or oily character when worked. Light-coloured heart-wood is known to be less durable than the darker type, in European larch.

Sitka spruce is traditional for spars, having one of the highest strength-to-weight ratios of any timber, and being available in long, knot-free lengths. But it is soft, holds a fastening badly, is rather prone to rot, and finds little application in joinery.

Good pines Several fine pines are available in different parts of the world, and local usage is a sound guide to their worth. Examples are Southern yellow pine in America (similar to pitch pine under which name it is sometimes exported), and Kauri pine from New Zealand; the latter is said to be one of the finest boat-building timbers, but do not confuse with Queensland Kauri which is a rather poor timber.

Poor pines, which should be granted only a grudging home aboard, include European redwood, alias Scots pine and red or yellow deal; whitewood, European, Finnish or Russian, also called deal and common spruce; Western white spruce; and Parana pine, which is not a species of pine at all. The principal drawback with all these woods is their susceptibility to rot, and they should all be well treated with Cuprinol. They also absorb water rather too readily.

ii. Hardwoods

Teak is unquestionably the prince of boat-building woods, because of two outstanding characteristics: it exhibits remarkable stability in widely fluctuating conditions, and it weathers extremely well, being capable of easy restoration to the original condition after years of neglect in the open. It is, therefore, the first choice for work exposed to the elements, like handrails, seat slats, cockpit gratings and, especially, sliding hatches, which demand a stable structure to function properly. Be it noted, however, that there is no wood, teak included, which is completely stable, as those who have sailed in the tropics can testify. Down below, it requires only sealing, or a rub of oil. Varnish does not hold very well on teak, and painting it is a crime.

Teak is also delightful to work, holds fastenings well, and is very durable. (Do not, however, believe those who insist that it is immune from rot and teredo. I have seen both.) The drawback with teak is its cost. Also, every other production boat has teak trim plastered around the cabin, and this has, to my mind, made teak-work sadly hackneyed.

Teak hails only from the Far East, the prime stuff coming generally from Burma. Beware of terms like 'African teak', (afrormosia or iroko). There is no such thing. Rhodesian teak is a rather splendid, red wood, but it too has no family connection with teak.

Afrormosia is probably the closest alternative to teak, being a notch or two down in every desirable property; it is cheaper than teak, though still very costly. Its usage is, consequently, parallel to teak, though slight brittleness and crossgraining make working more difficult. Being less oily than teak afrormosia takes varnish well.

Iroko has a variegated grain, ranging from yellow to dark brown, and varnished is, to my taste, one of the most attractive woods of all, though it weathers grey if untreated. It is often difficult to distinguish from teak—until you start working it. Then you will find its tendency to reverse grain and blunt tools only slightly less infuriating than its nomadic qualities. In short, though some iroko is stable, it tends to move, and continues to move even when seasoned. Consequently, I strongly recommend that any iroko you use be either laminated, or fastened down in some manner, when it will be found very satisfactory for duties ranging from varnished trim to heavy-duty rudders, and it makes excellent laminated beams.

Iroko possesses two major advantages, which have led to its widespread use in boats. It is, currently, one of the cheapest of the quality hardwoods suitable for boats; and it is very durable indeed. In fact, I have never seen a piece affected by rot or water softening.

Mahogany covers several species of wood. African mahoganies (Khaya) are, perhaps, the poorest, and certainly the most variable in quality. In general, they are light to medium weight, low to medium strength woods. Easy to work, except for reverse grain, mahogany takes a fastening well, does not warp excessively, and is moderate in cost. Its principal attraction is visual. It is pink, darkening to red-brown, with a figured grain, and it takes varnish very well. Its durability is not good, however; in damp conditions it will succumb to wet rot, and under water it tends to become soggy. Use it in cabin joinery but treat it with Cuprinol. I do not recommend it for exposed usage.

American—i.e. Brazilian, Peruvian, Honduras—mahoganies are similar in every way to the African variety, but superior, except for appearance which is straighter in grain and rather bland. They are often used on coamings, hatches, and other exterior fitments if better woods are not available but should always be well protected with varnish or paint.

Philippine mahogany covers a number of species of *Shorea*, known variously as lauan, meranti, and seraya, none of which are mahoganies, and few of which are from the Philippines. Of the three types sold—yellow, light red, and dark red—the latter is preferred for its better strength and durability, though none is exceptional. Appearance is not especially attractive, but as these timbers are available in long, clear lengths, they are used for planking and stringers. Philippine mahogany is prone to worm attack and timber should be carefully inspected before purchase.

Utile and sapele are somewhat similar in appearance and behaviour, both looking like a mahogany. Utile, however, is the superior wood in every respect, and all remarks about it apply to sapele to a lesser degree. Utile is a stronger, denser, and harder wood than mahogany, and, most important of all, it is more durable. It can be used in exposed conditions, if painted or varnished, and will not rot in damp interiors to the same extent as mahogany. Utile works and screws well and planes to a characteristically glossy surface. It is especially suited to good-quality joinery, as it is arguably the most beautiful of the red woods, displaying a rich, sometimes highly figured grain when varnished.

Sapele has a straighter grain, striped with wavy lines. Being only moderately durable, its use is mainly in the cabin. In veneer form, it is used widely in plywood and cold-moulded construction.

Oak, traditionally the top timber for boat building, in fact, leaves a lot to be desired for joinery and general work. With the exception of properly seasoned oak, and preferably American white (both of which are difficult to get), oak is alarmingly prone to dry rot. Under varnish it has a habit of blackening right through when damp, or in the vicinity of steel fastenings which are often attacked by the acid in the wood. This acid also affects urea glues. Japanese and American red oaks should be avoided.

Elm is another traditional boat wood, now little used. Imports of rock elm, excellent for bending and framing, are banned because of Dutch elm disease, and ordinary elm is not a good timber. Wych elm could be used more widely; it is strong and has attractive markings, but all elm has rather poor durability.

iii. Other Woods

There is, unfortunately, no space here to discuss the many other interesting and beautiful species which find application in boats; a more comprehensive list is given in Appendix A. It is worth mentioning, however, a few types that are defective in some way, though they may be available and cheap.

Such a wood is *beech*, close grained, strong, and exceptionally warp free, but, unfortunately, susceptible to dry rot in unventilated places. This is a weakness also of *ash*, which should, therefore, not be used down below. Outside it is often used for tillers, oars, and frames in open boats, applications which take advantage of its high strength-to-weight ratio and excellent bending properties. Ash is attractive to look at and a delight to work.

Keruing is one of the cheapest hardwoods, but it is very heavy, coarse-grained and unattractive. It can be used for structural bearers and the like, but, despite the exudation of resin that gums up tools, it is not particularly durable, and gradually breaks down when exposed to the weather. *Ramin*—available everywhere in D.I.Y. shops—exhibits very high moisture movement, is not at all durable, and should not be used unless well treated with preservative, which it takes well.

E   BUYING WOOD

There are basically two ways of buying wood. The first is to buy the cross section you actually need, the second to buy the timber in bulk and cut it to suit. If the planned job is anything but a minor one-off, and if you have a circular rip saw, buying in bulk has every advantage. It is a great deal cheaper, not only in terms of cost per cube, but also you can cut exactly what you need, when you need it; small stuff has a habit of warping if not used quickly. The only problem about buying in bulk is planing the plank, and it is usually worth getting the timber merchant to push the order through his thicknesser.

Timber is sold either in finished, i.e. planed, sizes, or 'rough sawn', and you should be clear exactly what sizes you are getting. Bulk stuff is nearly always 'rough sawn', and, if very large, may not even be square edged, i.e. it may still be the shape of the tree. Allow from $\frac{1}{16}$ in to $\frac{3}{16}$ in (1.5 to 4.5 mm) on the thickness, depending on the quality of the plank, for finishing from rough sawn. Standard thicknesses are 1, $1\frac{1}{4}$, $1\frac{1}{2}$ and 2 inches; 1 in (2.5 cm) will cover all general work (fiddles, tables), $1\frac{1}{4}$ in (3.2 cm) is the ideal width for most trim and surrounds, and 2 in (5 cm) is needed for handgrips and special work. Make sure they are 'thick' (slightly more than the stated size), and these sizes will serve most purposes. A distressing proportion of the wood you buy will be wasted—ends of planks are often checked, saw cuts are at least $\frac{1}{8}$ in (3 mm) wide, edges are not straight, offcuts are the wrong size, and so on. Allow twenty to thirty per cent wastage for finished wood, cut to size, and at least forty per cent for timber in bulk.

Actually selecting the timber is a job demanding patience and tenacity, for changing economics are causing timber merchants to become wholesale traders rather than selective purveyors. Also timber is a natural product, which is not constrained by engineering specifications, so that great variations in properties within the same species are normal. Furthermore, a common name sometimes covers several species. For quality joinery, each plank must be individually examined for knots, worm holes and other defects, trueness and shakes. Longitudinal shakes are fairly obvious but those running across the grain are tiny thunder cracks (mahogany may have this), that render the wood useless. Grain marking is important for brightwork and, as the wood is usually weathered grey, I make a practice (not always popular), of taking along a plane to clean off a patch of surface. Examine the wood carefully for sapwood, which should never be used in a boat, likewise splintered heartwood. Quarter-sawn wood, identified by the end grain showing straight across through the thickness of the plank, is best, but almost unobtainable. Again, economics demand that logs be sliced into full-width planks, termed 'sawn through and through'.

Rare also is properly seasoned wood. Instead, a great deal of timber sold is kiln dried, and, as already noted, this is to be avoided if possible. Unless used immediately, or stored in a warm, dry shed, air-dried wood is likely to prove superior. One way of insuring properly air-dried timber is to purchase several months in advance, and store the timber flat, each plank separated from the one above by wooden slats, called dunnage, spaced about 3 to 6 ft (1–2 m) apart, and all exactly one above the other to avoid warping. Paint the ends to stop checking. The timber pile should be shielded from the rain, yet allowed plenty of ventilation. If, when you cut the wood, conditions are damp, allow the pieces a day or so to surface-dry indoors; in this way you will get timber that is roughly in equilibrium with the prevailing climate, yet dry enough to glue.

F PLYWOOD

Since the grains of laminations in plywood cross at right angles, the sheet has the same strength in either direction, and laminations are balanced so that warping is hardly a problem. Furthermore, ply comes in handy, big sheets, usually 8 ft × 4 ft (244 × 122 cm). All tremendous advantages. But, remember that ply is only half as strong in any one direction as solid wood, and so totally unsuited in strip form for supporting loads. You still cannot screw into end grain edges (twice as many as in solid wood), and it still moves with moisture, albeit less than the solid.

The top grade is Marine Ply to British Standard 1088, kitemarked, but unless the job is structural or exterior, the considerably cheaper 'exterior' grade (also called 'weatherproof' and WBP) may be perfectly adequate. The principal difference is that core laminates in proper marine plywood, as well as the face veneers, are carefully selected and joined, whereas the core of an exterior grade can be real rubbish. Before buying cheap ply, examine the edges all round for 'holidays' in the core; these not only reduce the strength dramatically, but are also inbuilt rot traps. WBP means that the glue used is equal or identical to the glue used in marine ply, but delamination can, nevertheless, occur in cheaper ply, due to poor quality-control during manufacture. The quality of the outside veneer cannot be concealed, but core material is often something of a mystery, especially in 'exterior' grades. Suppliers are often hard to pin down, and vague terms like 'Malaysian hardwood' should be treated with suspicion. In short, if you buy cheap ply, you take a chance, but one that may well be justified by the job and the cost. Many production boats use 'exterior' grade for interior work.

Scores, if not hundreds, of trade names abound in plywood supply, and since these fluctuate continually it is pointless trying to list them with their properties. It is advisable, I feel, to stick with the better-known hardwoods, among which are mahogany (khaya), makore, luan and meranti; veneers can be almost anything you fancy, from sycamore to sapele, but if you propose to paint, any reasonable-quality veneer will do. Douglas fir shuttering ply is used sometimes on boats, but it absorbs water, takes a poor finish and is not recommended.

Standard thicknesses are in millimetres—4, 5, 6, 9, 12, 15, 18, 22 and 25, except in North America where the equivalent in inches prevail. 6 mm is only for very light work, like locker floors. 9 mm covers low- to medium-strength applications, like shelves, while 12 mm can be used for most general joinery. 15 mm is suitable for bulkheads and locker faces, where rigidity as well as strength is important, and 18 mm is generally reserved for heavy-duty work. Weights of average hardwood ply are given in Appendix B.

Certain other boards, notably WBP blockboard, can be used where thickness cum stiffness is more important than strength. An example is cabin doors.

2. Joining Wood

To the practical yachtsman, joints are like knots. There are hundreds of sophisticated sorts, but you have to know only a handful thoroughly to do everything that is needed.

All the joints illustrated can be made without special machine tools, dowelling systems or training. They are practical and strong, and, in consequence, most of them look right. Of course, there is no substitute for good workmanship, but modern glues have made things a hundred times easier (see Section I 7). This is not merely a matter of adhesion. A gap-filling resin ensures perfect contact between the faces of the most indifferent joint, by setting to a rigid solid. The effect is to boost the frictional and location forces, so that even without adhesion, the joint would be considerably stronger. Nevertheless, the basic joint design must be right, even with the strongest of glues. First, the contact area should be generous; one would never think of sealing an envelope by gluing the paper edge to edge, for instance. Secondly, the contact area should be as far as possible at right angles to the forces trying to pull the pieces apart; glues are weaker in tension. Thirdly, fastenings should penetrate across the grain, not into end grain. A rough test of design is this; if you take away the glue, will the shape of the joint, or the position of the fastenings, still tend to hold the

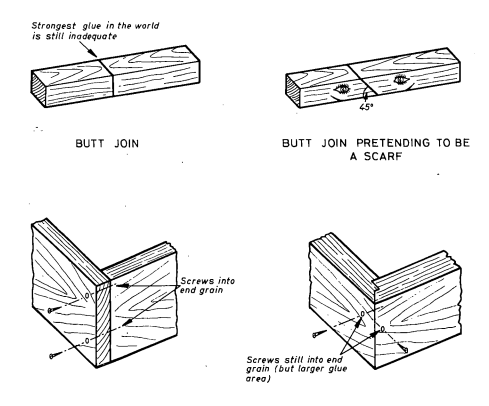

Figure 3. POOR JOINTS

pieces together? Fig. 3 illustrates the sort of joint that fails the test.

The most common joints are those that cross at angles (Fig. 4). In solid timber, the half-cut joints illustrated are simple and sturdy, and all that is required to make them is a tenon saw, a chisel and some accurate measuring, preferably with a combination square. The invisible 'T' is especially neat for such jobs as letting a piece into a beam, as no end grain is visible.

Mitre joints also hide ugly end grain, but they are intrinsically weak; this is of no consequence in picture frames, but on boats they are best limited to trim, which takes little load and is reinforced by the backing material, as illustrated. Many people find it difficult to make a hairline joint, certainly a skilled task without the right tools. One method is to cut the pieces as accurately as possible, clamp them both snugly in position, then saw down the joint with light, steady strokes of a tenon saw. Since any false movement of the teeth will affect both faces in exactly the same way, the faces will mate perfectly when brought together, though it may take several cuts to achieve. The technique is particularly useful when the mitre is at an odd angle. The pieces cannot, of course, be fixed or cut to length until the joint is made.

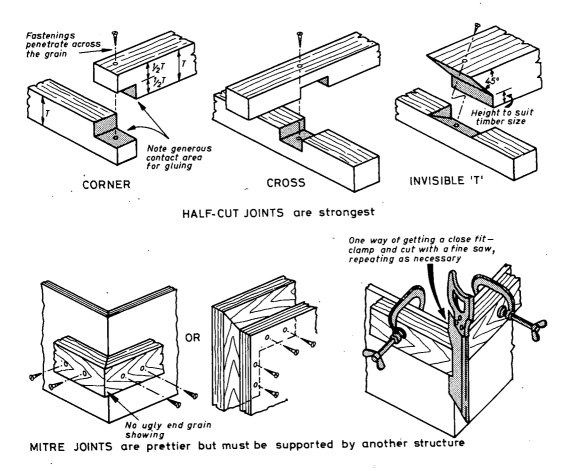

Fastenings penetrate across the grain

Note generous contact area for gluing

Height to suit timber size

CORNER   CROSS   INVISIBLE 'T'

HALF-CUT JOINTS are strongest

One way of getting a close fit — clamp and cut with a fine saw, repeating as necessary

OR

No ugly end grain showing

MITRE JOINTS are prettier but must be supported by another structure

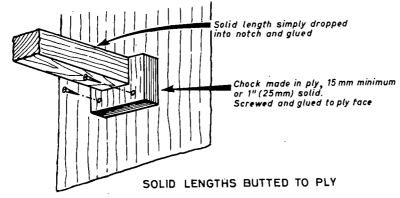

Solid length simply dropped into notch and glued

Chock made in ply, 15 mm minimum or 1" (25 mm) solid. Screwed and glued to ply face

SOLID LENGTHS BUTTED TO PLY

Figure 4. CROSSING AT ANGLES

Butting a length of solid to a plywood face (Fig. 4) is frequently necessary when building something out from a bulkhead. A quick method is to make a chock in solid timber or heavy ply, position it accurately with the solid length in place, and mark the two screw points with an awl pushed through the holes already drilled in the chock. The chock can then be screwed and glued in the right position, and the timber length dropped into place with a spot of glue afterwards.

Joining pieces end to end is illustrated in Fig. 5. The odd scarf can be made by the technique described for mitres, of repeated clamping and sawing, but for any quantity of straight scarfs, a scarf box, (the one in Photo 2 is made from 15 mm ply and 2 in iroko sides) is essential for rapidity and accuracy. The timber pieces are first marked and cut roughly with a saw. Each one is then in turn clamped rigidly in the scarf box and planed, using the sides of the box to guide the plane. In order to prevent the plane nicking the box sides, I use a $\frac{1}{2}$ in (12 mm) softwood spacer between the wood and the box. For the highest precision, true off by scraping with the plane iron, sighting the light under a steel straight-edge placed on the face to ascertain the

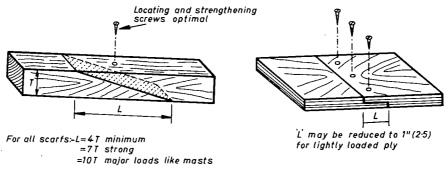

For all scarfs:-L=4T minimum
=7T strong
=10T major loads like masts

STRAIGHT SCARF

'L' may be reduced to 1"(2·5)
for lightly loaded ply

STEPPED SCARF

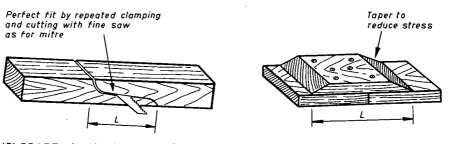

Perfect fit by repeated clamping and cutting with fine saw as for mitre

Taper to reduce stress

'S' SCARF—for the fancy worker and BUTT STRAP for the rough one

Figure 5. LENGTHS and SHEETS JOINED END TO END

2. A scarf box made of a pair of 15 mm plywood boards, fitted with hardwood guides for planing. Taper (scarf ratio) is 7 to 1.

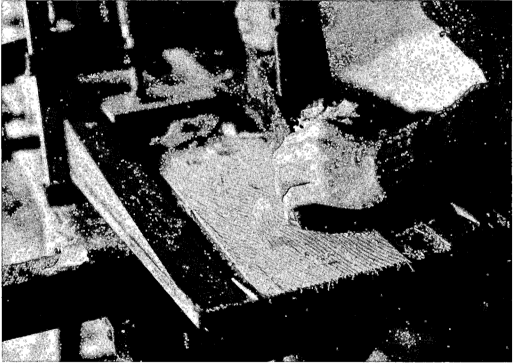

3. Scarf box in use. The wood is clamped firmly both down and across the plane guides. Note the softwood spacer between the workpiece and the guides, to avoid cutting the latter.

4. Scarf bed in heavy-duty angle iron. Note how a flat has been tack-welded on to the bottom flange to achieve a perfect inside right angle.

high spots. When gluing, make sure that not only the scarf but both lengths of timber are clamped to a rigid base if you want a straight join. One of the most useful jigs I have is simply a length of heavy angle iron, 4 in × 4 in × 4 ft 6 in (10 × 10 × 140 cm)—Photo 4—which produces a true scarf from the most warped rubbish. Highly economical.

A scarf box cannot be used on ply edges, which are best prepared in a process of repeated planing, and measurement by straight-edge and the eye. This is not so difficult as it sounds, because a kink in the line of the laminates instantly points up a jolt in the workmanship. Naturally, the length of the scarf must be marked first, and the ply must be clamped to a firm base plank, the edge coinciding exactly with the edge of the ply. A belt- or orbital-sander is helpful in the final stages, to obtain a perfectly flat, even finish. The scarf is glued by pressing between two heavy timbers that stretch across the ply and are strongly clamped at both ends; a few small fastenings are needed through the joint, to prevent it slipping.

A stepped scarf is simpler, and is acceptable where the ply is not under bending stress. Bulkheads, for example, are only in compression, and can be joined with a step, whereas seat tops are better straight scarfed. The step is easily made with a rebate plane, guided against a straight-edge; even easier is to make a number of closely spaced parallel cuts, using a hand-held power saw set to the correct depth, then finishing off with a rebate plane.

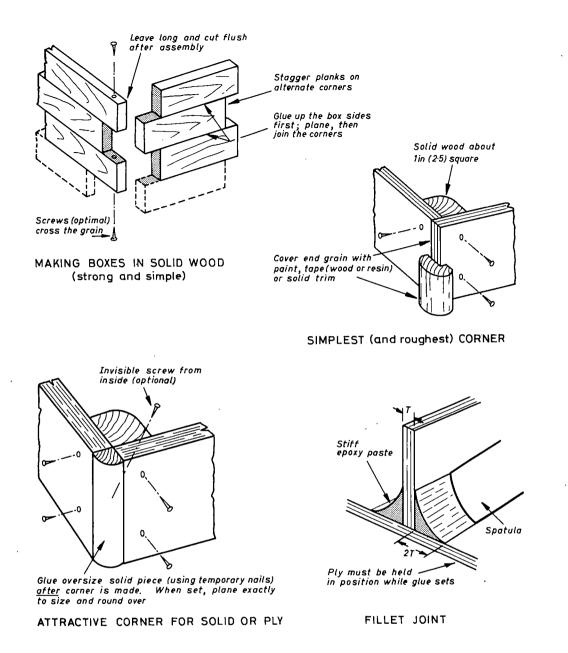

Leave long and cut flush
after assembly

Stagger planks on
alternate corners

Glue up the box sides
first; plane, then
join the corners

Solid wood about
1in (2·5) square

Cover end grain with
paint, tape (wood or resin)
or solid trim

Screws (optimal)
cross the grain

MAKING BOXES IN SOLID WOOD
(strong and simple)

SIMPLEST (and roughest) CORNER

Invisible screw from
inside (optional)

Stiff
epoxy paste

Spatula

Ply must be held
in position while glue sets

Glue oversize solid piece (using temporary nails)
after corner is made. When set, plane exactly
to size and round over

ATTRACTIVE CORNER FOR SOLID OR PLY

FILLET JOINT

Figure 6. CORNERS

Different corner jointing is shown in Fig. 6. The common method with ply is to screw up to an inside corner post; the end grain can be hidden by mitering, by covering with trim, or simply with paint (not varnish, which merely highlights the amateurish appearance), or by fixing an outside cornerpiece as well. This latter method, illustrated in the drawing, looks very professional, especially if the outer piece is a darker coloured wood. An extremely strong way of building up boxes in solid timber strips is shown in Fig. 6. The system is really a laminated variation of half-cut joints, which lends itself to strong constructions, like hatches. The sides are first laminated and planed to flat planks when the glue is set, then the corners are joined, allowing the planks to protrude. The protrusions are flushed off and rounded over if desired, after the glue has hardened.

This method of flushing off after a joint has been made, rather than trying to pre-measure, gives superior results on any construction, and should be used wherever possible.

Finally, though the all-glue fillet joint in Fig. 6 looks easy, it is messy and time-wasting, since the parts must be held while the glue sets. It might be justified in cases where you want to fix something that is suitably jammed, like a bulkhead in a small boat.

3. Laminating

Just as modern glues have simplified jointing, so have they revolutionised the compositing of wood—especially for the yacht fitter who, like the housewife, can achieve the most amazingly professional results by simply adding water and mixing . . . Well, not quite perhaps, but by clamping together lots of thin slices, various shapes can be constructed that are true, attractive, and more stable than solid wood. They are generally stronger too, and, for the amateur at any rate, steaming boxes are things of the past.

Typical examples of laminated structures are shown in Fig. 7. For the most part, the jobs are straightforward. First the desired curve is laid out on a strong board, with a string of stout lugs; alternatively, a rigid template can be used. The laminates, with true, fresh-cut surfaces, are then simply clamped up firmly over a polythene release sheet, until the glue has cured, when they can be shaped and smoothed as

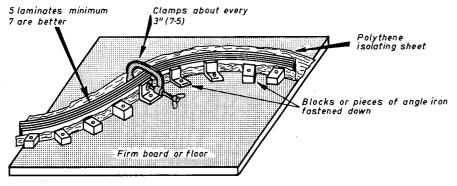

LAMINATING A CURVED PIECE

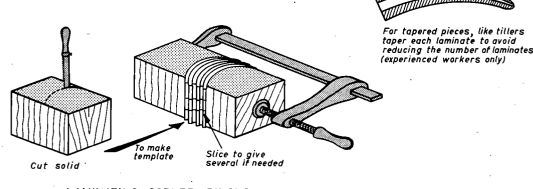

For tapered pieces, like tillers
taper each laminate to avoid
reducing the number of laminates
(experienced workers only)

To make
template

Slice to give
several if needed

Cut solid

LAMINATING CORNER PIECES

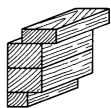

Stepped shapes, eg. hatch coamings,
are economical and strong

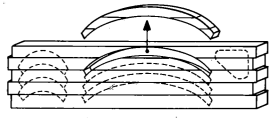

Slicing shapes out of straight laminations saves wood
and is quick.
Not as strong as a curved lamination

STRAIGHT LAMINATIONS

Figure 7. GLUED LAMINATIONS

required. Use as many clamps as you have, at least one for every 3 in (7.5 cm) for $\frac{1}{2}$ in (1.3 cm) laminates, and more for thinner strips; the edges of the laminates may have to be hammered flush onto the board, if they are slightly warped. To allow for edge and end imperfections, always make the laminates slightly wider and longer than the finished piece. Laminate thickness is important; five laminates are the minimum needed to hold a shape, while seven will spring back hardly at all. More may be needed if the work is very large—like a stem-piece—or highly curved.

Laminated pieces need not be curved. Straight structures have many advantages over solid lumps of wood; better stability, complicated step sections, without the need for grooving or routing, and often a big saving in wood. An example is given in Fig. 7, and another—the solid wood box—in Fig. 6. Strictly speaking, no template is needed, but clamping up inside a length of angle iron (Photo 4) will give truer results. Laminate thickness is not critical, being best decided by the shape of the piece and the wood to hand.

5. Laminating curved shapes from flat strips. Every frame on this boat has been laminated, likewise all the deck beams and the heavy curved stem piece.

6. Laminating a big 'un. Here a 14-foot rudder is being laminated from straight strips, using both sash cramps and internal bolts, which will later be cut to length and become part of the structure. The wood is iroko, the glue resorcinol.

Glues are discussed in Section I 7, but for durable laminated structures, there are really only two alternatives: resorcinol gives a stronger, more weather-resistant job, provided that the joints are perfect, the wood is dry and clamping pressures good. Epoxy types are much more forgiving, but the right resin must be used; I have had disappointing failures after only a couple of years, because the glues were too rigid for wood. Fastenings are not needed, unless laminates are few and thick, as might be the case in a straight piece. They may, however, be useful for extra cramping if you are short of cramps, even if they are later removed.

4. Joining Wood to Other Materials

Most boats nowadays are not made of wood, but of GRP, metal or ferro. Yet much of the fitting is still done in wood, and certainly, most of the additions or alterations you do to the fitting of your own boat will be in wood. Consequently, you will often be faced with the problem of joining wood to some other material.

The problem, in a nutshell, is this: wood moves with moisture, while other materials (especially metals and ferro) expand and contract with temperature. So in hot, dry weather, the steel deck (say) expands and the wood trim shrinks, while in damp, chilly conditions, the opposite occurs. Inevitably, the joint will be subject to alternating stresses and, if not properly done, may crack. Fortunately, there are many satisfactory solutions, a selection of which is illustrated in Fig. 8. All embody one or more of the following points, which amount to a sort of commonsense code of practice—condemnation enough, it seems, for all too many designers and boatyards.

- Wherever possible, wood should be fixed with fastenings, as these hold right through the boat material and across the wood grain, and are, therefore, less likely than glue to give way, even if there is differential movement. Where unavoidable, glue-only fixing must be very carefully designed for minimum movement and maximum load-spread; even so, it seldom lasts for exterior wood.
- Vertical fastenings exposed to bad weather are bad news. Not only are they potential leak points, but they also conduct cold quickly, and cause condensation—and hence rot—inside the wood. Wherever possible, you should screw into exterior wood from underneath or from the side. Through-bolts ought to be capped, or at least plugged and sealed with a coating of paint or varnish. It is good practice to fit wooden cleats (strips) to the other material first, then fasten the new fitting, a dorade box, say, to the cleats. Between cleats and hull a flexible sealant is better than glue. When obliged to use glue for strength reasons—an epoxy is the only possibility for dissimilar materials—try and use a slightly flexible type. If the fit is rough, sealant alone will not perform well and you must use both glue and sealant in the following manner: first, bed the wood

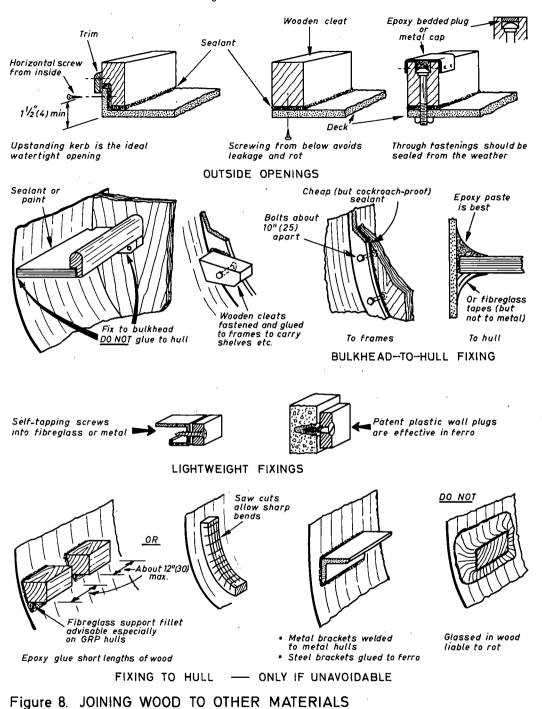

Upstanding kerb is the ideal watertight opening

Horizontal screw from inside

Trim

Sealant

$1\frac{1}{2}''(4)$ min

Wooden cleat

Deck

Screwing from below avoids leakage and rot

Epoxy bedded plug or metal cap

Through fastenings should be sealed from the weather

OUTSIDE OPENINGS

Sealant or paint

Fix to bulkhead
DO NOT glue to hull

Wooden cleats fastened and glued to frames to carry shelves etc.

Bolts about 10" (25) apart

Cheap (but cockroach-proof) sealant

Epoxy paste is best

Or fibreglass tapes (but not to metal)

To frames   To hull

BULKHEAD–TO–HULL FIXING

Self-tapping screws into fibreglass or metal

Patent plastic wall plugs are effective in ferro

LIGHTWEIGHT FIXINGS

Saw cuts allow sharp bends

OR

About 12"(30) max.

Fibreglass support fillet advisable especially on GRP hulls

Epoxy glue short lengths of wood

DO NOT

• Metal brackets welded to metal hulls
• Steel brackets glued to ferro

Glassed in wood liable to rot

FIXING TO HULL — ONLY IF UNAVOIDABLE

Figure 8. JOINING WOOD TO OTHER MATERIALS

7. A wooden sternplate about to be bedded and bolted on to a ferro deck. To achieve a perfect fit the sternplate has been bedded first on to an epoxy/cement mix covered with polythene film, then removed for final bedding on mastic.

down on stiff epoxy paste, with an isolating polythene sheet between glue and wood to make a perfect fit (Photo 7); then, when the epoxy has set, remove the plastic and bed the wood down on sealant. I have used this method with excellent results, particularly on ferro and steel, which are less even than GRP gelcoat. When fixing shelves and so on inside, don't fix directly on to the hull. Hulls are prone to pant, and in any case, drilling through them is not a good idea. Generally, the bulkheads are fixed to the hull, and the furniture should be fixed to the bulkheads: drilling and fixing to frames and beams is also quite permissible. If you have to fix to the hull, then use one of the methods in Fig. 8. It is most convenient, incidentally, that steel and ferro have the same expansion characteristics, so fixing one to the other is good practice.

Techniques of working materials other than wood are discussed in Part V.

5. Fitting Queer Boat Shapes

Boats are curved in queer ways, and fitting something to them is not straightforward. In fact, a surface is seldom even straight, much less horizontal, and if you find a right angle, you are lucky. Most of the problems stem from either multiple angles or curves.

Multiple angles occur when the joint is not at right angles in either direction. The technique illustrated in Fig. 9 is to measure each angle separately, using an angle gauge (or sliding bevel), together with levels or straight-edges. The correct lines can

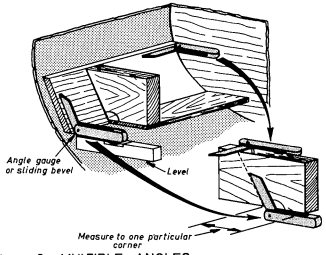

Angle gauge
or sliding bevel   Level

Measure to one particular
corner

Figure 9. MULTIPLE ANGLES

then be marked on the piece for cutting. Distance measurements need careful thought, because they vary according to their position along the angled edge. The shipwright's tenet for this, and every other fitting job, is: 'Measure twice and cut once!' which one might usefully prefix with, 'Think thrice!'—as bitter experience has taught me.

There are three useful techniques for shaping to curves. The spacer spiling method is a quicky for shapes that can be offered into position and nearly fit. The measurement spiling version is for pieces that can be offered into position, but don't fit the curve at all. And the tick stick method is for pieces, usually large ones like bulkheads, which cannot be offered up even near position.

In the **spacer spiling method** (Fig. 10a) the wood is fitted up as snug as possible, and a line parallel to the hull is drawn along it, by keeping the pencil hard against a spacer, and the spacer hard against the hull. The spacer can be a wooden block or, with practice, simply a finger. Sometimes a wheel is used, a pencil point being poked through the centre.

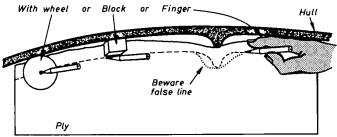

With wheel   or   Block   or   Finger   Hull

Beware
false line

Ply

Figure 10. (a) SPACER SPILING

32

8. Spiling a plywood shelf to the hull using a stick, notched to receive the pencil point. A square keeps the stick at a constant angle.

Measured spiling is merely a variation of the above technique, used on ply that cannot be fitted close; it is also needed where there are projections, like frames, that stick out more or less at right angles to the curve, since spacer spiling gives a false line at the side of the frames. The technique is illustrated in Photo 8. The distance piece here is a length of wood with a point at one end to follow the curve of the hull, and a notch in the edge for the pencil point. The measuring stick is maintained at a constant angle by means of a set square, or similar. The ply itself must, of course, be in the correct position to slide into place when cut to shape (it is no use having the right shape in the wrong place) and must also be flat all over. The reason for this can be seen in Photo 8: here the hull lies at a sharp angle to the ply, so that if the ply sagged in the middle, say, the measuring stick would trace a lower position on the hull, and consequently a different shape. Note also that in this case the ply would have to be cut at the hull angle, as well as hull shape, for a perfect fit.

The **tick stick technique** is a cunning method of measuring random shapes without actually taking any measurements. Fig. 10b shows how. Suppose you want to fit a bulkhead (or shelf or a cabin sole). Clamp any sort of flat board with a reasonable drawing surface—the tick board—in the same plane. The tick board can be placed anywhere in this plane, but you will find it much easier if you can place it with one straight edge exactly in the same position as you plan for the ply edge, and a known position along that edge (Fig. 10b(i)).

The next step is to take a stiff, pointed stick (I use a length of alloy angle, cut off obliquely) and place it on the tick board with the point touching the hull. Draw a line on the board, then tick both the stick and the board at the same place, and mark both ticks (Fig. 10b(ii)) ①. Move the point along the hull, and repeat, marking the new line and tick ②. It does not matter where you draw the line or the tick. Carry on with as many points as are needed to delimit the hull shape, making sure you touch every corner; the greater the number of points, the more accurately the ply will fit.

When you have finished, remove the board and lay it flat and in position alongside

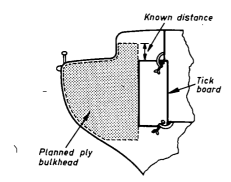

(i) Clamp tick board in position

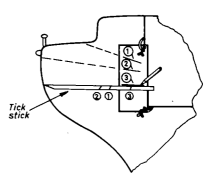

(ii) Mark lines and tick with tick stick touching hull

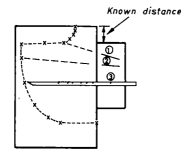

(iii) Place tick board against ply and match ticks and lines to get hull shape

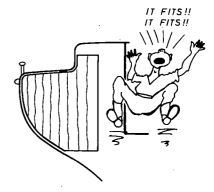

(iv) Cut ply and install

(b) THE TICK STICK TECHNIQUE

Figure 10. FITTING TO CURVES

the ply sheet. Lay the tick stick along line ①, and match the two ticks marked ①. The tip of the stick will then be in the same position as it was on the hull, and you can mark it with a cross (Fig. 10b(iii)). Repeat for every tick position, and you'll end up with a path of crosses, which are joined up using a thin batten guide, to give a smooth hull curve. Cut, and with a bit of skill and judgement, it should fit first time (Fig. 10b(iv)). In fact, the fit should be very good, provided enough points have been used.

There is a fourth technique, really just a variation on the other three, and that is to **cut a hardboard template first**. This is worth the extra trouble if the area is bounded by opposed edges, so that trimming the one only creates a gap on the other. In other words, the fit must be exact first time. Making a template is also worthwhile if you are working in expensive materials and you are not sure of yourself.

6. Tools

'A bad craftsman', chant the ignorant, 'blames his tools.' Well, so does a good craftsman, if his tools are no good, and perfectly right too. Both, in fact, would do better with better tools. For, the better the quality and quantity of tools, the more professional the work, and the wider its scope. Tools, in short, are an investment in every sense, for they can always be sold later to other handy-minded yachtsmen.

But tools are wickedly expensive, so you have to trim your investment to the sort of work you plan. Rather than simply reeling off lists of tools, therefore, it is more useful to tackle the matter from the usage end, i.e. what tools are needed to carry out the various operations. I have attempted, in Table 1, pp. 36–7, to list tools in rough order of sophistication. Column 1 covers hand tools, essential for anything more than routine maintenance. Column 2 contains what is needed in addition for the practical yachtsman wishing to construct and alter a variety of items aboard, though not necessarily continuously. And column 3 covers sophisticated tools, mainly powered, which would make a major fitting-out job quicker and better. The list is not exhaustive, for power tools are cheaper now, relative to hand tools, than they have ever been, and buying specific tools for specific tasks is easier to justify. Most of the tools listed are illustrated in Photos 9–14.

A   WORKPLACE

Professionals use splendidly long workbenches, which are worth their weight in teak, if not gold. When we lived aboard, cruising, I had to make do with a tiny vice clamped to a bread-board. Somewhere between the two extremes lies the ideal. For my money, the Black & Decker Workmate takes some beating; bench and vice combined, it grips almost any shape, and can be folded for stowage. For a boat, the smallest bench W400, is the handiest, especially if you are going to leave it aboard. But you will, in any case, need another, more solid work surface of some sort for hammering; a proper work bench, 3 in (7.5 cm) thick, is best, but a railway sleeper

Table 1

(Dimensions are guide figures only)

	1. Essential	2. Progressive	3. Sophisticated
WORKPLACE	Rough bench with some sort of vice.	Black & Decker Workmate or equivalent.	10 ft (3 m) min. bench with carpenter's vice. Trestles.
MEASURING	10 ft (3 m) steel tape. Set square. 4 ft (120 cm) straight-edge. Many pencils.	Angle gauge (sliding bevel). Spirit level. 3 ft (90 cm) and 9 ft (2.75 m) straight-edges. Combination square.	Plumb line. Fairing battens. Scribe.
DRILLING	$\frac{1}{2}''$ (13 mm) hand drill. Set twist drills, $\frac{1}{16}''/\frac{1}{2}''$ (1.5/13 mm). Bradawl.	$\frac{3}{8}''$ (10 mm) min. 2-speed electric drill. Ratchet brace & set of bits $\frac{1}{4}''/1\frac{1}{4}''$ (6/32 mm). Expanding bit to $2\frac{1}{2}''$ (65 mm). Spade bits for wood $\frac{1}{2}''/1\frac{1}{2}''$ (13/40 mm). 3 in 1 Stanley bits. Rose bit.	Drill stand. Plug cutters—selection. Hole saws—selection. Flexible or right-angle drive.
SAWING	Hand saw, cross-cut 8 teeth/inch. 12'' (30 cm) hacksaw. Junior 6'' (15 cm) hacksaw.	Jigsaw (power). Hand rip-saw 5 teeth/inch. Keyhole saw. 5'' (12.5 cm) circular saw (power)—may be drill attachment. Coping saw.	Saw table 3'' (7.5 cm) depth-cut. Band saw, 12'' (30 cm) throat. Guillotine.
PLANING & SHAPING	$2\frac{3}{8}'' \times 9''$ (6 × 22.5 cm) smoothing plane. Half-round Surform. Flat spokeshave. Selection chisels $\frac{1}{4}''/1\frac{1}{4}''$ (6/32 mm). Knife.	1'' (25 mm) bullnose rebate plane. 14'' (35 cm) jack plane. Block plane. Rounded spokeshave.	Power router with cutters: rounding over, 3 off. straight, 3 off. 45° chamfer, 1 off. 22'' (55 cm) try plane. 3'' (7.5 cm) power plane, or 6'' (15 cm) bench plane. Compass (adjustable curve) plane. Adze. Draw knife.

	1. Essential	*2. Progressive*	*3. Sophisticated*
SCREWING, CLAMPING & HAMMERING	3 screwdrivers. 6″ (15 cm) adjustable spanner. 4 clamps, 4″ & 6″ (10 & 15 cm). 1 lb (½ kg) claw hammer. Nail countersink punch.	Specialist screwdrivers (Philips, dwarf, large etc.). Yankee screwdriver. Screwbits for brace. Selection spanners (wrenches). Clamps—variety 3″ to 12″ (7.5 to 30 cm). Mallet. Punches, selection.	Screwdriver attachment for drill. Heavy adjustable wrenches. Sash cramps. 4 lb (2 kg) sledge hammer.
SANDING & FILING	Selection files: flat, half-round, rat tail. Selection rasps. Sandpaper: 80-grit coarsework. 120-grit fine work.	Disc sander on drill. 1 or 2 rotary files for drill.	Belt sander. Orbital sander. Bench disc sander (alternative to guillotine).
FINISHING & PAINTING	Scrapers—selection. Putty knives—selection. ½″, 1″, 1½″, 2″ (13, 25, 40, 50 mm) paint brushes.		High-quality brushes, different one for each colour paint.
VARIOUS	Pliers & vicegrips. Cold chisel. Saw guide 45°/90°. Bench hooks.	Glue mixing: small plastic containers, mixing sticks, 100 ml syringes. Cold chisels—selection. Wire cutters. Sheet metal snips. Trailing multi-socket & lead. Light with wandering lead. Vacuum cleaner. Crowbar. L-iron clamping bed.	Small pop riveter. Hollow punch. Grommet punch for fitting brass eyes. ¼″ (6 mm) chuck for drill. Scarf box. Saw bench roller trestle.
TOOL HUSBANDRY	Oilstone. Saw file.	Oilstone guide.	Saw tooth setter. Bench grinder (may be drill attachment). Drill sharpener. Selection power tool spares, brushes, drill key, jigsaw blade guide, etc.

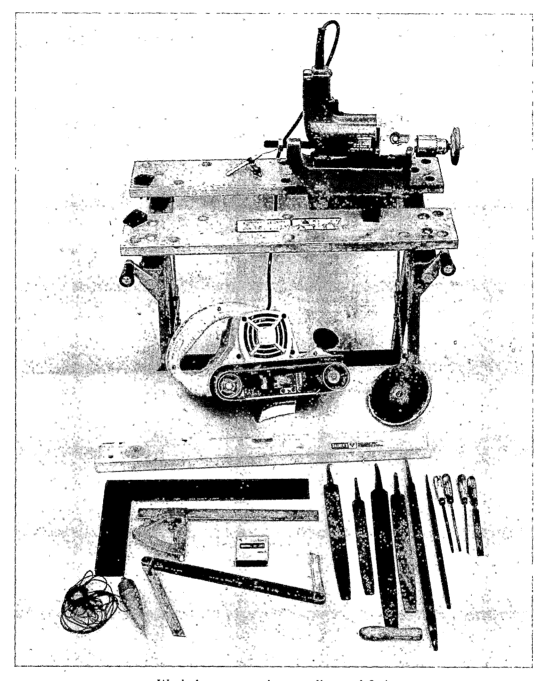

9. Workplace, measuring, sanding and fitting.
From top and left to right. Grindstone from drill in horizontal stand, Black & Decker Workmate bench, belt sander, sanding disc for drill, level, square, adjustable square, 10-foot tape, plumb line, angle gauge, rasps and files.

on trestles will do. You will also need, mounted on this, a 4 in (10 cm) steel vice, if you intend to tackle anything more than light joinery. A couple of trestles, incidentally, are a good investment anyway.

B MEASURING

A steel tape, minimum length 10 ft (3 m) is the first necessity. A broad, good-quality tape, that will reach out 4 foot and more without flopping is a great advantage if you work on your own, and it should have a lock to prevent it rolling back. For fine work, some people like a folding rule, but the tape does equally well. In the same way, I have found that ordinary pencils are just as good, if not better, than flat carpenters' pencils.

Every other cut in boat joinery is off-square, so you cannot do without an angle gauge or sliding bevel. Another near vital measuring tool is a combination square, i.e. one which slides along a steel rule. It can be used for measuring, marking and scribing without actually reading off any figures, and is usually fitted with a bubble level and 45° edge as well.

Straight-edges, 3 ft and 9 ft can be of timber (good-quality clear pine), and if you can run to the cost of a 3 ft (1 m) steel rule, so much the better. I have also found that a straight-edge of Formica sheet, 3 in (7.5 cm) wide, finds many applications, as it will curve to the boat in one direction, but remain straight in the other.

C DRILLING

An electric drill is far and away the most important power tool. It should, preferably, be a ½ in (13 mm) size, consuming about 400 watts, and with two speeds, the higher one roughly 2000 r.p.m. for wood, and the lower, 1000 r.p.m. or less for metal. Numerous attachments are available, but these are generally much inferior to separate power units. Of most use are the various bits: a set of twist drills, obviously; spade bits for easy wood drilling; hole saws; a rose bit (countersunk); and, above all, for rapid screw-sinking, 3 in 1 Stanley bits, each bit being specific to one size of screw (see Fig. 14, p. 60). Plug cutters are also specific to screw size, but Nos. 8 and 10 will cover nearly all work. Plug cutting really demands a drill stand, which is handy too for metal drilling and other jobs; a light, D.I.Y.-type stand is fine. Another useful drill attachment is a right-angle or flexible drive, as boatwork often demands drilling in constricted corners. An alternative is the 12-volt Versatool drill which is compact enough to be held in one hand. Hand drills should likewise be short, and half braces, comprising only a palm pad and ratchet handle, can occasionally be found.

D SAWING

The quality of hand saws ranges from the superb to junk that should be directed to the nearest dustbin before it can damage any wood. Pointers to quality are: when

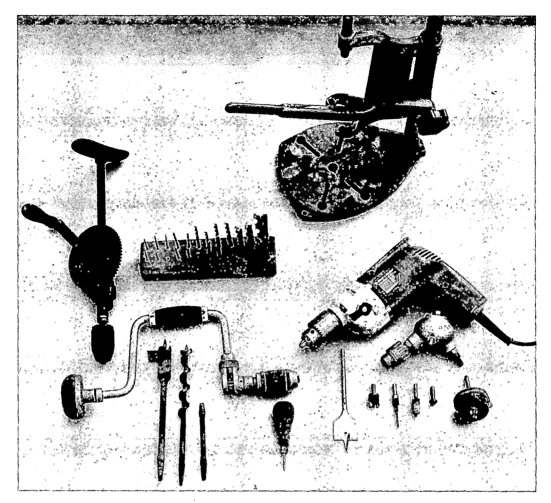

10. Drilling.
From top and left to right. Drill stand, hand drill, set of twist drills, brace with
(underneath) adjustable bit, wood bit and screwdriver bit, bradawl, $\frac{1}{2}$-inch power
drill and (underneath) spade bit, plug cutter, Stanley 3 in 1 countersink, rotary
file, rosebit, hole saw.

grasped by the handle and tapped at the end of the blade, a good spring steel will ring
clear for a long time; good steel will also spring back quickly after being bent; the
finest blades are thinner at the top than at the teeth, making for easy cutting; handles
should be good-quality, and fixed with at least four rivets; plastic, anti-stick coating
is of no advantage, as it rubs off in due course. Ideally, you need a cross-cut saw of 8
to 9 teeth per inch, a rip saw of about 5 teeth per inch (cross-cut and rip teeth are

differently shaped), and a tenon saw of 12 to 14 teeth per inch, for jointing. Keyhole and other saws are listed in Table 1, p. 36.

Skill in using a saw is something one acquires with practice, but I pass on one, little known technique for ripping long, thick planks. You stand behind the saw, i.e. with the teeth facing away from you, and drive it with long, slightly circular strokes, both hands clasped on top of the handle, and the blade working between your legs. It is a powerful and tireless action, compared with the usual kneeling posture which twists the spine. Furthermore, cutting is more accurate, as you can see exactly where you are going. The first couple of inches, incidentally, should be started in the usual way. In point of fact, though, the greatest skill in sawing is keeping a really sharp, correctly set saw. Sharpening should be done frequently, with a triangular saw file, clamping the blade just below the teeth between a pair of hardwood strips. Frequent

11. Sawing.
Rise and fall 12-inch circular saw table with fence and mitre guide. Behind the table, support roller, height-adjustable with G clamps on legs. On the table *l. to r.* Cross-cut saw, rip saw, jigsaw, tenon saw in Jointmaster jig, coping saw, junior hacksaw and hacksaw.

41

setting is also well worth the trouble; it is done gently, using a small hand setter which can be bought at modest cost. From time to time the saw should be sent off to the saw doctor for a complete level, sharpen and set.

Of the power saws, a jigsaw is the one to buy first. With it you can cut ply over your knee, in a confined space, rapidly chop battens to length, and cut curves. Because of queer boat angles, the table *must* tilt. For a big job, a circular saw bench will pay for itself in wood costs alone; you buy in bulk and cut exactly what you need. The saw must rise and fall, preferably tilt too, though that is not essential, and be able to cut to a minimum depth of 3 in (7.5 cm), i.e. about a 10 in (25 cm) blade. A tungsten-carbide-tipped blade is very expensive but pays for itself on a long job, particularly with hardwoods, and like some other, no-set blades, it gives a narrow cut, and a virtually planed finish. A home-made roller trestle with height adjustment, of the type shown in Photo 11, is invaluable when handling large timbers. A circular saw will groove and rebate as well as rip; for this, a wobble blade is useful but not essential. The same can be said of a band saw, which should again have a tilting table. Guillotines are now available to cut wood mitres and ends with impeccable accuracy, but they are only really justified for a professional.

Safety. It is perhaps, prudent at this point to mention safety, power woodworking tools being highly dangerous machines, as the number of fingers missing in any large joinery shop will testify. The circular saw is one of the most lethal, and even spinning slowly with the power off, is able to slice off a finger before you can feel it. The basic rule is *never to lean past the blade*. Use a notched stick to push the work through, and walk round to retrieve it. The roller trestle, mentioned above, is a great aid to keeping the timber under control from the front of the bench. The other danger arises from cross-cutting large pieces, with hands placed either side of the saw; the blade is likely to snatch the wood and hurl it at you. This can also happen if ripping without a splitting knife behind the blade.

E PLANING AND SHAPING

The common feature of all planing and shaping tools is some sort of cutting blade, and if you are working with hardwoods, make every effort to get tungsten vanadium steel (not tungsten-carbide-tipped). Only a high-quality steel will hold an edge. Essential tools are a general-purpose, 9 in plane, a set of chisels, a spokeshave, and a half-round Surform for hollows. For joinery work, a bullnose rebate plane is indispensable, and further planes are needed for more advanced work. Top of the list is a 14 in (35 cm) jack plane, for straightening longer edges. Next, and much cheaper, is a block plane, with an adjustable throat; this is a small, single-handed plane, with no capping iron, used on edges and on end grain, for which work the throat is adjusted to a fine gap. For straightening long plank or plywood edges, a try plane of about 22 inches (55 cm) is needed; these are very costly, so it is worth looking for an old wooden one.

12. Planing.
From top and left to right. Hand power-plane upside down in stand and fitted with fence, chisels, curved Surforms, wooden jack plane, wooden try plane, spokeshave, smoothing plane, bullnose plane, power router with bits.

The adjustment of planes is a subtle affair. The distance that the cutting edge projects beyond the capping iron affects the coarseness of the cut; a large projection ($\frac{1}{16}$ in or 1.5 mm) is suitable for softwood and deeper cuts, while for end grain and hardwoods with wild grain (mahogany, especially, has a nasty tendency to reverse grain) the projection should be reduced to a hair's breadth. The same conditions demand that the throat be narrowed, which is done on a normal smoothing plane by moving the frog (on which the plane iron rests) forward, with the adjusting screws provided. The plane iron on a smoothing plane can also be angled sideways, to ease one corner clear of the wood for trimming edges (see Fig. 11a), and for working your

43

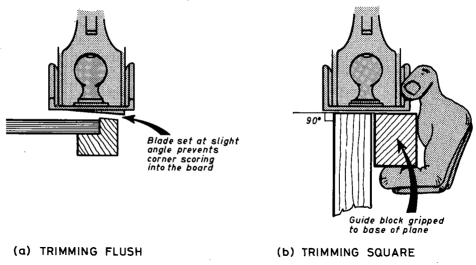

Blade set at slight angle prevents corner scoring into the board

90°

Guide block gripped to base of plane

(a) TRIMMING FLUSH   **(b) TRIMMING SQUARE**

Figure 11. PLANING

way across a wide board; this avoids score marks. Fig. 11b illustrates how to square off an edge, using a wooden block as a guide.

Using a plane correctly is a skill that takes some time to acquire, but here are a couple of points. Stand in a relaxed and easy position, twisted spines inevitably resulting in twisted work; correct height for planing is about 3 ft (90 cm). Plane with the grain. When planing end grain, work towards the centre, to avoid splintering the wood off the far edge. If you want to peel off large quantities of material from a wide plank, plane mainly directly across the grain; this also keeps the plank flat in both directions. It helps a lot when planing the stickier woods to rub the sole of the plane with a candle. Above all, keep the iron SHARP, see *Tool Husbandry*, below. A plane that is hard to work, sticks, or chatters, is either blunt or maladjusted.

Many people still use old-style wooden planes, which are relatively light and don't rust. To adjust the blade, first jam it in an approximate position with a rap on the wooden wedge, turn the plane over, and sight along the bottom surface. To reduce the cut, tap the back of the plane sharply with a mallet, to increase the cut, tap the blade in; blade angle is adjusted by tapping the blade sideways.

A hand power-plane is a fine tool for gouging away quantities of wood, rather like a mechanical adze; but a bench type, or a hand plane clamped upside down, is needed for quality work. However, top of my power list would not be a plane, but a router, a tool that spins differently-shaped cutters at about 20,000 r.p.m. The most important cutters for boat work are rounding-over ones (self-guiding by means of a pin running along the edge of the wood), which give really professional edges to fiddles, trim, handgrips and so on; three sizes are needed, with radii of $\frac{1}{4}$, $\frac{3}{8}$ and

44

½ inches (6, 10, 13 mm). Straight cutters of ⅛, ¼ and ⅜ in diameter (3, 6, 10 mm) are used mainly for gouging out holes to exact depths, but do not expect a low-power router to groove long lengths. There are many more cutter shapes, but the frightening price of these prohibits proliferation.

F   SCREWING, CLAMPING, HAMMERING

The tools here are all fairly self-evident (and all for joinery, notwithstanding the title). It seems that one never has enough clamps, so it's a good idea to look for second-hand ones. By far the handiest kind for joinery are the sliding cramps (Photo 13), which can be operated rapidly, and with one hand, but you also need a few 'G' cramps, which do not vibrate loose. Sash cramps can be bought complete, or you can just buy the ends for fitting to lengths of wood or piping.

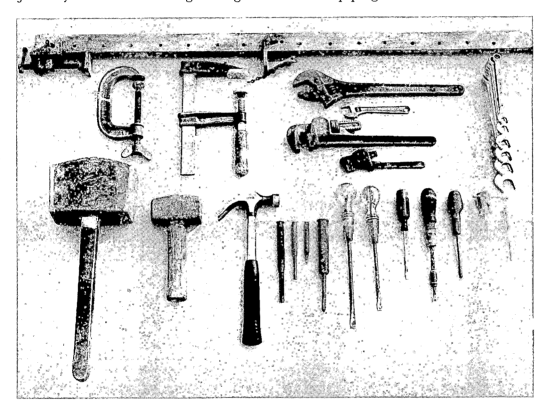

13. Screwing, Clamping, Hammering.
From top and left to right. Sash cramp (on wood bar), G cramp, sliding cramp, adjustable spanners, set spanners, wooden mallet, small sledge hammer, claw hammer, flat punches and centre punch, screwdrivers, yankee screwdriver, Philips and tommy bar screwdrivers.

G SANDING AND FILING

Again, a self-evident set of tools except perhaps for the power sanders. There are four types—the disc, orbital, belt, and bench disc. The **disc sander** removes a lot of material, but leaves an uneven finish, and for the rare occasions when it is needed, a disc stuck into a drill is adequate. It absorbs a lot of power, however, so be on guard against burning out the drill. An **orbital sander** is purely a finishing tool, but even so a finishing touch by hand is needed, to obliterate the whorls that show up under varnish. A few machines are fitted with an alternative to and fro motion, for wiping out the whorls and sanding hard up to edges. An orbital machine should run at a speed of not less than 6000 oscillations per minute.

Belt sanders are, by comparison, powerful machines for flattening and smoothing. They smooth the most cross-grained wood, and are undoubtedly one of the most useful of power tools. I also find them invaluable for flushing off and rounding over joinery after gluing, especially when end grain has to be removed. In addition, chisels, plane irons and so on can be ground roughly but accurately, by clamping the sander upside down, and fitting a metal sanding belt. Best sanding-belt grades are 40-grit for heavy work, and 100-grit for fine finish.

A **bench disc sander** consists of a vertical sanding disc, abutted by a horizontal table, which is adjustable and fitted with a sliding mitre. Consequently, the end of timber pieces can be flatted perfectly to any angle, as well as rounded over, smoothed, etc. If you are intending to do a lot of joinery, this is a machine to consider seriously.

H VARIOUS

Certain additional tools—pliers, cold chisel, small punch for counter sinking panel pins—are essential right at the start. Others, like tin snips and pop riveter, are needed as one's scope expands. A selection is given in Table 1 (p. 37), but it is impossible to cover them all, as ingenious new tools are always appearing on the market. Some—a small rotary sander attachment consisting of a sheaf of tiny sandpaper squares, and an adjustable template made of little sliding pins, to mention but two—I have found all but worthless. Others, like the stubby screwdriver with a mini crowbar through the handle for getting into tight corners, have become indispensable. In this latter category, two things are worth special mention. First, a proper wandering lead attached to a multi-point, 13 amp socket head, with at least 3 and preferably 4 sockets. It only needs a wandering light, a drill, jigsaw and sander to occupy 4 sockets, and the growth of adaptor upon adaptor, with the accompanying worm's nest of wires, is both inconvenient and dangerous. Although for safety's sake all power tools must be double insulated—particularly important in a marine environment—the multi-socket should be fitted with an earth and its own 13 amp fuse. Secondly, an old vacuum cleaner of the cylinder type is a tremendous

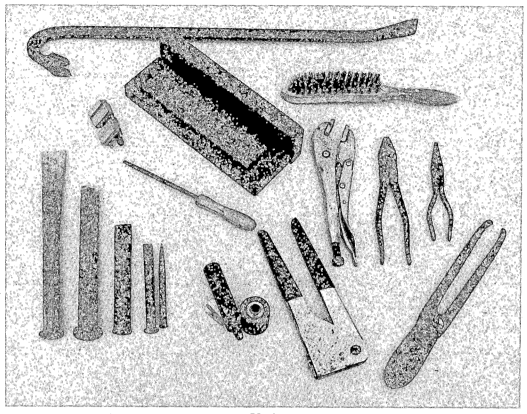

14. Various
From top and left to right. Crowbar, honing guide, oilstone, wire brush, saw file,
vicegrips and pliers, cold chisels, setting punch for brass eyelets, pop riveter,
tinsnips.

asset in the limited confines of a boat, for maintaining an orderly work area. With a
reversed tube, it can also be used to dry out damp spots, or to warm glue in dark
places on a cold day.

Included in this heading are jigs. The scarf box and angle-iron clamping bed have
already been described, but even more essential is a saw guide for accurate cutting
with a tenon saw. Guides range from a simple, open wooden-box type with 90° and
45° cuts in the sides to guide the saw, to sophisticated cast iron affairs, which clamp
the saw on a sliding traveller. I have found the Joint Master a handy and versatile jig,
though a trifle on the light side for serious use; it wears quickly, and if you intend to
work it hard, it is advisable to have a set of spares to hand.

Though not strictly a jig, a bench hook is a must (Fig. 12). It provides a stop to
hold the workpiece against, protects the bench, and is used for both chiselling and

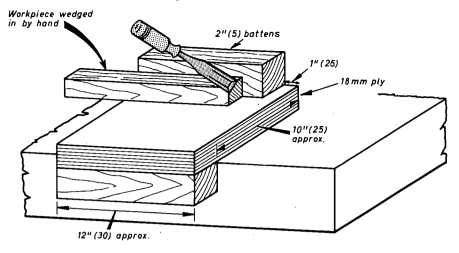

Figure 12. BENCH HOOK

sawing. As can be seen from the illustration, it can be knocked up in a few minutes from off-cuts.

I TOOL HUSBANDRY

'Just keep your tools sharp', is the advice shipwrights tend to hand out on almost any kind of problem. It sounds trite, but never was a truer word spoken. You ought to be able to shave with your chisels, using your saw blade as a mirror. Sharpening saws has already been discussed (p. 41); for chisels and plane irons, proceed as follows.

Use a combination fine and coarse oilstone, keep it in a tailor-made wooden box, and lubricate with light machine, household type oil. Wipe it clean after use, and if it shows signs of clogging, sponge it down with paraffin.

Place the chisel, or plane iron, on the stone at the correct angle, about 25° for plane irons and fine paring chisels, 30° for average chisels (Fig. 13). The angle will often be stamped on the iron. If the bevel is already at the correct angle, rock the iron slightly, until a bead of oil, squeezed out along the edge, shows that the bevel is flush on the stone. Then, pressing down as close to the edge as possible, rub in a circular, scribbling track, the purpose of which is to wear the stone evenly and keep it flat. The difficulty is to maintain the same angle all the time; I find it helpful to keep the wrists and forearms stiff. When you can feel a slight burr along the edge of the flat side of the iron, turn it over, lay it flat on the stone, and rub the burr off. If the burr re-appears on the reverse side of the edge, repeat the whole procedure with a few light strokes. The edge will then be literally razor sharp. The final touch is very slightly to round the corners of a smoothing plane iron. An iron that is very blunt needs honing on the coarse stone first, and if it is badly mauled, or off-square, some power treatment

48

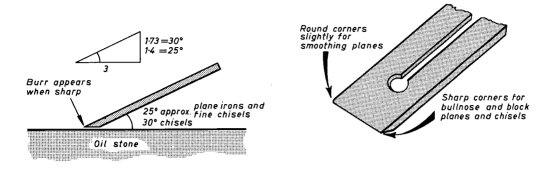

Figure 13. SHARPENING PLANES AND CHISELS

beforehand. As noted above, a belt sander, clamped upside down, is a convenient tool.

Little wheeled guides are sold, which keep the iron at an accurate angle while sharpening, and they certainly make for a good edge. But they wear a hollow in the stone, and I use mine only for a periodic tune up. If the stone develops hollows, it can be levelled by rubbing on a flat, concrete floor, swabbing repeatedly with paraffin (kerosene).

Not only plane irons need constant attention to keep them in fettle. Screwdrivers must be regularly honed to terminate in a square, level end, with sharp edges that fit snug in the screw slots. Twist drills are usually sharpened on a bench grinder, though a fine-grit, metal sanding disc, or even a belt sander, will do. If you feel flush, you can buy an electric twist-drill grinder, or at least a special sharpening guide. Router bits present problems: flat-edge ones can be laboriously honed on an oilstone, but normally it is advisable to send dull bits to the saw doctor. Hammers become pitted and rounded over with long use, and need to be trued on a grindstone, as do punches. Power tools also get tired, and demand attention. And everything should be regularly cleaned and oiled.

All in all, tools need constant maintenance if they are to give the best results, and their husbandry is an integral part of joinery and other handiwork.

7. Glues and Sealants

Fish glue or boiled hooves? That, roughly, was the choice in days gone by, and for sealant you used linseed putty and red lead. Glues today are infinitely superior, but there is a penalty. They are also infinitely more complex, and a complete description of the thousand and more formulations available in Britain alone (there are many more in the U.S. and elsewhere) would be neither possible nor useful. Instead, I have looked only at those glues which could be useful on boats, classified them into general types, and described their general properties. Appendix D summarises the most important of these properties, and gives a number of trade names, but the fact that a glue is mentioned does not imply that it is the only, or indeed the best, of its class.

For further aid in the selection of glue types, refer to Table 2, which matches the adhesive to the adherend. If there are two adherends—say, wood and fibre-glass—choose the adhesive which best applies to both, in this case an epoxy.

Table 2 – Adhesive Selection

Adherend

Adhesive	Wood	GRP	Metals	Ferro	Rubber	Fabrics & Foam	Plastics*
Resorcinol	A		C	B		A	C
Urea	A					B	
Epoxies	A	A	A	A	B	A	B
Reactive Acrylics	B	A	A	B		Y	B
Cyanacrylates		B	C		A		B
Anaerobics		C	A				C
PVA	Y			Y		A	
Contacts	C		B	C	A	Y	B
Hot melt (veneer strip)	B						

* (N.B. Polythene, Teflon and some other plastics can only be poorly bonded)
A – excellent
B – good
C – moderate
Y – good bond but has other limitations

A   USE OF GLUES

Unfortunately the selection of glues cannot be separated from their properties in use. If you are gluing in the bilges, in winter, a high-performance glue that needs precise temperature control will fail before a lower-grade, but less sensitive glue. Gluing is one of the nastier aspects of joinery, and a messy glue will usually result in a worse job than an easily handled one, whatever the other properties. Also, cost, strength, storage life and many other aspects affect the choice of adhesive. Listed below are the principal factors to be considered when gluing.

i. Setting Action
Glues are applied and set in six different ways:

- Liquid loss, where the liquid part of the glue is absorbed to leave a solid glue line (e.g. PVA). This type is very easy to use, but may shrink as it sets. It will only work if at least one adherend is absorbent.
- Contact, where the liquid is allowed to evaporate first, before the two glued surfaces are pressed together. This has the advantage of instant bonding. Adhesive tapes are a variation.
- Liquid setting, e.g. cyanacrylates, where the glue reacts with the atmosphere, or the joint itself, to set solid. Again, easy to use, but the range of glues is rather limited.
- Multipart, where the setting reaction is initiated by mixing two (sometimes three) components. Sometimes, the components are applied separately to each surface. Multipart glues are by far the most difficult to use, but also, unfortunately, there is a great range, possessing properties which make them indispensable.
- Hot melt is a solid, which is melted in place, and solidifies almost immediately afterwards, an action which has advantages for certain applications.
- Solid two-part, where both parts come ready mixed as a powder, and are activated by heating, or occasionally by wetting. The first type is used only in high-performance engineering applications. The second is a urea, like Cascamite.

ii. Gap Filling

The ability of a glue to bridge gaps without weakening or crazing is a most important requirement for boat work, where joints are often irregular. Gap-filling ability varies from a few thousandths of an inch for cyanacrylates, to half an inch or more for epoxies. Average values are indicated in Appendix D.

It is worth noting that the thinner the glue line, the stronger it is (provided the joint is not starved by overclamping), because a thin line will flex, where a thick one would crack.

iii. Strength

High strength seems obviously desirable, but it is one of the most difficult properties to define in practice. Paper glue, for instance, is feeble stuff, yet an envelope seal is stronger than the paper itself, and using a costly resorcinol would not improve the strength of the envelope one whit. In other words, strength of bond must be related to joint design, in this instance strength being derived from a generous overlapping bond area.

Joint design should always aim at as large a glue area as possible, and this should be at right angles to the forces trying to pull it apart, because glues are strongest under a sliding (or shear) action. When pulling apart directly (tension), glue is weaker, and under cleavage (as when breaking a butt joint) weaker still. The feeblest glue action is against peeling; if you bond something, like a strip of wood to GRP, it is wise to bolt or pin the ends somehow. The peeling action then cannot start, and the bond will endure. Another precaution is to avoid abrupt changes in the thickness of material; a butt strap joint, for instance, should be chamfered, as shown in Fig. 5, p. 22.

To return to our envelope, in a steamy atmosphere the paper glue would fail, so again, strength is dependent on service conditions, and in boats, it is the glue strength after several years in a marine environment that matters. To complicate matters further, there are two other qualities that affect strength, viz:

(a) Flexibility is extremely important with wood, and especially on a boat, for a flexible glue will give and redistribute stresses, whereas a brittle glue will simply crack. This is the theory underlying the new 'toughened' glues, that incorporate certain rubbers within the chemical structure to act as molecular shock absorbers. Many epoxy failures on wood joints are due to excessive brittleness, and you should use glues that are as flexible as possible.

(b) Structural adhesives are those which can carry heavy permanent loads, like laminated beams, without distortion. They are generally *thermosetting* glues, i.e. they set by chemical reaction, and cannot be softened by heat or solvents and then allowed to harden again. They are typically two-part adhesives.

Non-structural adhesives, (contacts, PVA) creep under sustained loads, but are perfectly safe for joinery subject to intermittent loads. These adhesives are normally *thermoplastic*, the opposite of thermosetting.

iv. Durability

Durability of wood adhesives is classified by British Standards (BS 1203 and 1204) as:

WBP: waterproof and boilproof. Highest resistance to boiling water, cold and exposure.

BR: boil resistant. Good resistance to boiling water and weather, but fail on long exposure to weather where WBP survives.

MR: moisture resistant. Survives exposure to weather for only a few years. Withstands long immersion in cold water but only limited immersion in hot.

INT: interior. Withstands some immersion in cold water, and need not, like the others, resist biological attack

All joints that are both exterior and structural on a boat should preferably be WBP. Only resorcinol and phenolic adhesives have this grading. For most others, BR is adequate, but for interior joinery not heavily loaded, MR is sufficient.

v. Workability

All the theoretical properties of a glue are eyewash if the man on the job (likely to be working upside down, in the dead of winter, or under a broiling sun) cannot apply it properly. Things to look for are:

Consistency. A thin glue is needed for large and/or close fitting areas, and a thick one for gap filling. It is essential that the latter is not only thick, but thixotropic, or non-slump, as well, especially for vertical surfaces. For some epoxies, both thick and thin are obtainable in the one glue by adding fillers (see p. 56).

Stringiness is a vile characteristic of some glues and invariably makes for messy and low-grade work.

Pot life is the time between mixing, or applying, the glue and setting. Sometimes you need instant setting, but with general and joinery work, a setting time of about four hours, and a life in the pot of at least two hours is ideal. This gives you time to glue up a job, clamp it overnight, and work on it the following morning. All reactive glues set faster the higher the temperature. The rule of thumb here is, a rise of 18°F (10°C) will halve the setting time, 36°F will quarter it, and so on.

Moisture and Temperature Tolerance. Different glues show different tolerance to damp and cold, both the enemies of good bonding. Ureas need drier wood than resorcinols, but will set satisfactorily at slightly lower temperatures. Epoxies vary widely in tolerance, some being able to glue wringing wet wood. PVAs are fairly tolerant all round, but contacts dislike moisture. And most glues are oil haters, except for acrylics, solvent cements, and anaerobics which can tolerate surface greasiness.

Clamping requirements are often closely related to gap filling. Urea is a poor gap-filling glue, and needs high clamping pressures to bond strongly, whereas epoxies fill well and need no pressure clamping at all.

Cleaning. Being able to wash hands and tools with water is a big plus. Not only is the glue easier to handle, but keeping things clean greatly boosts the quality of the work. Glues that need special solvents to clean them off—this is a drawback with many epoxies—are messy, unpleasant, more costly, and bad for the skin.

Hazards. Toxicity, odour and flammability are all factors that affect your work, and a glue might well be unacceptable on account of its foul smell alone.

vi. Safety

But most modern glues are hazardous to some degree, and it is prudent to pay close attention to the manufacturer's warnings and recommendations. Some manufacturers issue safety manuals, and a brochure on safe handling can be obtained from The British Adhesive Manufacturer's Association, 20 Pylewell Road, Hythe, Southampton. In general, precautions amount to care and commonsense in use, but the following is worth noting:

Anything containing solvents is likely to be flammable or toxic or both, and the work space should be well ventilated. Eyes are especially vulnerable. I also keep a couple of aerosol, BCF-type of fire extinguishers handy, as much for wood shavings as for solvents. The chlorohydrocarbons—trichlorethylene is a common one—are not especially flammable, but prolonged inhalation can permanently damage your kidneys.

Epoxies, and more particularly their hardeners, are generally dermatitic—some authorities even say carcinogenous—and contact with the skin should be minimal. This applies to a lesser degree also to resorcinols and ureas, both of which tend to give off acid fumes which sting the eyes. Cyanacrylates bond strongly to skin. Finally, precautions should be taken against inhalation of glue powders and fillers.

vii. Other Properties

Colour is important, as dark glue lines are frequently unacceptable. Resorcinol is often rejected for this reason. The ideal colour, I have found, is a clear amber, which blends nicely with all brownish woods, to camouflage my poor workmanship. Alternatively, use a colourless glue.

When set, the glue must be capable of being planed and sanded. Most glues pass muster, exceptions being rubber-base glues, hot melts, and epoxies heavily filled with silica that set bone hard.

Finally, cost and storage life must be considered, and clearly, the cheapest glue you can get that will do the job is the one to use. The unavoidable wastage, when using two-part glues, adds greatly to their cost, and when you use this type, try and get one where the mix ratio is a straight 1:1, and non-critical at that.

All these points are pertinent to the choice and use of glues, and as far as possible I have tried to cover them in the following discussion, and in Appendix D.

B TYPES OF GLUES

Adhesives are such a cookbook technology, that there is no universally accepted classification; setting action, however, provides a convenient basis for grouping.

i. Chemical Setting

All these glues set to a solid by changing their chemical composition. They are all thermosetting and structural, and comprise most of the modern, high-performance adhesives.

The first two are basically wood glues; when they set, they release water, which must be absorbed by the wood.

(a) Resorcinol-formaldehyde is one of the two most durable glues known (phenol formaldehyde is the other), and will powerfully bond wood-to-wood, provided that temperatures are above about 50° F and preferably 60° F (10°–15° C), moisture content of the wood below 18 per cent and clamping is strong and even but not too severe. Gap filling is moderate—20 thousandths of an inch (0.5 mm) and up to 50 thou. (1.25 mm) at a pinch. Resorcinol is a thick, red-brown resin, fairly easy to apply with paint brush, and to wash off with water. The two parts are either liquid to liquid, ratio 1:1, or liquid/powder, and setting time is around 4 to 8 hours. I find the liquid to liquid easier to use. Cost is relatively high, and storage is at least one year.

The main use for resorcinol is in laminated wooden structures and high-class joints, but it will also stick plastic laminates, expanded polystyrene, asbestos board and concrete, nylon and leather.

(b) Urea-formaldehydes are less durable glues (usually MR or, at the most, BR), but much cheaper than resorcinol. Ureas survive longer immersed in water than when exposed to the weather. Gap-filling ability is less than half that of resorcinol, and close-fitting joints with high clamping pressures are needed. Wood must be drier—preferably no more than 15 per cent moisture—but many ureas will set satisfactorily at $40°$–$50°$ F ($5°$–$10°$ C).

Ureas are usually white powders which are mixed into a colourless, thick liquid with water. The hardener is either an acid, painted on the opposite face (Aerolite 300), or it is incorporated in the powder (Cascamite). Both types are fairly easy to use applied with a toothbrush, the Aerolite being better for large jobs, and the Cascamite for small ones. In fact, the main application for Cascamite is probably in cabin joinery, a spot of glue being quick to mix in a little plastic pot, where it remains usable for several hours.

Ureas will also glue plastic laminate.

There are two other condensation wood glues, blended sometimes with those above, but not generally available because of usage problems. One is phenol formaldehyde, used to glue all marine and WBP plywood. The other is melamine formaldehyde, used largely to upgrade ureas to BR durability.

(c) Epoxies cover such an enormous range of formulations that it is difficult to generalise. Their main attribute is that they are 100 per cent solids (no liquid or gas emissions), setting to a stable resin. Their capacity for gap filling, therefore, is theoretically infinite, though in practice one should not exceed about $\frac{1}{4}$ in (6 mm), because of joint movement. Pressure clamping is not required, though the pieces must, of course, be held rigidly in position until the glue has set. The other characteristic of epoxies is that they form strong bonds with most materials, so they are very suitable for gluing dissimilar materials. For gluing wood to GRP, ferro and metals, epoxies are the first choice. On steel and ferro, epoxies perform particularly well, having similar expansion characteristics. GRP may present problems, and you should be certain that the epoxy used is recommended for the job. Bonds with rubber and plastics are moderate to poor. Polythene, Teflon and, to a lesser extent, Delrin, can only be bonded very badly.

But how do you set about choosing an epoxy from the bewildering variety available?

There is no easy answer. You can listen to recommendations by other yachtsmen/builders/salesmen; you can ponder the desirable properties listed above, matching them to available glues, but in the long run personal experience is what tells. There are some further guide lines, however. If the glue has a non-critical mix ratio, about 1:1, and a faintly sweetish, inoffensive smell, then it is likely to be a polyamide. These have excellent, all-round adhesion, high moisture tolerance and a reasonable flexibility. But their resistance to water is generally lower than other types, and they may cure slowly at low temperatures.

Epoxies with simple mix ratios, around 30 or 40:100, and a strong solvent smell, are probably aromatic amine-based. They set well at low temperatures, and are very durable, but tend to be too brittle for general boat use.

Epoxies with exacting mix ratios, around 10:100, are probably aliphatic amines, with durability and curing temperatures intermediate between the other two.

Rapid-setting (5 minutes) epoxies have poor bond performance, and should be used only for quick repair jobs.

Epoxies are costly glues, but have a long storage life. Certain epoxies are sold specially for boat use. West claims to be a complete system for gluing and stabilising the wood by sealing it. It is not easy to use, having a critical 20:100 mix ratio, and a short, even violently short, pot life in hot weather. It sets brittle, and adhesion to GRP is poor. Peredite is, in many respects, ideal; a 1:1 mix ratio, a clear amber colour, strong adhesion to most materials aboard, and a good flexibility. Peredite has the great advantage that it can be washed off with water before setting. In fact, it is water miscible, i.e. it will glue damp materials, and can actually be mixed with cement to upgrade the mortar—very useful on a ferro boat. The drawback with the glue is that, like all polyamides, resistance to water may be slightly lower than in other epoxies.

Fillers can be used with many epoxies—some, like West, are sold with fillers, to adjust gap-filling and flow properties.

Cellulose microfibres and wood wool are used for bridging gaps in wood-to-wood joints.

Microspheres and microballoons provide a stiff, lightweight paste for filling and fairing. Easy to sand when set.

Colloidal silica, used in small amounts with other fillers, helps prevent the paste slumping.

Talc powder and Portland cement are cheap materials which, when mixed together, make a paste for gap filling and fairing in non-critical places.

Metals. Aluminium, steel, brass, etc. in flake or powder form are used to ward off degradation by sunlight, or make a simulated metal.

(d) Epoxy blends. Epoxies are blended with other materials to improve certain properties. The three that concern us are:

Epoxy tars are low-cost, and lower-performance, adhesives suitable for rough jobs only. They have high water-resistance, but tend to be brittle. But epoxy tar paints form an excellent protective barrier on steel and ferro hulls.

Epoxy polysulphide is a very flexible and strong adhesive, but has a foul smell. It might be justified in certain big jobs, like gluing a moulded deck to hull.

Toughened epoxies incorporate the rubber monomers, mentioned above, which give them high bond strengths, especially in peel. They are especially suitable for GRP, and especially old GRP which may be difficult to bond.

(e) Reactive acrylics. These are clear, two-part glues, with a bond performance somewhat similar to epoxies. But since the resin and the hardener are applied separately to each surface, and set in less than 20 minutes, these glues are suitable for quickie jobs. They have a high tolerance to grease, and adhere well to metals, so can be used to repair fuel pipes and engineering bits. Drawbacks are gap filling, limited to 20 or may be 50 thou. (0.5 to 1.25 mm), extreme stringiness, strong smell and lower durability than most epoxies. They are also more expensive than epoxies. Toughened types are also available.

(f) Cyanacrylates are the so-called 'wonder glues', which are activated by the adherend itself to set almost instantly. Gap-filling ability is terrible, normally less than 12 thou. (0.25 mm), the glue is extremely brittle and not resistant to moisture. Consequently the main application of cyanacrylates is tiny instant repair jobs, with very close fitting joints. An interesting property is that cyanacrylates bond very powerfully to rubber, and are, therefore suitable for fixing rubber strips to metal and GRP (hatches etc.), and for temporary repair of rubber dinghies. The glue is extremely expensive and stores badly. Two final points: use only minute amounts for proper bonding, and keep it off yourself. It glues flesh most effectively.

(g) Anaerobics set in the absence of oxygen, e.g. a closefitting joint. Used mainly for engineering applications in locking nuts on threads, repair of pin holes in welds, *in situ* gaskets, and fixing bushes in place.

ii. Water Base

PVA emulsion—ordinary white, creamy wood glue—is the only type of water-base glue of interest to us. In most respects PVAs are ideal for joinery: single-part, ready for instant use, not noxious, cheap, and they bond wood very strongly. Gap filling is about 20 thou., but only modest clamping is required. The only drawbacks are that they are not resistant to moisture, and creep under load, so must only be used for lightly loaded interior joinery, that is both fastened, and painted or varnished afterwards. PVAs are resistant to biological attack.

A new breed of reactive PVAs is appearing, with high moisture resistance, but, to date, these glues are neither suitable for general handiwork, nor widely available.

iii. Solvent Base

Solvent based glues applicable to boatwork are mainly contact types, which have the great advantage of instant bonding without clamps or fastenings, essential when veneering with plastic laminates. They are also used for gluing rubber, fabrics and foam plastic (not polystyrene). There are many contact formulations suited to different jobs, among which are rubber inflatables, temporary repair of sails, and bonding rubber to metal. Contacts are generally nonstructural glues, and are not moisture tolerant. Though not really suitable for joinery, a good, general-purpose-type like Bostic No. 3, is handy to have around. Certain high-performance contacts are two-part, and may be applied and allowed to dry, and reactivated with heat or solvent. Handy too, sometimes, is a double-sided tape for holding bits temporarily in place.

iv. Hot Melts

Wooden veneer strip is sold, backed with a hot melt, so that it can be simply ironed on. (Photo 37, p. 132). The glues have fairly good moisture resistance, but are not structural. Small, handyman electric application guns are now available, so the use of hot melts for general joinery may become more popular.

v. Solvents

Solvents can be used as glues with certain plastics. Simply dissolve some plastic chips in the solvent, and use. Perspex, Makrolon (the high strength, polycarbonate hatch 'glass') PVC, ABS and Polystyrene can all be bonded with methyl ethyl ketone (MEK) or, failing that, ethylene dichloride or chloroform.

Polythene, Teflon (Fluon) and Delrin cannot be bonded in this way.

vi. Poor Glues

Ordinary polyester resin used in GRP is not a good adhesive. It is brittle, shrinks badly, and bonding is uncertain. If employed at all, it is best used in conjunction with glass fibre matt or cloth, placed as a fillet, e.g. when bonding bulkheads to hulls.

Animal and vegetable glues are subject to biological attack, and are obsolete.

C   CLEANING

For optimum bonding, a properly cleaned surface is essential, and Appendix D gives the cleaning schedules for various materials.

D   TYPES OF SEALANTS

The dividing line between glues and sealants is rather vague, and products can sometimes be used for both, an example being polysulphide rubber. The number of sealant formulations is again enormous, but the three groups most used on boats are butyl, polysulphide and silicone. Polyurethanes are also used.

i. Butyl Rubbers

Butyl rubber is my recommendation for all general work—bedding down hatches, portholes and so on, to provide a watertight, durable seal. Some manufacturers do not recommend butyls below the waterline, but it is frequently used in closely fitting joints. Butyls are reasonably priced mastics, usually white, supplied ready for use in tubes or gun cartridges, the latter being more economical for anything more than an occasional squirt. Their great advantage is that they never set beyond a certain point, remaining always in a pliable, rubber state, which will always rejoin to itself like chewing gum. They stick well to anything, but cannot be sanded smooth. Do not use them, though, where there is likely to be much fuel or oil about. Their other disadvantage is that they shrink and pull away from gaps of more than about ⅛ in (3 mm).

ii. Polysulphide Rubbers

These are normally two-part sealants (one-part types are available, but slightly inferior), which set to a firm rubber which can be sanded. As such they are often used for caulking decks, but once set, they will not rejoin as will the butyls. Durability is fair, and adhesion is good with the correct primers; but in my experience, the bond with wood tends to fail after a few years. Polysulphides are costly (and you have to mix the entire pack), unpleasant to use, and take several days to set.

iii. Silicone Rubbers

These are usually single-part mastics in tubes or cartridges, that set in a few hours, without shrinkage, to firm and very stable rubbers that are highly weather-resistant. Some can be used under water (refer to manufacturer's recommendation). Their adhesion varies from poor (especially with oily woods) to adequate, and the primers recommended by manufacturers should always be used. Silicones are costly, and their appropriate use in boats is for making a variety of perfect-fit gaskets—port-holes, hatch sealing, instrument dial seating and so on. Encasing electrical connections is another use, as they are excellent insulators, and they can also withstand temperatures as high as 480° F (250° C).

iv. Other Sealants

Like adhesives, a vast range of other sealant formulations is sold, some of which may well find application in interior joinery, because of their lower price. For example, wood bolted to an irregular ferro frame needs only a low-grade sealant. It must, however, be both waterproof, and proof against insect and fungus attack.

8. Fastenings

A SCREWS

Wood screws are the usual type of fastening used in general joinery work. The shank is tapered, with the unthreaded portion designed to pass relatively easily through the top part of the joint. Unless this is drilled to the correct size, therefore, the screw will not squeeze the two parts together. Consequently, screw holes should always be drilled in two sizes, though with small screws and soft wood the minor, bottom hole need be no more than a stab with a bradawl. The appropriate sized holes for different screw sizes are given in Table 3.

As an alternative to twist drills, which have to be changed over every few moments, the 3 in 1 Stanley bit, illustrated in Fig. 14, is more convenient, more rapid and much more accurate. Since these bits are costly, and have a high death rate, it's a good idea to standardize on a few sizes. It makes sense for buying screws too. The

Table 3 – Wood Screws

Size Gauge	Drill sizes (see Fig. 14) inches				Suggested Standard Lengths inches
	1	2	3 Hard woods	Soft woods	
4		$\frac{7}{64}$	awl	awl	$\frac{1}{2}$ $\frac{5}{8}$
6	$\frac{17}{64}$	$\frac{9}{64}$	$\frac{3}{32}$	awl	$\frac{3}{4}$
8	$\frac{5}{16}$	$\frac{11}{64}$	$\frac{3}{32}$	awl	1 $1\frac{1}{4}$
10	$\frac{3}{8}$	$\frac{3}{16}$	$\frac{7}{64}$	$\frac{5}{64}$	$1\frac{1}{2}$ 2
12	$\frac{27}{64}$	$\frac{7}{32}$	$\frac{1}{8}$	$\frac{1}{8}$	$2\frac{1}{2}$
14	$\frac{1}{2}$	$\frac{1}{4}$	$\frac{5}{32}$	$\frac{5}{32}$	3
16	$\frac{17}{32}$	$\frac{9}{32}$	$\frac{3}{16}$	$\frac{3}{16}$	4

most commonly used screws in general joinery I have found in practice to be very roughly as follows: $1\frac{1}{4}$ in × 8, 40 per cent; $1\frac{1}{2}$ in × 10, 25 per cent; 1 in × 8, 20 per cent; 2 in × 10, 5 per cent; $\frac{3}{4}$ in × 6, 5 per cent; the remaining 5 per cent covers usage of this and that. One can, therefore, conveniently get away with two, or at most three, Stanley bits.

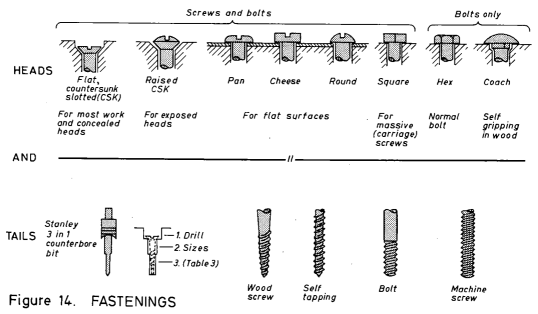

Figure 14.   FASTENINGS

Self-tapping screws have parallel, fully threaded shanks designed to cut threads in thin walled material, and the harder the material, the thinner it must be: steel, up to about $\frac{1}{16}$ in (1.5 mm); aluminium, up to $\frac{1}{8}$ in (3 mm); and GRP to $\frac{1}{4}$ in (6 mm) or thicker. Stainless steel is not suitable for self-tapping. The hole should be fractionally larger than the diameter at the root of the threads. In my experience, however, self-tapping screws hold every bit as effectively in wood as wood screws themselves, provided that two sizes of holes are drilled, as outlined above.

The different types of head and their usages are shown in Fig. 14. Speciality screws, like the square driving slots of Philips, Pozidrive and Supadriv, have been excluded.

B   BOLTS

Bolts are usually used only for heavy structural duties; not only are they stronger, but they pass right through the joint, and do not rely on a thread cut into a weaker material. 'Bolt' in trade jargon means the type where only the end of the shank is threaded; if you want a fully threaded type, which has the advantage that it can be cut to length if too long, ask for 'machine screw'.

Types and sizes of thread are terrifying, in both their multiplicity and their erratic availability. The supply situation in Britain is still in a state of flux, as the changeover to metric takes place. Unlike screws, however, the changeover on bolts is now nearly complete, and I strongly recommend that only I.S.O. metric (coarse thread) bolts are purchased, for reasons of spares and interchangeability. Metric is denoted by the prefix 'M', e.g. M12 × 100, means 12 mm dia. and 100 mm long.

The commonly available metric sizes, together with the older, Whitworth equivalents, are given in Table 4; 6, 10, 12, and possibly 8 mm diameter will cover nearly every application in a boat.

The various head designs are shown in Fig. 14. It is advisable to use washers on non-countersunk types, and under every nut.

If you only use the occasional bolt, it is hardly worth while laying in a stock of odd sizes on the off-chance that they will one day find a home. The best thing here is to buy threaded rod, and make your bolts as required, using a nut for the head. Pein the rod end over slightly with a hammer, to prevent the nut unscrewing; to prevent it screwing down the rod, pop three holes with a centre punch round the junction of nut and rod at the top. Locktite anaerobic glue will do the same job.

Table 4 – Bolts
Metric Sizes (Whitworth Standard Equivalent)

Length mm (inches)	Diameter mm (inches)				
	6($\frac{1}{4}$)	8($\frac{5}{8}$)	10($\frac{3}{8}$)	12($\frac{1}{2}$)	16($\frac{5}{8}$)
10($\frac{3}{8}$)					
12($\frac{1}{2}$)					
16($\frac{5}{8}$)					
20($\frac{3}{4}$)					
25(1)					
30(1$\frac{1}{4}$)					
35					
40(1$\frac{1}{2}$)					
45($\frac{3}{4}$)					
50(2)					
55(2$\frac{1}{4}$)					
60					
65(2$\frac{1}{2}$)					
70					
75(3)					
80					
90(3$\frac{1}{2}$)					
100(4)					
110					
120(4$\frac{1}{2}$)					
130(5)					
140					
150(6)					
up to 500(12) occasionally					

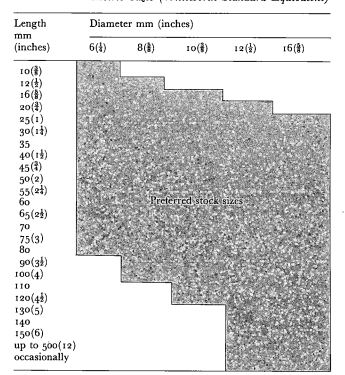

Preferred stock sizes

C NAILS

Ordinary steel wire nails must never be used anywhere on a boat, as they rust like the devil, but hot-dip galvanised nails are permissible in rough work and in conjunction with glue.

Serrated bronze and occasionally Monel nails ('Gripfast' or 'Anchorfast') can be used instead of screws, provided that one can hammer home on a solid base wi'h no 'bounce'. In hardwood, and for larger sizes, pilot holes, about half the nail diameter, must first be bored. Like steel nails, 'Gripfast' are sold in diameters from $\frac{1}{16}$ to $\frac{3}{16}$ inches (1.5 to 4.5 mm), and in lengths from $\frac{1}{2}$ to 3 inches (1.3 to 7.5 cm), and occasionally up to 6 inches. While used on structural work, they find only certain application in joinery. Old-fashioned copper roves and iron dumps find virtually no application at all in joinery.

Of much greater importance are brass panel pins, used usually in conjunction with glue, for fastening wooden trim in place. The pins are lightly countersunk with a small punch, after which they are hardly visible under varnish, thereby saving a good deal of fuss with plugging or drilling. You will need two sizes: ¾ in (18 mm) and 1 in (25 mm), both approximately 18 gauge. An alternative to brass pins is the galvanised, square steel type, available at builders' merchants. Being stronger, they are suited to heavier work and to very hard wood which buckles brass pins.

D   MATERIALS

Taking into account considerations of strength, corrosion resistance and availability, stainless steel is probably the best all-round material for fastenings in joinery, and should be used whenever your pocket permits. Having said that, stainless steel should not be regarded as a panacea to all your fastening problems, for there are several important qualifications in its use.

First, though costly and often difficult to obtain, only the molybdenum, or marine grade, Type 316 (also called EN58J) is properly resistant against marine conditions. For most duties, however, the usual 18/8 variety—the numbers refer to percentage chrome and nickel respectively—will serve. Never use marstonitic stainless steel, easily detected by a magnet.

Secondly, even Type 316 can suffer serious corrosion under water when part of the fastening lies in stagnant water trapped in a hole while the head is exposed to open water. Since stainless steel relies on a supply of oxygen dissolved in the water for its corrosion resistance, the concealed portion will be attacked. Shielding corrosion, as the phenomenon is known, can be particularly serious just behind bolt heads and for fastenings in damp wood.

Monel, an alloy containing mainly nickel and copper, is a wonderfully resistant alternative, but it is very difficult to obtain in any range of fastenings and very expensive.

Bronze, too, is a splendid fastening material, being extremely durable and nearly as strong as steel, but it is now hard to obtain. By definition, bronze is an alloy containing copper and tin, and there are many types, including gun metal, naval bronze, aluminium bronze and silicon bronze which is used to make 'Gripfast' nails. Manganese bronze is *not* a bronze at all, but good quality brass. Everdur is a silicon copper with excellent properties, used widely in the U.S.A.

Brass, an alloy containing copper and zinc, is, in contrast, an inferior material in respect of both strength and corrosion resistance. Again, there are many types, but the commonly obtainable brass screw is a poor thing ideed, apt to sheer when being driven home, and prone to dezincify in a marine environment. The result is that, after a year or two, it takes on a coppery appearance and crumbles. In fact, I refuse to use brass screws anywhere on a boat, except for fixing brass catches and the like where appearance is more important than strength.

Galvanised steel is the most viable alternative to stainless for bolts, but it must have been hot-dipped and spun, i.e. centrifuged to throw off surplus zinc which would otherwise clog the threads. To ensure easy screwing, threads are undercut before galvanising, and the nuts are retapped afterwards. Because of the thread proportions, 8 mm is the minimum diameter that will function satisfactorily after the dipping and spinning process. Proper hot-dipped galvanised bolts are also becoming scarce, and zinc-plated ones, easily recognised by their bright appearance, are replacing them. This is a pity, because, while galvanised bolts, snugly bedded in sealant, will last many years on a boat, zinc plating is usually so thin as to be virtually useless as a defence against corrosion.

With screws, zinc-plated (or, even worse, cadmium-plated ones) are now the only type obtainable. But if you cannot afford stainless, or bronze, they are the only alternative. In which case, I have found that dipped in molten, anhydrous lanoline, or more tediously bedded in epoxy, properly filled and painted over, they give no trouble inside the cabin for many years. They may rust-stain eventually, but will not give way like brass. The anhydrous lanoline is also an effective lubricant for driving them home easily.

PART II

The Shape of Things and Humans

.The art of building things that fit comfortably to the human frame is well, but not perhaps widely, known. It is important not merely for comfort in the luxurious sense, but also to avoid unnecessary strain and to promote safety aboard. This section outlines the properties of the principal artefacts aboard, using an articulated model man, scaled to the average adult of 5 ft 10 in (1.78 m), see Photo 15. Things made specially for larger or smaller people—women are some 4 inches (10 cm) shorter on average—should be adjusted accordingly.

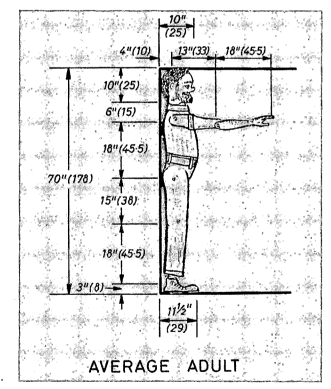

15.

But on a yacht, where space is so tight, it is often the boat that dictates the sizes, and compromises are necessary between, say, elbow room in the galley, and length of a bunk. Whether there is a problem or not, it is prudent, when planning a construction or modification, to make a scale man of cardboard, and move him around the drawings. Scale models can be purchased, or a cardboard model made using the proportions in Photo 15. *All metric dimensions—the ones in brackets—are in centimetres.*

1. Lying

Photo 16 shows a bunk in side view, and three figures are given for the length. Here, as elsewhere in this section, 'A' is the smallest dimension that is usable without acute discomfort. 'B' is an acceptable figure, and often found in yachts. 'C' is the dimension at which real comfort begins.

Bunks, especially quarter berths, are often tucked wholly or partly under things, so minimum heights are given too. These are important to comfort, particularly at the shoulder, and should be kept as large as possible if you want to avoid that troopship feeling. Ideally, you should be able to sit up in bed without bumping your head, as shown in Photo 16.

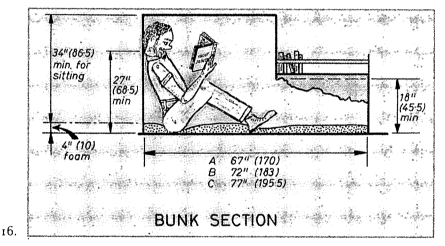

16.

BUNK SECTION

34" (86·5) min. for sitting — 27" (68·5) min — 4" (10) foam — 18" (45·5) min

A 67" (170)
B 72" (183)
C 77" (195·5)

While a bunk cannot be too long, it can certainly be too wide. Something the width of a domestic bed (say 36 inches) is impossible to jam oneself in, and can murder all sleep in a following wind, when the ship is rolling (Photo 17). For this reason a double bunk should have some sort of centre board if it is to be used as a single at sea. A double bunk need not be twice the width of a single, i.e. 2 × 24 = 48 inches. 42 inches (107 cm) is sufficient to make a very pleasant double berth.

Bunks can often be made narrower at the feet, with a useful saving in space, provided that one can lie on one's side with knees drawn up.

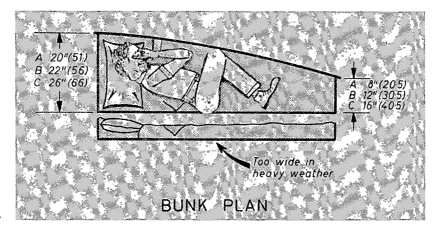

A 20"(51)
B 22"(56)
C 26"(66)

A 8"(205)
B 12"(305)
C 16"(405)

Too wide in
heavy weather

BUNK PLAN

17.

2. Sitting

In Photo 18 our man is sitting at a standard table-and-seat arrangement. But an 18 in seat height is more of a maximum than average, and can be reduced to increase the comfort provided there is space to stretch one's feet out a little more. A seat height of 13 inches is not unreasonable, though it then becomes a trifle difficult to use the table. The level of the top of the table must naturally drop with the seat, the 11 in difference being quite critical. Incidentally, if you drop the seat, you will probably lose valuable locker space, but life is not perfect. . . .

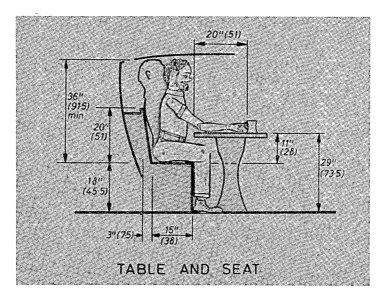

20"(51)

36"
(915)
min

20"
(51)

11"
(28)

29"
(735)

18"
(45.5)

3"(75)   15"
(38)

TABLE AND SEAT

18.

19.

Sitting in the cockpit (Photo 19) is rather a special case, because you must brace your feet on the opposite side. Spacious cockpits are stylish in port, but a curse at sea, where one day they may lead to a broken bone. The tiller is shown at a height of 32 inches, because that is what is needed when you stand; but a height of 27 inches is much more comfortable when sitting. Many tillers hinge up, thus accommodating both heights, but unless they are provided with a stop, they are wearying to use. Alternatives are a vertically forked tiller, practical though not very becoming, and a curved tiller which can be turned upside down to curve up instead of down.

When you are standing at the tiller (Photo 20), you may hold it just behind you (the height then is not too critical) but it is pleasant to lean back and steer confidently with the coccyx, leaving hands free to light a leisurely pipe.

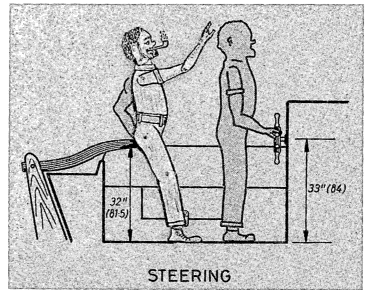

20.

The best height of a wheel depends mostly on its shape (spokes or not) and its diameter, but a general guide is that the hands should be between 4 and 8 inches below the level of the elbows for a comfortable steering posture.

3. Standing

Headroom is too obvious to need comment, except that beams a whisker too low are much worse than something that must obviously be ducked under. For this reason, doorway heights A and B, in Photo 21 are at, or below, eye level. If a step down in headroom is necessary, and a step in the sole level is possible, then that step should be well before the doorway, as people always lean forward when they move forward.

Doorways need not be the same width all the way down. They can narrow below hip level, and floors as narrow as 11 inches are not too inconvenient.

While on the subject of standing, one often sees safety lines which could, more properly, be called trip lines (Photo 22) being exactly the right height to catch you below the knee caps, and tip you into the briny.

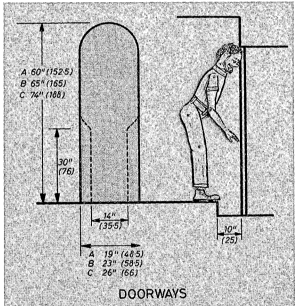

A 60" (152.5)
B 65" (165)
C 74" (188)

30" (76)

14" (35.5)

10" (25)

A 19" (48.5)
B 23" (58.5)
C 26" (66)

21. DOORWAYS

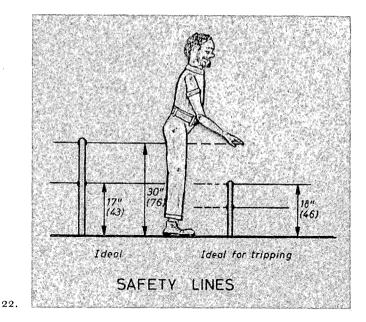

22.

4. Worktops

The height of worktops is critical, if one is to work at them without strain. 36 inches is the standard height for sinks, cookers, workbenches and so on, but if the former are to be used mostly by women, then dropping the top an inch or so may be advantageous. For close eye work that is not strenuous on the muscles, like a stand-up chart table, 42 inches is comfortable, while for certain other work that involves a great deal of hand movement and muscular effort but not much eye strain, a lower than average worktop is called for. The most comfortable height for sawing, for instance, is 31 inches for the average man.

Whatever the height, the front edge of the top should stand forward of the toes by 3 to 4 inches (Photo 23). This is not easily done on a boat, but if the top is much used, the result is worth it. The strain of leaning forward slightly against a straight up-and-down front creeps up on you slowly, first tiring out the muscles of the back, then the leg, then the neck and finally the whole body.

The other clearance to watch is the headroom when you lean forward (as you always do when working); sinks and cookers are often placed under the decks, and the edge of deck and coachwork often sits at a nasty height.

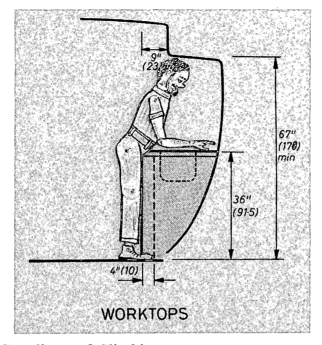

WORKTOPS

23.

5. Reaching, Crawling and Climbing

Reaching (Photo 24) is not generally tiring, as it is only done for brief periods. Kneeling to reach into lockers, the limit of stretch is about 25 inches from the shoulder. Note that our man cannot actually see what he is doing, and it would be better if there were space for his head in the locker too, calling for an opening height of about 12 inches. Standing, one can reach a height of 6 feet with ease, even allowing for a good reach forward.

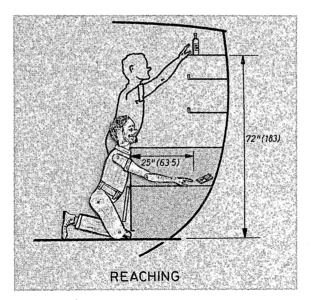

REACHING

24.

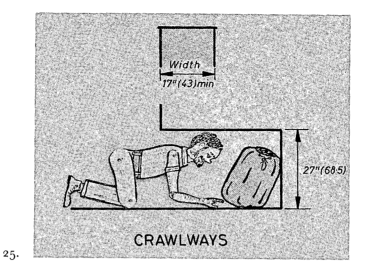

25.

Crawling also is not something in which one indulges day and night, but it is done more often on boats than anywhere else, and Photo 25 gives a rough idea of what is possible. Hatches are a kind of crawlway, and 16 × 18 inches is about the smallest you can use without squashing through, although I have successfully tested a hole 10 × 14 inches, and I am of depressingly average proportions.

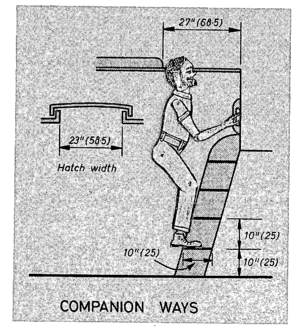

26.

Photo 26 illustrates a companionway of sound and comfortable dimensions. Steps may be pitched an inch or two less than the 10 inches shown, preferably not more, though 12 inches can be regarded as a maximum. The step width is not critical; 10 inches is the optimum, but less than half that width is still pleasant to use, provided that one's toes do not come up hard against the bulkhead behind. Similarly, the slope of the ladder is not too critical, a rise of about 3 inches for every 1 inch stepped out being common. Less than this is awkward, as one is prone to fall backwards. In any event, handgrips, either on the ladder or on the bulkhead, should be provided in generous measure. The hatch opening is important, as one must not only be able to leap up the ladder without clocking the back of one's head, but also to descend, clutching a box to one's chest. The 27 inches shown must, therefore, be regarded as a minimum for the slope of ladder indicated; clearly the further the ladder juts into the cabin, the deeper the hatch.

6. Hands

The average hand, or, more accurately, a standard hand around whose proportions you can design things, is shown in Fig. 15. Obviously, the most important aspect of the hand is gripping, and Fig. 15 shows a round bar grip, 1⅛ inches being the most comfortable diameter. In fact, a perfectly round bar does not lie as well in the hand as a rectangular cross section (rounded over), with the flat, long side against the palm. The reason is that the main gripping muscles draw the fingers, rather than the thumb, down to the palm. A shape 2 inches by a maximum of 1 inch wide, with well rounded corners, is good to hold, and nearly twice as strong as a round bar of 1⅛

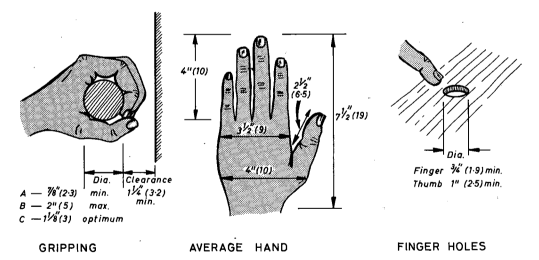

GRIPPING · AVERAGE HAND · FINGER HOLES

Figure 15. HANDS

73

PART III

Designs and Dimensions

1. Design Thinking

Any handy yachtsman will confirm that an astonishing proportion of the time needed for a job is spent simply thinking about it. But it is not time wasted. This technical daydreaming is the stuff that inventions are made of, and while we may not aspire to emulate Edison, it pays, before getting materials and charging at the construction, to peer at a project inside and out, turn it this way and that, consider how to build it and how long it will stand up to hard use. Everyone scribbles on the back of envelopes through this stage, but whether you proceed to proper drawings or not is a matter for personal taste.

For those who lack practical experience, **drawings** are safer. They should be as detailed as possible; lay out three or more views (it's surprising what shows up when you look at the work from a different angle), and proceed to a sketch of each separate piece. All the pieces can then be shaped ready for assembly like a kit. This classical engineering approach is particularly suited to rather complicated but separate units, like a saloon table or companion steps. But take care to make pieces oversize whenever they can be trimmed after assembly, for wood is not like steel. It moves. Drawings must, of course, be done to scale, and suitable scales are roughly $\frac{3}{4}$ in to a foot for something boat size, 3 in to a foot for something table size and 6 in to a foot for details; the metric equivalents are usually 1:20, 1:5, and 1:2. A scale rule is a must.

The opposite extreme is '**eyeball design**', and one man I know went as far as to determine the height of a doghouse by building the sole, then standing upright and placing three fingers on top of his head. (I seem to recollect, though, that he forgot the beam depth.) In fact, eyeball design is satisfactory provided you have sufficient practical experience, but even then sketches showing the outline dimensions are usually necessary.

The third alternative is to use **existing designs**—in the flesh, by visiting other boats, or on paper—and here this book is intended to provide as much information as possible.

Whatever method or methods are used, design thinking should take into account several factors. The first is obviously that **the object should do its job properly**. Sliding hatches should slide both in fog and in sunshine and not leak; Dorade ventilators should allow the passage of air but not water; and everything that needs to fit people must do so, a topic that has been discussed in Part II.

75

The most common defect I have come across—and this applies more, if anything, to professionally built boats than to amateur ones—is that things are built to work in a horizontal position. Designers draw things level and yards build them that way on flat, concrete floors. Often only perfunctory concessions are made to the probability that for some of the time the boat will be heeled at 45°, at which point it becomes a matter of personal taste whether you walk on the floor or the wall. Most of these defects arise from liquid flow—bilges drain properly only in harbour, while at sea the fresh water empties itself through the tap, sea water gushes up the plughole and toilets do horrible things. But there are frequently other defects—inadequate fiddles, doors that fly open, and chart tables that decline to retain charts in anything stronger than a Force 3. It is important, therefore, to visualise what may happen at sea and design accordingly. Guidelines are: it is easiest to do nearly everything facing fore and aft rather than sideways; stowage needs to be heavily restrained sideways by fiddles, etc., slightly forward and virtually not at all facing aft; drainage is best done fore and aft, remembering that the drainage path will shift as the boat heels.

Secondly, **the object should continue to do its job for a long time**. Designing for strength and durability is a tricky task for the layman since it demands a knowledge of material properties and how stresses are distributed; one can only try and imagine how something is likely to fail and beef it up accordingly. For instance, stresses concentrate towards the supporting base—a fold-out seat must be very strongly secured at the root but can be lightly made at the tip, hand grips need wide, thick bases but can be relatively thin in the middle, and so on. Stresses also concentrate at abrupt change of sections, so every change of size should blend rather than jump. And it hardly needs saying that materials must be suited for the job in hand not only for strength but also for resistance to wear and corrosion.

The third design consideration is **how you are actually going to make the object**. Your skills, your tools, the materials to hand, and cost will often decide the design. It is much better to make a thing simple but accurate rather than complicated and rough, and it is certainly cheaper to glue together two-1 in pieces of timber that you have, than to buy one 2 in piece.

The appearance of a finished article is extremely important and should never be far from your mind when designing. It must look right and match the style of the boat, and while beauty lies largely in the eye of the beholder, there are certain helpful rules observed by architects. Ellipsoidal curves—i.e. French type curves—are prettier than circles, and rectangles look nicer than squares. Wherever possible outlines should be blended, one into the other, for softened shapes suit a ship, but where it is difficult to blend—often the case where two pieces fit on top of or at right angles to each other—make a decisive step at the junction. A feature like this looks much better than a fumbled attempt to blend. Edges should be well and clearly rounded over or alternatively sharp-edged or sharply bevelled; edges that are somewhere between look amateurish. Colour is largely a matter of personal taste but generally red woods clash with light brown ones. The contrast between white paint and varnish always looks attractive.

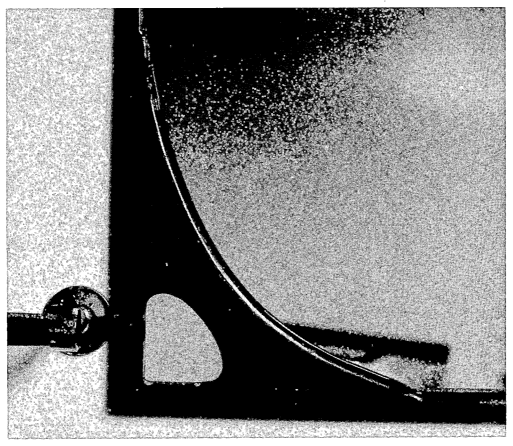

27. Combination grip and corner reinforcing—design that is practical, rugged yet pretty.

The corner grip in Photo 27 is a simple illustration of the points discussed. It fits the hand perfectly and, as both a corner reinforcement and a handgrip, it is immensely strong without being clumsy. (Note how the grain runs across the corner.) It was also straightforward to make and looks attractive, rounding off an otherwise ugly corner.

Finally, one of the main aims of design thinking is to **simplify** to the nth degree the building, the shape, the function, everything. As the sage once observed, 'Any fool can make a complicated thing, but it takes a genius to make a simple one.'

2. Designs

A FOUNDATION WORK AND LAYOUT

While certain aspects of foundation work—i.e. soles, bulkheads, cockpit support-beams and the like—are touched on elsewhere in this book, it is useful to look here at the overall design considerations.

If you start work in an empty hull, you will immediately discover that you and all your tools slither repeatedly and infuriatingly into the middle. The temptation is to lay down the cabin sole in one dance-hall expanse, and build everything on to it, as in a house. Resist! Though some authorities do recommend this, I consider the technique very bad practice, mainly because it is essential to be able to reach every part of the hull for maintenance and repair, and a one-piece sole, even with numerous access hatches, is bound to obstruct some areas. Also, fitting a bulkhead accurately between sole and deckhead is difficult, and the junction between sole and bulkhead is a moisture trap which is likely to rot. If rot does set in here the whole interior is in jeopardy, for repairs are nearly impossible.

So, lay a temporary floor of old planks and fit the bulkheads first, either by glassing in or by fixing to frames. Professional yards will often fit not only bulkheads but the whole interior before fitting the deck, but this is generally beyond the scope of amateurs and one-off yachts. Bulkheads are nearly always in plywood between 12 mm and 18 mm thickness depending on size. Cleats, $1\frac{1}{2} \times 1\frac{1}{2}$ inches (4×4 cm) can then be screwed to the bulkheads for the sole to rest on, with intermediate cross beams about 2×3 inches (5.0×7.5 cm) where necessary. These should be at maximum intervals of 3 feet (90 cm), and longitudinals half-jointed in to correspond to sole hatches and the furniture above. When planning the size of hatches, remember that small is beautiful; this goes for locker lids and any other large area of wood that must be taken, or hinged, out of the way in the cramped confines of a boat. You will end up with a grid, looking rather like that illustrated in Fig. 16a. It can get quite complicated because the grid must match not only the furniture above but the tankage underneath (future replacement is important), and space must be allowed for pipes and possibly cables. The result is worth it, for you will have proper access to everything below the sole and be able to replace the latter if need be.

The sole material is, again, normally plywood, around 15 mm thick. Planking can be used, but it swells a lot across the grain and jams. For gap widths around hatches, and lifting of same, refer to Section G below; and for finish of soles refer to Section IV 3.

You will then have vertical and parallel plywood faces on which to hang the furniture. This is done by screwing and gluing support cleats to the bulkhead (Fig. 16b) and other verticals, supplemented as necessary with the minimum attachments to hull and deck as indicated previously. Access, particularly to the hull but also to seacocks, plumbing and cables, is of prime importance. You will need reasonable

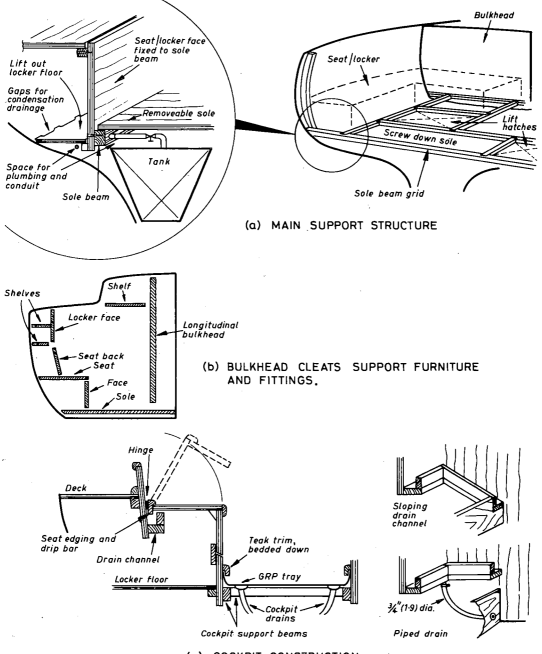

(a) MAIN SUPPORT STRUCTURE

(b) BULKHEAD CLEATS SUPPORT FURNITURE
AND FITTINGS.

(c) COCKPIT CONSTRUCTION

Figure 16. FOUNDATION WORK

79

access for cleaning regularly, and painting occasionally, and construction must be planned so that, before final assembly, every part can be painted separately all round, thus coating areas which will never again be painted.

Whether the construction will be assembled with or without glue also merits some thought. One's first instinct is probably to glue and screw everything together for maximum strength. But one day you may have to dismantle a section for maintenance, or perhaps just to alter a layout, and you don't want to do that with a crowbar. The answer lies in a judicious mixture of properly glued smaller structures (including as many of the cross joints as possible), which are then screwed together to make the whole, but with bedding compound in lieu of glue. Stainless or bronze screws, with a spot of lanoline for easy removal in years to come, are best for this duty.

One final point on construction is that horizontal surfaces like shelves and locker bottoms should follow the hull shape neatly but should not make perfect contact, and should certainly not be bedded or glued against the hull. The reason is that such a horizontal joint constitutes a nasty water trap for condensation forming on the hull and trickling downward towards the bilge.

All in all, a good deal of thought on the minutiae of construction is required on a first class job; such points are not generally shown in the architect's drawings.

Constructing a cockpit from scratch presents rather different problems from interior furniture. The fundamental support structure is generally a beam grid, rather than end plates (bulkheads), although the coamings often provide extra longitudinal strength. But the main difference is, of course, that the cockpit must be designed to operate wet. Designing locker lids and floor hatches to seal perfectly is seldom successful, in my experience. Instead, they should be designed to leak slightly—into a drainage channel. To minimise the effects of dirt, and to make certain that water gets away, internal channel dimensions should not be less than 1×1 inch (2.5×2.5 cm). Drainage on the leeward side can be effected either with a channel sloping back into the well, as is done in most GRP boats nowadays, or with a $\frac{3}{4}$ in pipe (Fig. 16c). The pipe is easier to make but less reliable.

Cockpit lockers are normally large (necessarily) so access should be large enough to get at least head and shoulders in, so as to reach to the back. Again, the GRP construction of a one-piece top/front lid can be imitated in wood, see Fig. 16c.

A cockpit floor made of plywood and screwed down on bedding is a frequent source of leaks and should be avoided if possible. One elegant solution is to mould a shallow bath floor in GRP, and hold it in place with teak cover-strips, screwed from the inside. There is then little chance of leaks, and the entire floor can be removed for repair or access to the engine. A further refinement is to make the floor in translucent GRP and flood the engine compartment, or whatever is underneath, with daylight—see Photo 43, p. 158. Fine, but remember to avoid illumination down below, else you will be ankle deep in an eerie glow on night watch.

B SEATS AND TABLES

The conventional arrangement for a built-in seat, also often a berth, is shown in Fig. 17. The seat board which retains the cushions is too small on many boats to do its job effectively and should properly stick up above the seat about 2 inches (5 cm) as

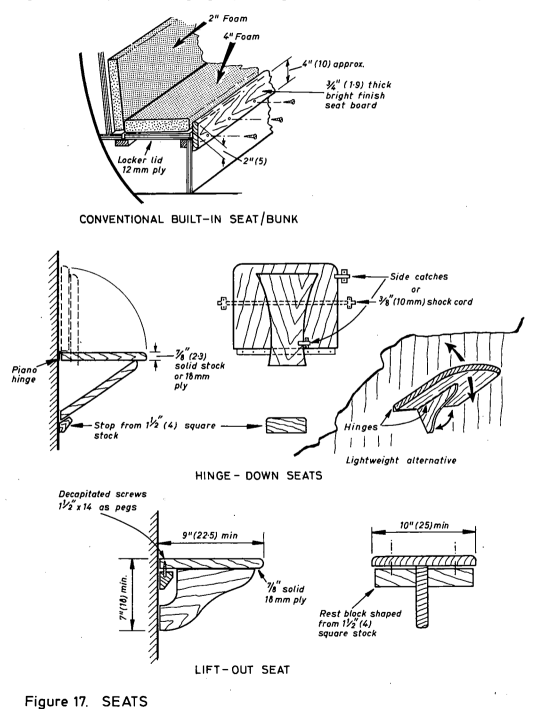

Figure 17. SEATS

illustrated. This means the total board height is about 4 inches, but on big yachts a larger board of 5 to 6 inches (15 cm) looks better. Foam seat cushions should be 4 inches thick (10 cm), never less as they gradually compress, but the backs need be no more than 2 inches thick. The lengths should be divided up to suit the locker lids underneath, say 2 cushions and 4 lids on a 6 ft (2 m) seat; it is always better to make lids smaller rather than bigger for handling at sea.

For those interested in adding things to existing yachts rather than building from scratch, the movable seats in Fig. 17 are of greater interest. A hinge-down seat will often be of use in places like the heads, the forepeak, the galley table and the chart area. It can be made in a variety of ways but the one shown is robust, practical and not difficult to make. Retaining it firmly in the folded position is important and this can be done with either shock cord (hooked or fixed) or catches; the latter have to be at the side if you value your spine and other anatomy. A lighter, but less robust, alternative is shown in the inset, and another (not shown) is simply supported by rope or chain. Yet another alternative is a hinge-up seat; the design illustrated for a bulkhead table in Fig. 19 can be simply adapted by replacing the fiddle box with a wooden cleat about 2 inches—i.e. the thickness of the seat with strut plus some —screwed to the bulkhead.

A lift-out seat is also shown in Fig. 17, and as there are no tiddly hinges or catches it is strong and easy to make. It is often more convenient as well not to have a permanent fixture. Considerable forces, both downwards and away from the bulkhead, are borne by the rest block which must, therefore, be beefy, likewise the pins which should be of stainless steel.

Tables come in so many shapes and sizes that it is not possible to describe them all. A typical good-quality saloon table is shown in some detail in Fig. 18. It incorporates a stowage box as well as a lower shelf and can have either one leaf or two. Construction may look a trifle complex at first sight, but all joints are of the simple butt type, screwed and glued; for this reason solid planks are somewhat easier to use (as well as more classy) but plywood is suitable provided that cleats are used to avoid screwing into end grain. Tables must be bolted—not screwed—to the floor because they bear the brunt of many a lurching yachtsman at sea. The hand pole—it can also be of 1½ in (4 cm) diameter wood—is an excellent strengthener and handy too for swinging oneself into the seats.

The leaves can be supported by either folding legs, unfortunately too long to stow under many tables, or the swinging strut shown. An important feature of the latter is the stop block, a wooden housing that positively locates the end of the strut. Without an end stop, the top of the table leaf is loaded and the bending strain will be taken by the strut hinge, which may give way or tear off eventually. If you want to avoid a stop block, then you must use not one hinge but two, and the distance between the hinges must nearly equal the horizontal distance over which the strut projects.

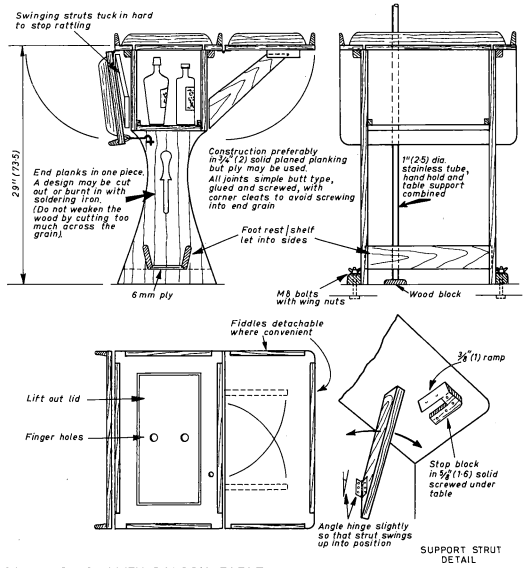

Swinging struts tuck in hard
to stop rattling

29" (73·5)

End planks in one piece.
A design may be cut
out or burnt in with
soldering iron.
(Do not weaken the
wood by cutting too
much across the
grain).

Construction preferably
in ¾" (2) solid planed planking
but ply may be used.
All joints simple butt type,
glued and screwed, with
corner cleats to avoid screwing
into end grain

1"(2·5) dia.
stainless tube,
hand hold and
table support
combined

Foot rest / shelf
let into sides

6 mm ply

M 8 bolts
with wing nuts

Wood block

Fiddles detachable
where convenient

⅜"(1) ramp

Lift out lid

Finger holes

Stop block
in ⅝"(1·6) solid
screwed under
table

Angle hinge slightly
so that strut swings
up into position

SUPPORT STRUT
DETAIL

Figure 18. QUALITY SALOON TABLE

Appropriate fiddles should be detachable, as they tend to be a nuisance in port. An elegant alternative to both hinging leaves and fiddle removal is illustrated in Fig. 19. The flop-over top is popular on several production boats and presents no constructional problems.

This is less true of the pole-mounted table, also used on many production yachts, mainly for lowering to seat level to form a double berth. I have also seen pole tables

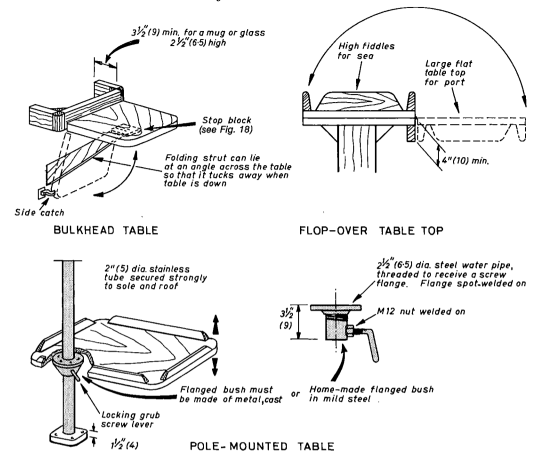

Figure 19. TABLE VARIATIONS

on a couple of traditional cruisers; here, however, the purpose was to lift the table to the roof when under way to clear the cabin space, on the assumption, presumably, that you have to hug your stewbowl to your lap anyway when crashing through mountainous seas. The constructional difficulty of the pole table lies in the flanged bush, which must be of metal. These can be purchased, but not at every corner shop, and you may find it quicker and cheaper to get one made as illustrated.

Finally, there is a hinging bulkhead table, sketched in Fig. 19. Since you need a ledge to fix to anyway, a neat idea is to turn this into a ditty box. The swinging strut is built as was shown in Fig. 18, but need not be central and square; it can slant across so that it tucks away when the table is folded. A bulkhead table can equally well, of course, hinge down, as shown in Fig. 17 for the seat.

C BUNKS

Whenever anyone comes aboard to look around, the first question is likely to be, 'How many does she sleep?' I have always thought this a curious, if not downright misleading way of gauging a boat. Do they sleep in hammocks? On a pair of oars laid across the cockpit? Can all the sleepers you have bunks for actually be accommodated when awake and active? Or perhaps the wakers have to sit on the sleepers, who are occupying the only seats. Whatever the sleeping arrangements, proper berth-design is an important aspect of seaworthiness, as well as comfort, for the berths are usually where the crew recoup when not doing useful things on deck.

i. Permanent Berths

These are used as bunks and nothing else, and are obviously the best if they can be accommodated in the layout. For one thing, you can have a solid, fixed bunk board, and a sound design of generous proportions is shown in Fig. 20. The board may be made either of 18 mm plywood, with edges trimmed, or of solid timber throughout. If the latter, it will probably be in the form of a single plank, and a couple of vertical pieces, about 2 × 1 inches (5 × 2.5 cm), should be glued and screwed to the inside to prevent bowing across the grain; the ends and bottom should also be well secured. The stormboard (see Photo 28) can be cut out of the bunkboard itself, and fitted with end pieces and barrel bolts as shown. Since most of the forces on the stormboard act outwards, the end pieces should be fixed on the inside with the grain running horizontally. The barrel bolts act mainly as retainers. Used in pilot berths (those

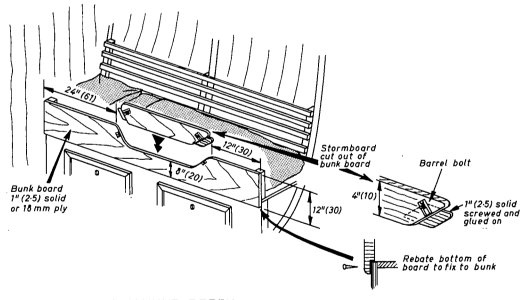

Figure 20. PERMANENT BERTH

28. Sliding double bunk, partially expanded. The bases 'finger' into each other.

against the hull, situated above and behind seats), and cabin berths, such a bunkboard arrangement will give a high degree of comfort and security; often a curtain may be hung across to provide privacy too. Fig. 20 also illustrates the use of slats running across the frames to keep the occupant away from hull condensation, and provide useful stowage at the same time.

Quarter berths are arguably the most seaworthy of all. The quarter sections of a boat have a comfortable motion, and since the berths are generally tucked in behind the cockpit seats, they are perfectly secure without the need for bunkboards.

Which way is it best to lie? There is little difference in my experience, but feet forward is perhaps slightly preferable. The reason is that, lying head forward when slamming into a head sea, one tends to press against the forward bulkhead and develop a crick in the neck. In any event, bunks should never slope down towards the head, and it is good practice to build in a 1 in slope the other way.

ii. Double Bunks

Only the larger boats will have permanent double bunks and, as pointed out in Part II, these should have a detachable dividing piece to prevent one from being thrown from side to side at sea. Bunks lying athwartships are an alternative, but you have to turn round every time the boat tacks, and sleeping across the boat when she is rolling downwind is an acquired taste.

Most double berths are of the occasional type, and the most common arrangement

86

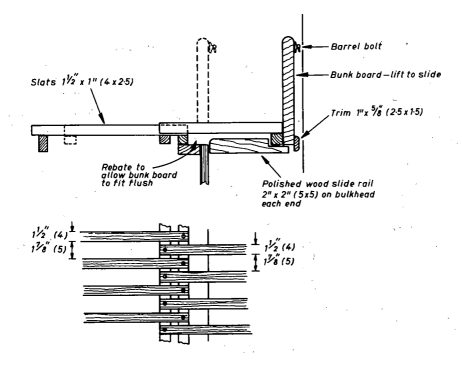

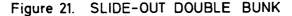

Figure 21. SLIDE-OUT DOUBLE BUNK

is to drop the table top into a U-shaped seat plan. The top can slide down a tube (Fig. 19), or sink on a leg hinged in the middle. If, however, you wish to make a double berth out of a permanent single one, then one of the neatest designs I have seen is that shown in Fig. 21 and Photo 28. The extension slats slide out from between the fixed slats, maintaining a flush surface and good ventilation. A hardwood rail, screwed to end bulkheads, is stepped to act as a stop in both the closed and extended positions; the bunk, therefore, has to be lifted to slide in or out. Barrel bolts, shot into the bulkheads, secure the top of the bunkboard.

The Root berth can also extend to a double, as shown in Fig. 22(b).

iii. Occasional Berths

In addition to the normal seat/bunk (Fig. 17), there are various types of occasional berth. One of the most popular is the pipe cot (Fig. 22a), best suited to the forepeak where it can be easily hinged out of the way, or used for sail stowage. Another virtue is that by hitching the rope or chain up, you can compensate for heeling.

The making of a pipe cot is often difficult because the corners are seldom at 90°; if you use, say, 1 in galvanised water pipe with standard screwed elbows, you will have to bend the pipes into peculiar curves. 1¼ in aluminium tube, on the other hand, can

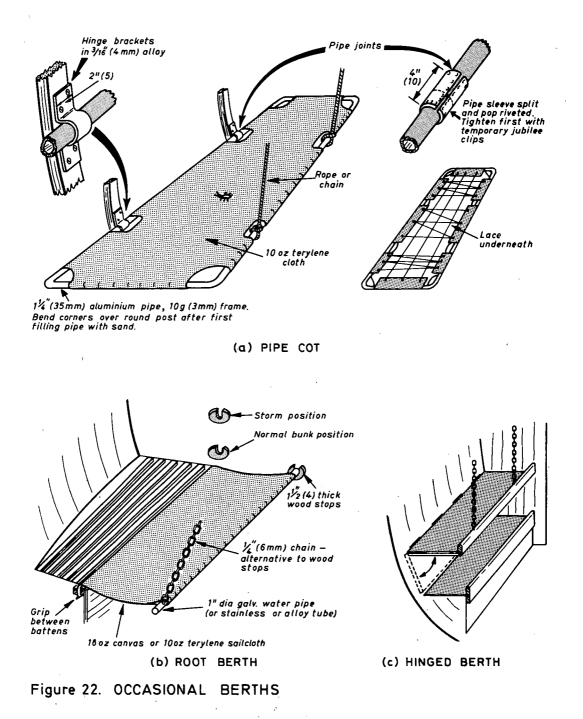

Hinge brackets
in ³/₁₆" (4 mm) alloy

2" (5)

Pipe joints

4" (10)

Pipe sleeve split
and pop riveted.
Tighten first with
temporary jubilee
clips

Rope or
chain

10 oz terylene
cloth

Lace
underneath

1¼" (35mm) aluminium pipe, 10g (3mm) frame.
Bend corners over round post after first
filling pipe with sand.

(a) PIPE COT

Storm position

Normal bunk position

1½" (4) thick
wood stops

¼" (6mm) chain –
alternative to wood
stops

1" dia galv. water pipe
(or stainless or alloy tube)

Grip
between
battens

18 oz canvas or 10oz terylene sailcloth

(b) ROOT BERTH

(c) HINGED BERTH

Figure 22. OCCASIONAL BERTHS

be bent fairly easily round a 3 in diameter post; but first fill the tube with building sand to prevent collapse, and, of course, remove the sand afterwards. Because tubing now comes in about 4 m lengths, two joints will normally be necessary, and these can be effected with short lengths of split tube as illustrated.

The Root berth is another good system, and if arranged as shown in Fig. 22b, the partly rolled bunk doubles as a lee cloth for the single, permanent berth. It need not, of course, be used in conjunction with another berth; it can be mounted as a straightforward single berth, and if one or two extra bulkhead chocks are fitted, the bunk can be tilted to accommodate different angles of heel. The cloth can equally well be stretched between two pipes.

Fig. 22c shows a fairly obvious way of using the back of a seat as a bunk. The bunk is best supported by chains on to the cabin beams, or alternatively by a leecloth on ropes.

iv. Bunk Bases

A sleeping person can release as much as $1\frac{1}{2}$ pints of perspiration in a night, and a good proportion of this will permeate through the mattress in the form of water vapour, cooling as it goes. If the air is cold enough, the vapour will condense at some point, and unless the underside of the mattress is well ventilated, water will accumulate. The problem can be quite serious if you are using the boat a lot in cold weather. In one boat on which we were living, the underside of a new, sprung mattress rotted away completely in just eight weeks. Even in warmer climates, it is good practice to construct the bunk base with adequate ventilation. Slats (clear pine is a good material) work well (see Fig. 23), and for ease of construction, these are normally laid flat. A refinement is to curve the bunk. It involves extra trouble and expense, but adds a lot to comfort and seaworthiness.

Plywood is the easiest base to make, but should, again, be ventilated; a simple method is to cut slots by drilling each end and joining the holes with a jigsaw or drilling holes with a holesaw. To avoid weakening the sheet, the slots must be carefully staggered, as shown. Another base, once very popular, is rubber webbing, which needs only a 2 in thick mattress. But it has a short life, and is seldom used nowadays. Foam plastic mattresses, 4 inches thick—6 inches (15 cm) for luxury— are virtually standard now, and give good service. Whatever you do, don't use an inflatable mattress. My first night aboard ever was spent on a lilo while rolling at anchor; it was like trying to sleep on a jelly, and eventually I opted for the floor.

v. Leeboards

Leeboards are essential on every berth used at sea. Solid boards are best, and these can either hinge up from under the mattress, or slot into end slides. The Root type described is also efficient. On the other hand, those modest triangles of canvas are not worth installing; like bikinis, they look pretty but offer little restraint. Proper leecloths are 12 inches (30 cm) high, they extend at least three quarters of the berth

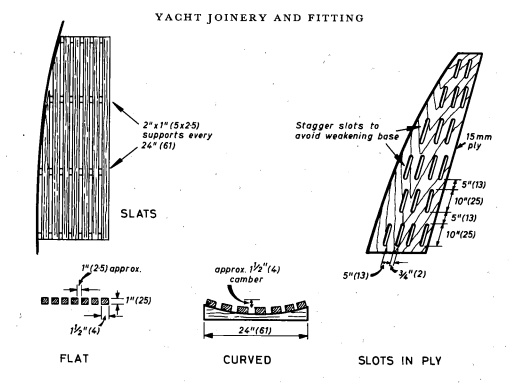

Figure 23. BUNK BASES

length, and are firmly secured along the entire base with a screwed batten. They are also roped to the coach roof or deckhead at maximum intervals of 18 inches (46 cm).

D STOWAGE

i. Fiddles and Shelves

With drainage, stowage is probably the most important aspect of seaworthiness in fitting out, and certainly one of the most neglected in production craft. Tiddly fiddles, that look terribly nautical at the Boat Show prove incapable of retaining anything in winds above Force 4. Everything, including shelves inside opening lockers, must have a fiddle to be seaworthy. Fiddle rails on tables and worktops should have dimensions no less than those shown in Fig. 24, although the precise design is a matter of personal taste. Several profiles are illustrated. Fiddles must be strongly fixed, because they are apt to be grabbed for support. For this reason, I dislike the taffrail style in Fig. 24, attractive as it is to look upon. Incidentally, there is a case for eliminating fiddles on tables (where they tend to be a nuisance in port) by using non-slip, plastic mats. These have an angle of friction greater than 45°, i.e. the cup tips over before it slips. A cheaper alternative is a damp towel. Personally, I have found that one really needs both towel and fiddle.

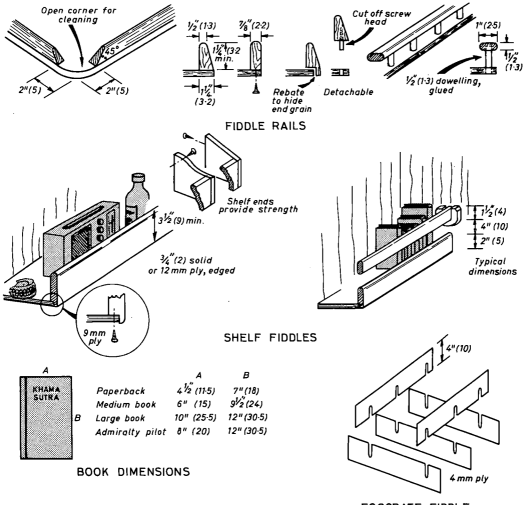

FIDDLE RAILS

SHELF FIDDLES

	A	B
Paperback	4½" (11·5)	7" (18)
Medium book	6" (15)	9½" (24)
Large book	10" (25·5)	12" (30·5)
Admiralty pilot	8" (20)	12" (30·5)

BOOK DIMENSIONS

EGGCRATE FIDDLE

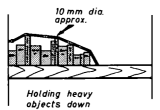

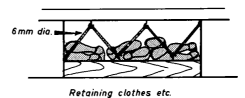

SHOCK CORD

Figure 24. FIDDLES AND SHELVES

Fiddles on shelves and lockers must be around 3½ inches for exposed shelves, and at least 2 inches (5 cm) for shelves inside lockers. Much, of course, depends on what the locker is retaining, and which way it is facing. Running fore and aft, the fiddle will have to retain stuff at angles up to 45 °; facing the bows the angle is only a few degrees, but things tend to jolt forward; facing aft the fiddle need only restrain the contents from edging off. Really effective fiddles often have to be so high that they block access to the shelf. One solution is to fit a detachable bar, as shown in Fig. 24. These are very practical for books. Another solution is to use shockcord, in one of two ways—either to hold things down, so that the fiddle can do its job, effective for heavy or large objects; or as a sort of girder, stitched across an opening to retain light objects. Shockcord strung across heavy stuff like books is seldom effective when the going gets rough.

Finally, there is the problem of what to do about numbers of objects sliding around large shelves. This is invariably a problem in the galley, and if I had a pound for every time I cleared up after jars of food had done each other to death in bumpy weather, I'd be as rich as Croesus. Cramming the shelf full of toilet rolls and dirty tea towels prevents the massacre, but it's hardly elegant. I confess I have not found the perfect answer. Long, athwartships shelves *must* be chopped up into shorter bits, with high fiddles, or even partitions. For other spaces I suggest the egg crate fiddle in Fig. 24. This is simply a number of plywood lengths, slotted to make into a convenient number of boxes, the whole crate fitting fairly accurately into the locker. It should not be permanently fixed, as it must be removable for cleaning, and indeed can be made fully dismountable for the same purpose. It is not very pretty, but does at least save the mayonnaise and mustard jars from mutual extermination.

ii. Lockers

Lockers, or to be precise, access openings to lockers, range from the very simple to the intricate. At the simple end is a hole cut out of the locker face. Edged with iron-on varnished trim, (see IV 1.A) this can be both attractive and practical, provided it faces fore and aft; facing inwards it may have to be uncomfortably deep to retain its contents.

Another simple locker, shown in Fig. 25, is the drop-face type. The one illustrated works like a washboard; the only point to watch is that the edges of the plywood lid must be thinned to prevent sticking.

Hinged lids can become quite sophisticated, but the design shown in Fig. 25 is not too difficult to make, and has other advantages. The overlapping frame will hide any imperfections, and it is attractive, especially with a dark varnished frame and light-coloured locker face. It is also robust, practical and utilises the cut-down from the face. The method is as follows: first cut out the required opening—using a jigsaw, you tilt the blade gradually through the wood and so avoid drilling holes. The opening and the lid edges are then planed straight, to leave a gap between the two of

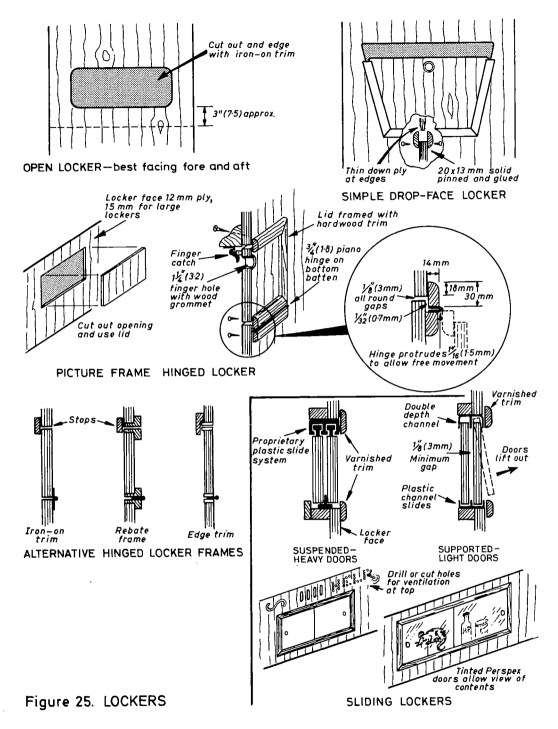

Cut out and edge with iron-on trim

3"(7·5) approx.

OPEN LOCKER—best facing fore and aft

Thin down ply at edges

20 x 13 mm solid pinned and glued

SIMPLE DROP-FACE LOCKER

Locker face 12 mm ply, 15 mm for large lockers

Finger catch

1¼"(3·2) finger hole with wood grommet

Cut out opening and use lid

PICTURE FRAME HINGED LOCKER

Lid framed with hardwood trim

¾"(1·8) piano hinge on bottom batten

14 mm

18 mm

30 mm

⅛"(3mm) all round gaps

¹⁄₃₂"(0·7mm)

Hinge protrudes ¹⁄₁₆"(1·5mm) to allow free movement

Stops

Iron-on trim

Rebate frame

Edge trim

ALTERNATIVE HINGED LOCKER FRAMES

Proprietary plastic slide system

Varnished trim

Locker face

SUSPENDED— HEAVY DOORS

Double depth channel

Varnished trim

⅛"(3mm) Minimum gap

Plastic channel slides

Doors lift out

SUPPORTED— LIGHT DOORS

Drill or cut holes for ventilation at top

Tinted Perspex doors allow view of contents

SLIDING LOCKERS

Figure 25. LOCKERS

93

29. Locker face with hinging lids ready fixed on. Note how the edges (and back) of the face have been painted prior to fitting.

about $\frac{1}{8}$ in all round. This may seem a lot, but anything much less and a combination of slight misplacings and paint thickness will cause the lid to stick. The lid is then framed with $1\frac{1}{4} \times \frac{5}{8}$ in hardwood, panel-pinned and glued to the ply with about $\frac{1}{2}$ in protruding all round. The frame is rounded over or chamfered on face edges, except for the outside of one edge, to which the brass piano hinge is attached. A piano hinge works truer and is stronger than separate hinges. The other leaf of the hinge is screwed to another hardwood strip, which is in turn glued and screwed to the locker face. To allow a clear 180° movement and to avoid strain on the hinge, care should be taken to arrange the gaps as indicated in Fig. 25. Lids may be hung vertically or horizontally, one or more in a locker face, and the whole is easier done before the locker face is finally fixed in place (Photo 29).

Several types of locker catch can be fitted, but none neater, I think, than the interior brass finger-catch, normally sold complete with turned grommet (teak or mahogany) for the finger hole. Fitting these catches presents no particular problem, but it is worth positioning them carefully for convenient use—normally slightly above and to the left of the hole, so they automatically fall under the finger of a right-handed person (Photo 30). It is this sort of detail that distinguishes good fitting

94

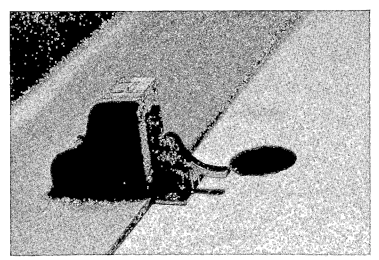

30. Finger-catch
mounting detail.

out from the merely adequate. The finished lockers are shown in Photo 31.

Despite its obvious advantages of simplicity and strength, this overlapping picture-frame technique is not common, and other types are shown in Fig. 25. The unframed type is simple, but difficult to make accurately, and the hinge must be fixed flat to avoid screwing into end grain. The result usually looks amateurish. A

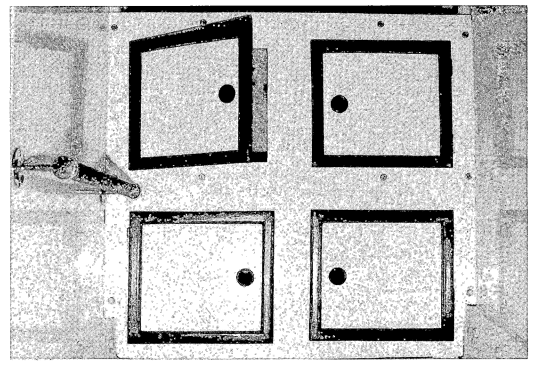

31. Finished locker face with overlapping lid trim. Trim is varnished mahogany
and ply is painted white, a practical and attractive scheme.

rebate frame, on the other hand, can look very professional, but it is tricky to make. The other type illustrated has wood trim only on the edges. It is commonly seen but often lacks elegance and strength.

Locker doors should not only remain closed when you want them to, but remain open as well. Otherwise, they are likely to bang about when you are struggling to remove things from the locker in a seaway. On vertically hinged lockers, a magnetic catch will generally be man enough. Alternatively, use a sprung ball-catch. Horizontally hinged lids opening upwards need something stronger, e.g. a short length of shockcord, with a hook which is strung out of the way on the inside of the lid when not in use. Horizontally hinged lids opening downwards need nothing at all.

Sliding locker lids are also a common sight aboard, and are certainly practical when sliding fore and aft. They look easy to make, but this is deceptive. To work smoothly, sliding things—this goes for hatches, doors, drawers and so on—must run between supports that are straight and parallel, and have the correct clearances. Sliding doors that warp may foul each other if too close together.

The larger locker doors—say, those more than about 18×18 inches (46×46 cm)—are preferably hung from slides to avoid sticking. This is best done using a patent slide system in plastic (there are many), available from a hardware store. Doors should not be less than 12 mm ply and, if the locker is a large one, the trim preventing the doors from breaking outwards must be sturdy. The plastic bottom guides alone are seldom adequate.

For smaller doors, a simple double channel in thick plastic is perfectly adequate. This can be screwed in with the doors in position (use brass screws well countersunk). The alternative is to arrange the channels so that the doors can be lifted in and out. If so, remember that the depth of the top channel must be greater than that of the bottom channel. Catches are not normally needed on sliding doors but, if preferred, a simple stop will suffice.

One excellent idea is to make the locker doors of transparent material, so you can reach the contents without scrabbling. Tinted Perspex is ideal, as it obscures the shambles within from all but a close inspection.

iii. Drawers

Drawers rate top marks for seamanlike stowage, for everything sits snugly in a box yet is completely accessible. They are admittedly somewhat wasteful of space, and also decidedly demanding to make properly. They slide, and sliding things, as previously remarked, are tricky. They are also boxes, which are surprisingly time-consuming to construct. Nevertheless, drawers are worth the trouble, and Fig. 26 shows an excellent drawer design I have seen, advocated too by naval architect Bruce Bingham.

The design is centred on a round dowel, over which the back of the drawer slides. This gives the drawer a three-point landing, thereby eliminating all misalignment

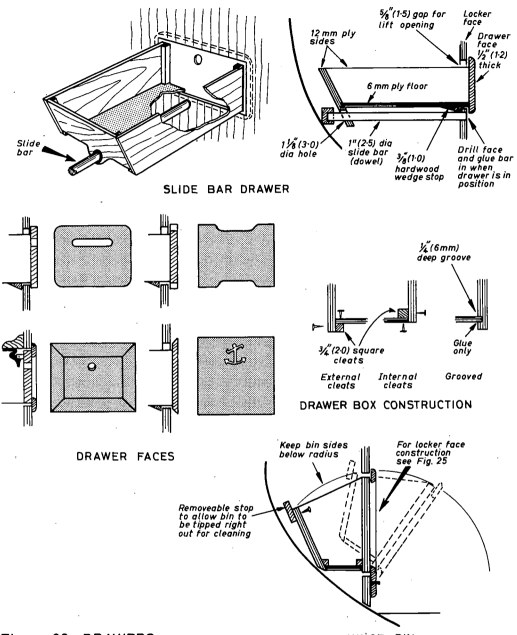

SLIDE BAR DRAWER

DRAWER BOX CONSTRUCTION

DRAWER FACES

Figure 26. DRAWERS

HINGE BIN

97

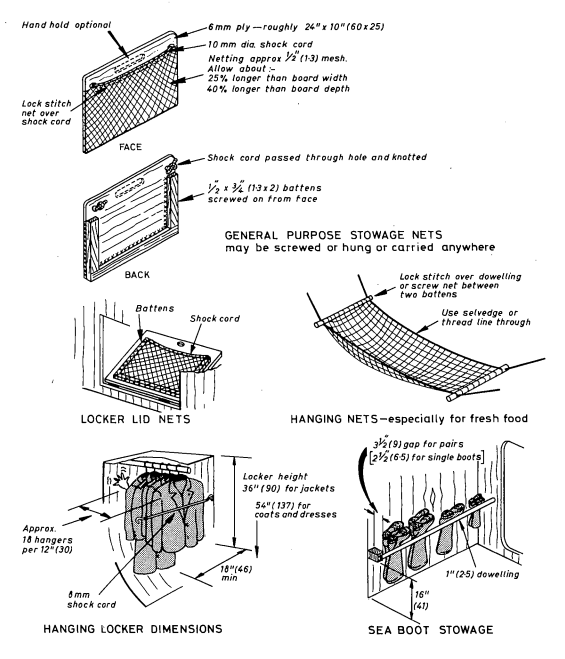

Hand hold optional

6 mm ply —roughly 24" x 10" (60 x 25)

10 mm dia. shock cord

Netting approx ½" (1·3) mesh.
Allow about :-
25% longer than board width
40% longer than board depth

Lock stitch
net over
shock cord

FACE

Shock cord passed through hole and knotted

½" x ¾" (1·3 x 2) battens
screwed on from face

BACK

GENERAL PURPOSE STOWAGE NETS
may be screwed or hung or carried anywhere

Battens

Shock cord

Lock stitch over dowelling
or screw net between
two battens

Use selvedge or
thread line through

LOCKER LID NETS

HANGING NETS—especially for fresh food

Locker height
36" (90) for jackets

54" (137) for
coats and dresses

Approx.
18 hangers
per 12" (30)

18" (46)
min

6 mm
shock cord

3½" (9) gap for pairs
[2½" (6·5) for single boots]

1" (2·5) dowelling

16"
(41)

HANGING LOCKER DIMENSIONS

SEA BOOT STOWAGE

Figure 27. SOFT STOWAGE

problems; furthermore, the drawer cannot lift or jump out of its hole. Obviously, the dowel must be secured firmly at each end, and it should be glued in after the drawer is in position. Construction of the box itself can be done, as shown, with inside cleats, outside cleats (certainly better for the side/bottom joint), or by grooving. Dovetailing is neat if you can do it.

More conventional wooden-rail slides are relatively straightforward to make. The main point to watch is that clearance is neither too great nor too small; $\frac{1}{20}$ in (1 mm) each side is about right. At the top sufficient clearance is needed to lift the drawer, but not so much that it jumps out of its rails. Another method is to use commercially available plastic slides. There is no reason why these should not be successful, provided that a locking mechanism is incorporated.

Drawer faces can be done in a variety of styles, a few of which are shown in Fig. 26. Points to consider are: drawers should match the style of the other joinery, particularly locker faces; if the drawer front stands proud of the locker face, a simple lift locking system can be used without leaving an unsightly gap at the top; flush faces demand a finger catch or similar; protruding knobs and handles are pretty but they tend to be dangerous at sea.

A sort of cheat drawer is the hinge bin drawn in Fig. 26. Hinge bins are secure, seaworthy and especially useful in those pyramid-shaped spaces between hull and locker faces that abound on boats.

iv. Soft Stowage

By this I mean nets, and stowage of soft articles like clothes. Unless you have actually used well-fitted side nets, it is difficult to appreciate how convenient and safe they are for stowage of clothes and small personal items. Easy to shove into, visible for quick retrieval, and open to ventilation, things stay put even in a knock down. Because they are not too large—two to three feet across by not more than 10 inches deep is about right (90 × 25 cm)—each crew member can have one.

To work properly, nets must be fixed firmly both sides and bottom, and have shockcord across the top. This is not always easy to do without marking bulkheads or fixing to the hull; hence the design in Fig. 27 for a self-contained net board that can be made on the bench.

The net is mounted on a plywood board of the correct shape, in the manner indicated, and the whole affair can then be fixed on with a few screws, or hung if the fixing is temporary, or even carried around by hand. You might, for instance, want to carry swimming costumes in the dinghy, or put safety harnesses near the companionway, or give each crew a net for his personal effects when there are not enough permanent bunks and everyone has to play musical chairs on change of watch (a disagreeably unseamanlike practice, incidentally). Another advantage of the boards is that they prevent condensation affecting the contents if used against the hull. The making of the netboards is straightforward enough, but ensure that you allow enough surplus netting for the stowage needed.

Another style of net is the hanging type used on long voyages, mainly for stowing fresh fruit and vegetables, but also for bulky things like toilet rolls and blankets. We used to string these nets anyhow, but the hammock system, using spreading battens shown in Fig. 27, is better. Yet another kind of stowage is that of nets fitted inside locker lids. These are practical stowage extenders, and handy too for items that must be reached quickly, like flares.

Also given in Fig. 27 are dimensions of lockers to accommodate clothes on hangers. Eighteen full hangers per foot is an average—heavy oilskins will occupy more space while cotton frocks will obviously take up much less. Finally we come to the problem of sea boots, always bulky, often wet and, therefore, best stowed heels up. I have tried upending the boot over a vertical spike, and explored other methods but with little success. The most workable is the simple bar illustrated, which is fixed alongside a convenient bulkhead. As the boots are jammed in upside down, they can be stowed under the oilskins without getting wet inside.

v. Miscellaneous Stowage

My experience of tools on boats is that they generally get chucked into a tool box or, at best, a drawer. Every time you want the green screwdriver with the pink neon light in the handle, you scrabble through the entire inventory barking, 'Someone has taken it! I know it was here. Come on! Who has it?' This is galling if you are a handy fellow who uses his tools a lot, and dangerous if you need something in a crisis. Tools, should, therefore, be readily accessible but, more than that, they should be stowed in such a manner that they stay dry, ventilated and cannot rattle or escape. The 'filing cabinet' rack in Fig. 28 does all these things, and does them well, as I have proved on a long voyage. The whole 'file' of spanners, say, can be taken to the job, and three or four 'files' will generally carry your entire tool stock. Tucked behind a companion-way, the system is economical in its use of space. One point is important; the canvases must be stitched together in pairs along the bottom, otherwise they become unstable and tilt their contents into the bilge.

The universal tool rack is more sophisticated and is the end product of several designs. You can carry it around easily, and stand it up *in situ* as a working rack (Photo 32). When stowed against the hull or a bulkhead, the tools are individually accessible (Photo 33). The construction is sketched in Fig. 28. Two 6 mm plywood boards are hinged together at the top, and each is fitted with canvas pockets and trays to suit. The pockets are made from a single strip of canvas, glued and pop riveted or bolted (screws would have to be too small) to the ply; make certain there is plenty of material allotted to each pocket, as neither the wood nor canvas yields. Hand openings are notched out of the top and one handgrip batten screwed to the face ply; do not use two battens as they will pinch your palm when you pick the rack up.

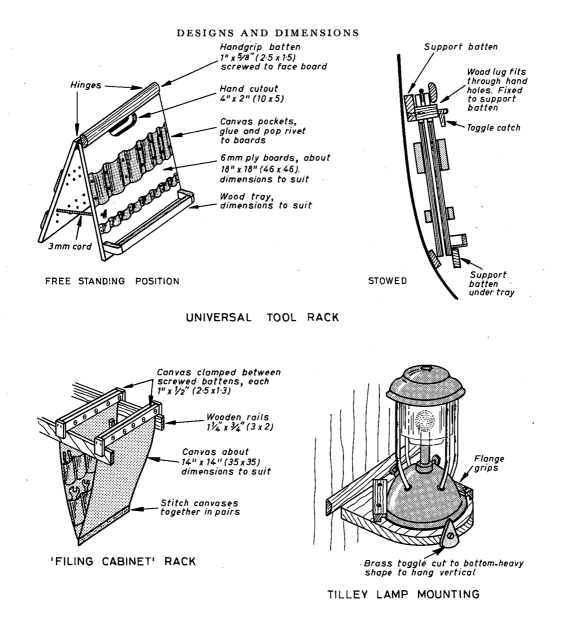

Handgrip batten
1" x 5/8" (2·5 x 1·5)
screwed to face board

Hinges

Hand cutout
4" x 2" (10 x 5)

Canvas pockets,
glue and pop rivet
to boards

6mm ply boards, about
18" x 18" (46 x 46).
dimensions to suit

Wood tray,
dimensions to suit

3mm cord

FREE STANDING POSITION

Support batten

Wood lug fits
through hand
holes. Fixed
to support
batten

Toggle catch

STOWED

Support
batten
under tray

UNIVERSAL TOOL RACK

Canvas clamped between
screwed battens, each
1" x 1/2" (2·5 x 1·3)

Wooden rails
1¼" x ¾" (3 x 2)

Canvas about
14" x 14" (35 x 35)
dimensions to suit

Stitch canvases
together in pairs

'FILING CABINET' RACK

Flange
grips

Brass toggle cut to bottom-heavy
shape to hang vertical

TILLEY LAMP MOUNTING

Figure 28. MISCELLANEOUS STOWAGE

Stowing the rack can be done in a variety of ways. In the one illustrated, the rack is fitted against the hull, where it takes up very little cabin space; the bottom both rests on and is jammed by a support batten fixed to bulkheads or frames. The top is held by another batten and an attached lug which passes through the hand hole. Examination of Photo 33 will clarify the design, which ensures that the rack is rigidly fixed in all directions.

32. A sophisticated tool rack. It can be carried about, stood up, and both sides carry tools.

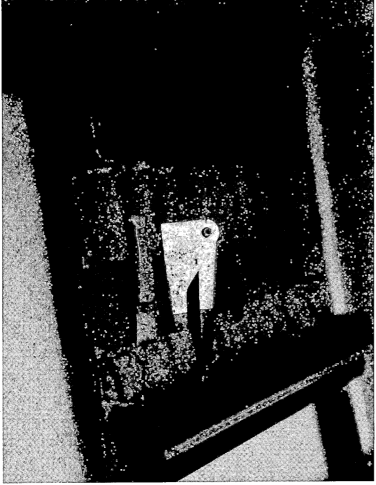

33. The rack fits on to the side of the hull, notching into the bottom batten and locking on to the top one.

When working aboard a good deal, one's tools tend to end up scattered around the floor, and an inordinate amount of time is wasted hunting for them. A simple little plywood table (not illustrated) is a great help. Roughly 12 × 18 inches (30 × 45 cm), drilled with various-sized holes and slots to take the tools, it stands on stubby legs about 15 inches (38 cm) high. No good for shipboard stowage, of course, but fine for fitting out.

Finally, plastic or stainless wire trays of the type used by supermarkets and laundries provide an excellent means of breaking down large stowage areas into more usable compartments. I have seen them racked on bunks as fresh-food bins, clipped behind the galley stove for general use or simply stacked inside over-large lockers. I have also seen them mounted on slides inside lockers where they become neat ventilated drawers.

103

E   THE GALLEY

The galley is the heart of a serious cruising yacht, and, therefore, merits close attention. Discussion of layout is outside the scope of this book, but in passing, certain desirable features are worth recording. The best layout, in my experience, is a U shape, providing the cook with a semi-enclosed and exclusive work area where he or she can reach stove, sink or work-top merely by turning. Stoves are virtually always gymballed (on a fore-and-aft axis) against the hull. In most cases this is a sensible position, but when the stove is large, problems appear; on one tack the cook is on top of the stove, and on the other tack, vice versa. When a deep stove swings out it is liable to hit the cook's legs. Photo 34 shows an alternative arrangement, where the stove is mounted against a bulkhead, in this case using the front wheel hub of a car to carry the cantilever load. The cook stands four-square in front of the stove and operates two-handed without the need to fend off the pots. The system is suitable only for a large boat. Motor boats can get away, at a pinch, without gymballing,

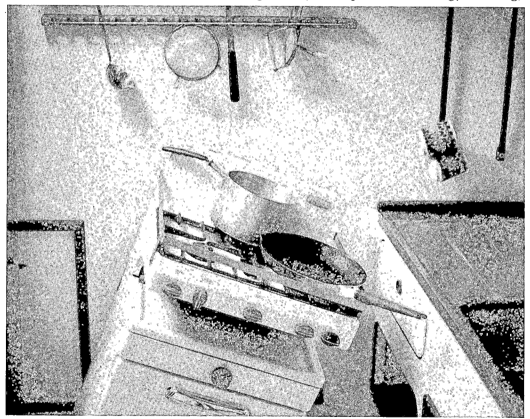

34. An unusual way of gymballing a stove on a bulkhead, so the cook faces the stove, both hands free. Practical for larger boats.

provided that a good fiddle rail is fitted. A tip on fiddles incidentally, is to build the rail—it can well be of ⅜ in bar—really high, say 3½ inches (9 cm), and make a valley dipping down to ¾ in (2 cm) for the frying-pan handle.

Galley sinks are all too often miserable little funnels under the tap, when what you sorely need is a damn great basin that will take all the washing up, retain the potatoes while you are peeling the onions, and hold the pot of beef Stroganoff safely while you are preparing the brandy mousse. For sinks are not merely water receptacles, they are important work units, as any seasoned sea-cook can testify. I never could follow the design logic of these tiddly sink covers. In short, you want the biggest sink that can be accommodated, and if the unit is lying athwartships, then a fiddle rail between sink and drainer will be found very useful; the drainer, in effect, becomes another holding area, leaving the basin free for washing. Another frequent defect is taps which are too low, or operated by hand. Taps should preferably be high enough to get a bucket under, and should be foot operated (or pressurised), leaving both hands free to wash. One final point—sinks with twin outlets that drain on either tack are a delight to work but unfortunately rarely seen. An effective home-made alternative used in the yacht *Meander* consists of a trough-like sink, running fore and aft and narrow at the bottom, which slopes down to the drain. This sink drains completely on either tack.

Galleyware stowage. Top of the galleyware list is the crockery, by no means easy stuff to stow. The common T front, cut-out lockers are difficult to use, difficult to clean, and hold only one size of dish that does not rattle and bang. Avoid them, if building from scratch. A more elegant and infinitely simpler idea is the peg stowage shown in Fig. 29. Half-inch dowels are fitted into holes drilled at the back of worktops, on shelves or in some other suitable location, and spaced to the dishes you have. They can be changed if any of the galleyware is changed, and are usable for pots, plates and most other galleyware, proportions of which are indicated in the drawing. The stowage, moreover, is easy to use and easy to clean.

The drainage cum stowage locker in Fig. 29 must usually be built into the galley from the start, but it approaches the ultimate in galleyware stowage. Essentially it comprises a floorless locker set above and behind the sink, with a sloping tray fitted underneath to conduct the drainage back to the sink. Inside the locker, the dishes are supported in a wire rack and/or wire trays, detachable for cleaning or replacement. The racks and trays may be of the ordinary household type, but must be carefully chosen for their ability to hold different things at large angles of heel. The beauty of the system is that it will not only drip dry and stow simultaneously, but will happily stow dirty dishes safely if you get into a blow and choose to postpone washing up.

Mugs and tumblers will generally (though not necessarily) be stowed elsewhere. Both are something of a headache. After a good deal of experimentation, I have found that mugs and cups hang quite nicely on a slightly springy wooden spike (Fig.

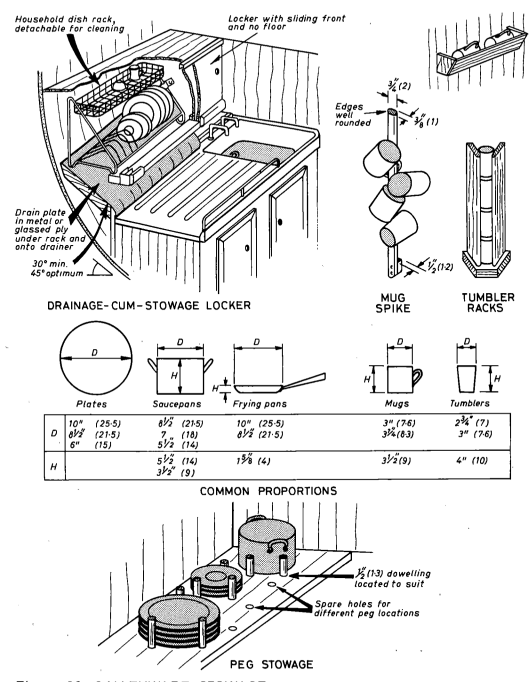

Household dish rack, detachable for cleaning

Locker with sliding front and no floor

Edges well rounded

$\frac{3}{4}''$ (2)

$\frac{3}{8}''$ (1)

Drain plate in metal or glassed ply under rack and onto drainer

30° min. 45° optimum

$\frac{1}{2}''$ (1·2)

DRAINAGE-CUM-STOWAGE LOCKER

MUG SPIKE

TUMBLER RACKS

	Plates	Saucepans	Frying pans	Mugs	Tumblers
D	10" (25·5) 8½" (21·5) 6" (15)	8½" (21·5) 7" (18) 5½" (14)	10" (25·5) 8½" (21·5)	3" (7·6) 3¼" (8·3)	2¾" (7) 3" (7·6)
H		5½" (14) 3½" (9)	1⅝" (4)	3½" (9)	4" (10)

COMMON PROPORTIONS

$\frac{1}{2}''$ (1·3) dowelling located to suit

Spare holes for different peg locations

PEG STOWAGE

Figure 29. GALLEYWARE STOWAGE

29) which is economical in space too. Tumblers, on the other hand, occupy relatively a lot of space, however stowed. The vertical rack illustrated is at any rate workable, and so too is the narrow shelf with a high fiddle. Individual stowage in holes cut out of a 4 mm plywood sheet is even more space consuming, but may be worth it for good glasses, and also, incidentally, for liquor bottles. A natty alternative for just a few tumblers is a gymballed tray, suitable for carrying around. Such a tray is fairly straightforward, though time-consuming to make; or it can be purchased quite reasonably from a chandler.

Several other stowage ideas for making the galley more seaworthy are shown in Fig. 30. The cutlery rack is a ridiculously simple idea for tools in frequent use, which I found aboard a Spanish trawler that rolled like a pendulum in a williwaw. The batten has to be fairly thin and springy. The utensil rack is designed to prevent the incessant swinging of hanging tools, and the spice rack is a particularly neat solution to the stowage of small jars. A properly placed trash bucket adds considerably to the seaworthiness of the galley, and an idea that seems to work well is to step the bucket on the back of a locker door. It can then be operated with the door open, or small trash can simply be pushed through the hand hole with the door closed.

Last, but not least, we come to the cook, often the most badly stowed item in the galley. While I have seen a safety harness clipped to the roof, the best system, I feel, is a bottom support, firm enough to lean against with complete confidence, which leaves the hands free for cooking. The support may take the shape of a piece of pipe, a wooden bar, or the strap shown in Fig. 30. The strap (it can be made from a car safety-belt) is clipped onto ring or U-bolts, which must in turn be backed with reinforcement that distributes the heavy loads involved. Do not mount the strap too high (32 inches or 81 cm, for the average person), as the torso must be free to swivel. The illustration also features a wedge bin—made in wood or bought in plastic—which will be found very useful for the stowage of bottles and utensils while working.

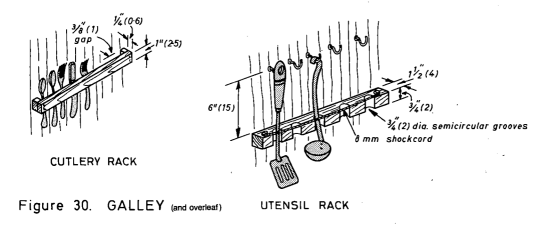

CUTLERY RACK

Figure 30. GALLEY (and overleaf)   UTENSIL RACK

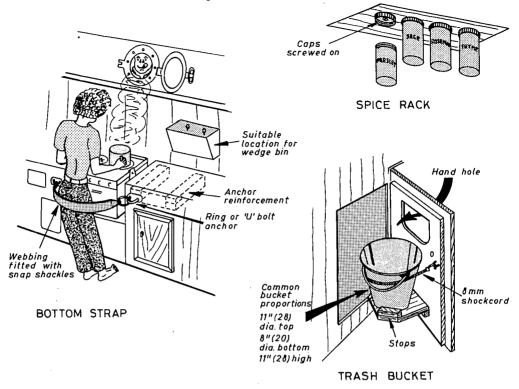

SPICE RACK

Suitable
location for
wedge bin

Anchor
reinforcement

Ring or 'U' bolt
anchor

Webbing
fitted with
snap shackles

BOTTOM STRAP

Caps
screwed on

Hand hole

Common
bucket
proportions
11"(28)
dia. top
8"(20)
dia. bottom
11"(28)high

6 mm
shockcord

Stops

TRASH BUCKET

Figure 30. GALLEY

F   THE CHART TABLE

Chart tables should preferably face forward, and this, in fact, is the case on most boats; the chart table is usually to one side of the main hatch (traditionally to starboard) and frequently at the head of the quarter berth, which serves as a seat. If facing sideways, the chart table is unlikely to have a seat, and should be 3 feet above the sole (see p. 71), but if facing forward there is normally space to sit. In which case, the table top should be no more than 1 foot above the seat, while the underside must be at least 8 inches to clear the knees. This gives a stowage case of around 4 inches in depth. If space is tight, there are various ways of stowing charts (other than under mattresses), two of which are shown in Fig. 31. The hull method is particularly compact and convenient—you can riffle through the charts and easily extract the one you want. Make certain, however, that the charts are kept clear of condensation with a plywood or rigid foam lining, and that the foot rack is well above the swash of the bilge.

The most frequent defect I have found with chart tables—and it is frequent—is their inability to retain a chart in rough weather. Fiddles, several times paper thickness in height, will not hold the paper, as their builders fondly imagine, because

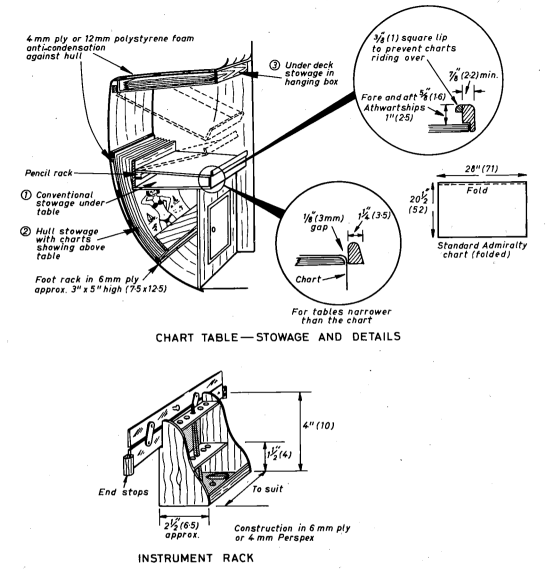

4 mm ply or 12mm polystyrene foam
anti-condensation
against hull

③ Under deck
stowage in
hanging box

3/8" (1) square lip
to prevent charts
riding over

7/8" (2·2) min.

Fore and aft 5/8" (1·6)
Athwartships
1" (2·5)

Pencil rack

① Conventional
stowage under
table

② Hull stowage
with charts
showing above
table

Foot rack in 6mm ply
approx. 3" x 5" high (7·5 x 12·5)

1/8" (3mm)
gap

1 1/4" (3·5)

Chart

For tables narrower
than the chart

28" (71)

Fold

20 1/2
(52)

Standard Admiralty
chart (folded)

CHART TABLE — STOWAGE AND DETAILS

4" (10)

1 1/2" (4)

End stops

To suit

2 1/2" (6·5)
approx.

Construction in 6 mm ply
or 4 mm Perspex

INSTRUMENT RACK

Figure 31. THE CHART TABLE

the chart bends up and rides over the top. A decent-sized fiddle with a lip to prevent
this is illustrated. Remember too that fiddles running fore and aft must be strong
enough to hold heavy books, RDFs, and people who grab them.

Sometimes a chart table large enough to accommodate a folded Admiralty chart
cannot be fitted, and the chart has to hang over the edge. To prevent it being worn
away by the navigator's belly, the offstanding fiddle, shown, is suggested. The

109

arrangement is also effective in holding the chart, provided that the gap is right.

Stowage of chart instruments is fairly simple, and an all-purpose rack is illustrated. Or you can buy something similar. But do have something, even if it is a couple of lengths of string to hold pencils and rubber.

G   HANDS AND FEET
i. Handrails and Finger Lifts

Every boat needs handrails and handgrips in every conceivable place where you might want to grab—galleys, toilets, companion steps, along the sides of the cabin trunk and outside along the coachwork are obvious examples. It is usual to cut handrails from the solid plank, and the method shown in Fig. 32 is simplicity itself. It involves merely careful drilling, sawing, rounding over and finishing, to make something that is beautiful as well as functional. You can save wood by cutting two rails from a wider plank, or by using a separate base, as shown. Use teak outside and any good hardwood down below, and attach with heavy fastenings, preferably bolts.

If you are willing to stand the extra expense, you can make handrails simply with the metal ring brackets designed to support a wooden rail. A very attractive rail, pictured in Photo 35, is made by threading heavy (20 mm) rope through bronze brackets.

Two finger lifts for sole hatches are illustrated in Fig. 32, and they have the virtue of requiring no fittings whatever. The rope ring is simple enough, but the finger

35. A rope hand-grab adds a nice touch to this lovingly fitted out interior.

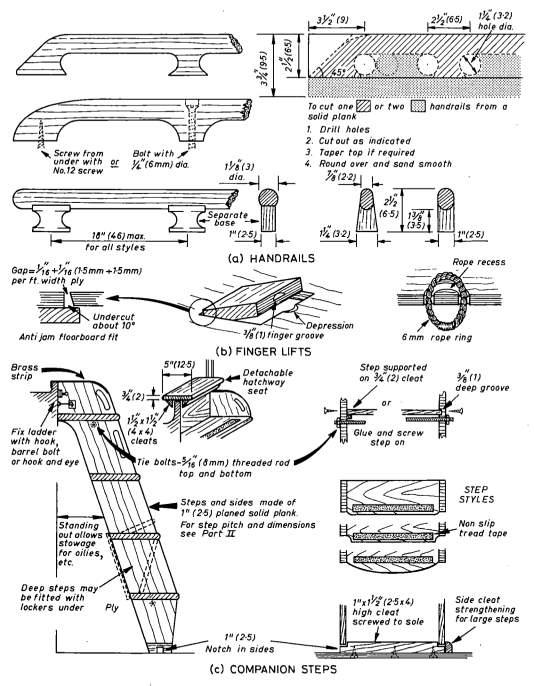

$3\frac{1}{2}''$ (9) $2\frac{1}{2}''$ (6·5) $1\frac{1}{4}''$ (3·2) hole dia.

$3\frac{3}{4}''$ (9·5) $2\frac{1}{2}''$ (6·5)   45°

To cut one ▨ or two ▦ handrails from a solid plank

1. Drill holes
2. Cut out as indicated
3. Taper top if required
4. Round over and sand smooth

Screw from under with or No.12 screw   Bolt with $\frac{1}{4}''$ (6mm) dia.

$1\frac{1}{8}''$ (3) dia. $\frac{7}{8}''$ (2·2)

Separate base $2\frac{1}{2}$ (6·5) $1\frac{3}{8}''$ (3·5)

18" (46) max. for all styles   1" (2·5) $1\frac{1}{4}''$ (3·2)   1" (2·5)

(a) HANDRAILS

Gap = $\frac{1}{16}'' + \frac{1}{16}''$ (1·5mm + 1·5mm) per ft. width ply

Undercut about 10°

Anti jam floorboard fit

Depression
$\frac{3}{8}''$ (1) finger groove

Rope recess

6 mm rope ring

(b) FINGER LIFTS

Brass strip

5" (12·5)   Detachable hatchway seat

$\frac{3}{4}''$ (2)

$1\frac{1}{2}'' \times 1\frac{1}{2}''$ (4 x 4) cleats

Fix ladder with hook, barrel bolt or hook and eye

Tie bolts—$\frac{5}{16}''$ (8mm) threaded rod top and bottom

Step supported on $\frac{3}{4}''$ (2) cleat $\frac{3}{8}''$ (1) deep groove

or

Glue and screw step on

Steps and sides made of 1" (2·5) planed solid plank. For step pitch and dimensions see Part II

STEP STYLES

Non slip tread tape

Standing out allows stowage for oilies, etc.

Deep steps may be fitted with lockers under   Ply

1" (2·5) Notch in sides

1"x$1\frac{1}{2}''$ (2·5 x 4) high cleat screwed to sole

Side cleat strengthening for large steps

(c) COMPANION STEPS

Figure 32. HANDS AND FEET

groove is more fundamental yet; a groove is cut in the hatch, and a depression rasped into the soleboard opposite. I have found it works perfectly well, provided that the hatch does not swell and jam, easily avoided by providing all round gaps when the wood is dry, no less than those indicated. For solid wood soles, the gap should be four times greater across the grain i.e. $\frac{1}{4}$ in per foot width.

ii. Companion Steps

The method of constructing wooden steps is essentially to place a plank each side to support the treads between. Solid wood, and preferably a good hardwood, must be used throughout, for during its long life the companionway will receive a battering as severe as any item aboard. I once estimated that during one year's living aboard, each step on our boat received some 40,000 blows from heel and toe. The treads must, therefore, be strongly attached to the cheeks; joiners like to rebate, but I consider the cleat support stronger (Fig. 32), with just a fractional rebate to neaten the appearance and discourage the tread from curling upwards. A strong mounting and a good wood are all the more important because screwing into the tread end grain is unavoidable. A structural glue must, therefore, be used, and tie rods should be fitted under at least the first and last steps to prevent the cheeks being pounded outwards over the years.

The steps must be firmly secured top and bottom, and an elegant base bracket is shown; consisting of only one cleat screwed to the floor, it nevertheless locates the step rigidly in all directions except upwards.

The proportions of steps have been treated in Section II 5, and within these proportions different styles are possible, some of which are shown in Fig. 32. The cheeks can also be curved, which looks very elegant but uses a lot of wood. Other variations include step lockers, and a broad top step (as drawn) to sit on. Any cruising yachtie will tell you that the favourite place for the night watch to sit is at the top of the companionway, so why not make it comfortable and secure?

If you cannot make a sitting step at the proper height, consider the little detachable hatchway seat illustrated. It is a delight on passage.

H   VENTS AND HATCHES

The purpose of a ventilator is to allow the passage of people and/or air, while barring the ingress of water. This statement of the obvious is merely to emphasise that fittings must be designed round the laws of fluid behaviour, rather than round considerations of cost, or more usually size. So, to keep dry it is worth taking a close look at the way Mother Nature has arranged for water to flow, before launching into design.

i. Air/Water Separation

Water is separated from a mixture of air and water flowing, say, through a ventilator, in one of three ways (Fig. 33):

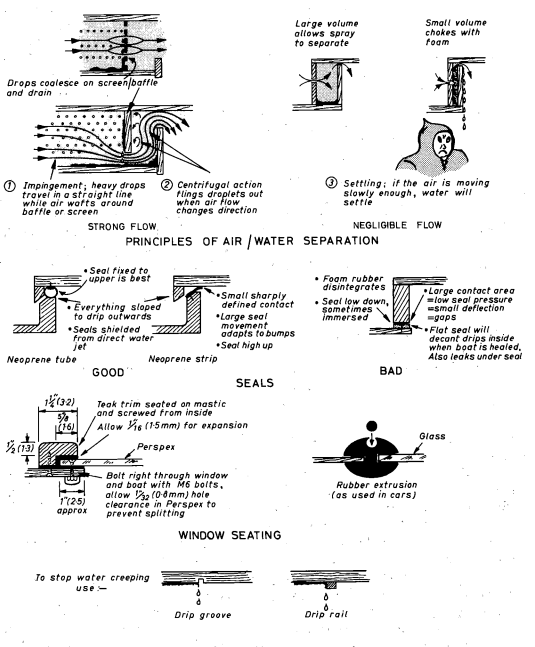

Drops coalesce on screen/baffle and drain

Large volume allows spray to separate

Small volume chokes with foam

① Impingement; heavy drops travel in a straight line while air wafts around baffle or screen

② Centrifugal action flings droplets out when air flow changes direction

③ Settling; if the air is moving slowly enough, water will settle

STRONG FLOW

NEGLIGIBLE FLOW

PRINCIPLES OF AIR / WATER SEPARATION

• Seal fixed to upper is best

• Everything sloped to drip outwards

• Seals shielded from direct water jet

Neoprene tube

GOOD

• Small sharply defined contact
• Large seal movement adapts to bumps
• Seal high up

Neoprene strip

• Foam rubber disintegrates
• Seal low down, sometimes immersed

• Large contact area = low seal pressure = small deflection = gaps
• Flat seal will decant drips inside when boat is healed. Also leaks under seal

BAD

SEALS

1¼"(3·2)
5/8 (1·6)
½" (1·3)

Teak trim seated on mastic and screwed from inside
Allow 1/16 (1·5mm) for expansion

Perspex

Bolt right through window and boat with M6 bolts, allow 1/32 (0·8mm) hole clearance in Perspex to prevent splitting

1"(2·5) approx

Glass

Rubber extrusion (as used in cars)

WINDOW SEATING

To stop water creeping use :-

Drip groove

Drip rail

Figure 33. FLUID MECHANICS or How to stay dry

(a) Impingement. If an obstruction is placed in the line of flow, the air will deviate around it but the momentum of the heavier water drops carries them straight on, and they strike the obstruction. There they coalesce into larger and larger drops, which finally drain away. It is obvious that the air must not be moving too slowly, else the fine droplets will have insufficient momentum; they will be deflected around the baffle by the airflow. It is less obvious that small baffles work better, if anything, than large ones, because the droplets are less prone to deflection. In fact, in industry, knitted mesh separators, made from microscopic wire, achieve 100 per cent separation efficiencies, yet hardly restrict airflow at all. Unfortunately, these are not suitable for boats, as the air velocity must be accurately controlled. The boat equivalent is screening, which is considerably less effective.

(b) Centrifugal action of air, swirling as it changes direction, flings out the drops. This is illustrated in Fig. 33.

(c) Settling is the most common way to separate air and water on boat fittings. It occurs when separate paths are provided for the air to rise and the water to fall, and when the air is moving slowly enough. To slow the flow up requires nothing more nor less than space, and the narrow, Maurice Griffiths type hatch illustrated, often leaks because it is too narrow.

The desirable points of a ventilator (or hatch, or cockpit seat, or whatever) can, therefore, be summarised as:

● Abrupt changes in direction of air flow, the more, the better (without restricting air flow unduly).

● Design which allows water and air to follow separate flow paths. *Height* is essential to permit the water to drain.

● Large volume for settling and draining. Here both height and width are needed.

ii. Seals

Seals are a positive means of excluding both air and water, but here again sound practice must be adopted to make seals effective.

The 'dos' and 'don'ts' of home-made seal design are summarised in Fig. 33, and there is little to add, except perhaps that the commonly available foam rubber strip should be avoided. It rots rapidly and tends to stick to the wrong surface and come away in bits. It also seldom seals properly, even when the cross-section is semi-circular. Neoprene, on the other hand, is highly durable if somewhat less flexible. It is readily available as tubing and sheet which can be cut into strips. It is best glued on (use a cyanacrylate on smooth surfaces, and an impact adhesive on absorbent materials) and pinned with small 'Gripfast' nails.

Another type of seal, particularly effective for portholes, is the type cast *in situ*. The best material for this is a silicone rubber (smells like vinegar when curing). Clean out the old seal and squeeze a generous beading of rubber into the groove. Allow a few minutes to skin over, then shut it lightly until cured. To prevent it sticking to the other face use grease or, better still, polythene film. The result will be a seal perfectly matched to the mating face.

iii. Windows

Non-opening windows require bedding rather than sealing and a couple of basic techniques are shown in Fig. 33. The rubber extrusion used to fit vehicle windows is neat and easy, and suited possibly to smaller GRP or metal boats, or perhaps to small windows. But for heavier work this fitting makes me uneasy, particularly when one considers the forces and flexures that can be imposed.

More reassuring is the simple overlapping of window on boat, as illustrated. The window is bolted through, and the trim, though mainly cosmetic, serves to conceal all fastenings from the outside and adds to the watertightness of the window. An alternative design is to rebate the pane flush with the outside of the boat and use flat trim; a frame can be used inside as well, to improve appearance. If the pane is horizontal, drain grooves must be cut in the trim to prevent the accumulation of water.

Armour-plate glass is more difficult to fit because it cannot be drilled (though you can specify holes if your glass is being specially made). The same designs can, nevertheless, be used, though it would be prudent to beef up the trim, if bolts are not used.

iv. Ventilators

The two ventilators drawn in Fig. 34 incorporate the various flow principles discussed, and the heavy-duty design should function under all but the most extreme conditions. Even then, the adjustable sleeve can be pushed up from inside the boat to seal against the top, and prevent a massive inrush of water when the Dorade is totally immersed, an important consideration if really heavy-weather sailing is contemplated. A cover to replace the cowl should also be kept handy. The top can be made of Perspex, if you want light as well as ventilation, and a nice touch is to sand the Perspex on the inside to make a translucent diffuser.

Flow areas are important. A 3 in diameter vent pipe is the minimum that will provide any worthwhile ventilation. A 4 in (10 cm) diameter is preferable for larger vessels, and to ventilate and light a large heads area you need something about 6×6 in (15×15 cm). If the cross-sectional area of the vent pipe through the deck is A, then the sectional area for flow anywhere within the box should be a minimum of $1\frac{1}{2} \times A$, and the cross sectional area of the cowl base $\frac{2}{3} \times A$ minimum.

Construction of the Dorade is straightforward, using either marine ply or solid timber. The cowl is best bought (I prefer the flexible plastic type, because it is less liable to damage), and only the vent pipe through the deck may give problems. Wood has to be too thick for most designs, so the pipe must be fabricated in metal or GRP, or a standard piece of plastic can be used—PVC drain pipe is an obvious choice, or a sturdy plastic container with the bottom cut out. The safest fitting is to

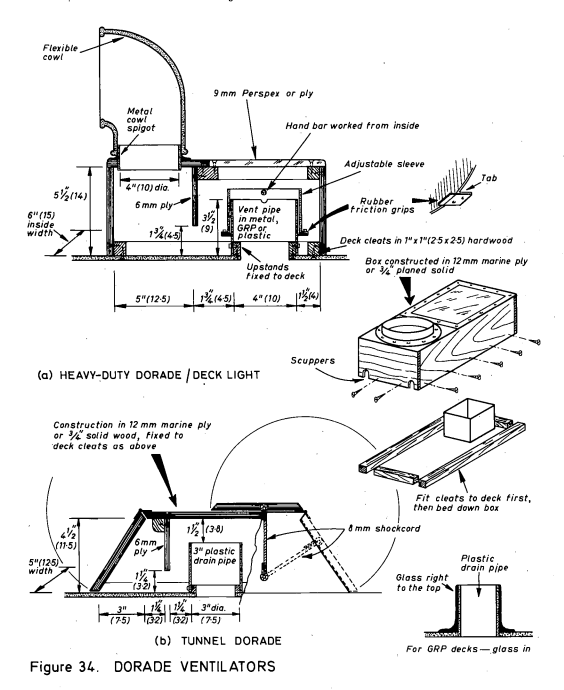

Flexible cowl

Metal cowl spigot

9 mm Perspex or ply

Hand bar worked from inside

Adjustable sleeve

Tab

4" (10) dia.

5½" (14)

6 mm ply

Rubber friction grips

6" (15) inside width

Vent pipe in metal, GRP or plastic

3½ (9)

1¾ (4·5)

Deck cleats in 1" x 1" (2·5 x 2·5) hardwood

Upstands fixed to deck

Box constructed in 12 mm marine ply or ¾" planed solid

5" (12·5)   1¾" (4·5)   4" (10)   1½" (4)

Scuppers

(a) HEAVY-DUTY DORADE / DECK LIGHT

Construction in 12 mm marine ply or ¾" solid wood, fixed to deck cleats as above

Fit cleats to deck first, then bed down box

4½" (11·5)

6 mm ply

1½" (3·8)

8 mm shockcord

Plastic drain pipe

5" (12·5) width

3" plastic drain pipe

1¼ (3·2)

Glass right to the top

3" (7·5)   1¼ (3·2)   1¼ (3·2)   3" dia. (7·5)

(b) TUNNEL DORADE

For GRP decks — glass in

Figure 34. DORADE VENTILATORS

bed the pipe over an inside kerb, but for GRP boats you can glass the whole pipe in as illustrated.

The tunnel Dorade has the virtues of simplicity and cheapness—there is no cowl and only two deck cleats are required. The box can be opened at either end—if the downwind flap is opened, air will be drawn out of the boat, and vice versa. Although upstanding flaps supported on struts would be somewhat more effective, they would also be very vulnerable to damage, and the simple shockcord snap is to be preferred.

All remarks already made concerning flow and vent pipes apply equally to the tunnel Dorade, and like the heavier-duty Dorade, a Perspex top can be fitted to admit light.

v. Hinging Hatches

The hinging hatch drawn in Fig. 35 combines the functions of a hatch, a ventilator and, if a Perspex top is used, a skylight too. Again, only straightforward construction techniques have been employed, and the design is centred around the flow principles discussed. The unique feature is the fabric spray curtain which deflects the spray and enables the hatch to be lifted nearly 2 inches before it admits the sea. Because of the large areas involved, a hatch is far more effective than a ventilator. For instance, a 2 ft hatch allows twenty times the air flow of your normal 3 in ventilator, and the design has been found effective in a 90-knot wind with heavy rain. If a lesser degree of ventilation is required, the spray curtain can be omitted, and the gap between the inner and outer coamings closed by $\frac{3}{8}$ in (1 cm). The hatch will still be highly waterproof.

Apart from being waterproof, hatches should also be very strong, and the design in Fig. 35 allows for three stiffeners over the top and a stormbar underneath. I consider the latter essential for heavy weather, and it is thief proof too. The construction of the outer coaming and the hatch itself should be in good-quality hardwood, half-jointed and glued.

A traditional skylight is not shown because it is so difficult to design one that is completely leakproof. In fact, my experience with these fittings is that they always leak, if not when new, then after rot has set up in one of the many crevices to which the design is prone. Instead, I would always opt for a hinging-type hatch with a transparent top—there is no joint whatever over the open hatchway, and note also how vertical fastenings penetrating from above have been largely avoided. Any leaks are designed to occur within the large drain channel between the two coamings. The only point with Perspex (or Makrolon) is that it expands and contracts a great deal, and this must be allowed for with generous gaps filled with mastic. For this reason, the alternative edge detail shown is preferable, though less attractive, and holes must always be drilled oversize.

One attractive feature of the traditional skylight is that it opens either side. This can be achieved with the hatch skylight by using reversable hinges (expensive and

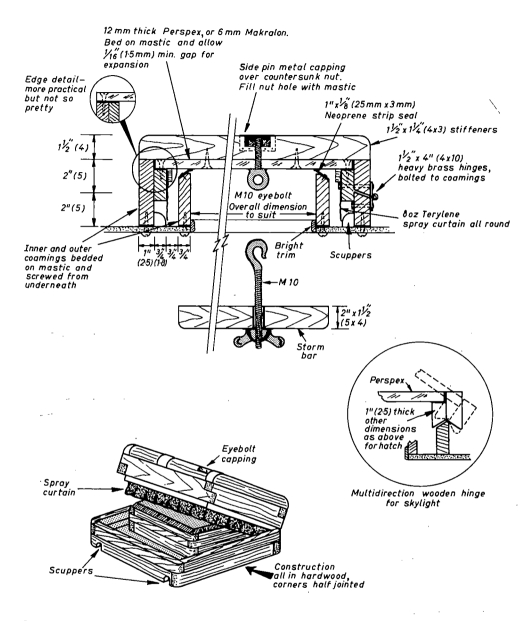

12 mm thick Perspex, or 6 mm Makralon.
Bed on mastic and allow
$\frac{1}{16}''$ (1·5mm) min. gap for
expansion

Side pin metal capping
over countersunk nut.
Fill nut hole with mastic

Edge detail—
more practical
but not so
pretty

$1'' \times \frac{1}{8}''$ (25mm x 3mm)
Neoprene strip seal

$1\frac{1}{2}'' \times 1\frac{1}{4}''$ (4x3) stiffeners

$1\frac{1}{2}'' \times 4''$ (4x10)
heavy brass hinges,
bolted to coamings

$1\frac{1}{2}''$ (4)

$2''$ (5)

$2''$ (5)

M10 eyebolt
Overall dimension
to suit

8oz Terylene
spray curtain all round

Inner and outer
coamings bedded
on mastic and
screwed from
underneath

$1''$ $\frac{3}{4}''$ $\frac{3}{4}''$ $\frac{3}{4}''$
(25)(1·8)

Bright
trim

Scuppers

M 10

Storm
bar

$2'' \times 1\frac{1}{2}''$
(5x4)

Perspex

$1''$ (2·5) thick
other
dimensions
as above
for hatch

Multidirection wooden hinge
for skylight

Eyebolt
capping

Spray
curtain

Scuppers

Construction
all in hardwood,
corners half jointed

Figure 35. HATCH — SKYLIGHT COMBINED VENTILATOR

hard to come by) or by making the wooden coaming hinge shown, the rest of the design being similar to the usual hinging type. The wooden hinge runs all the way round, to allow opening all four ways, and the skylight can be removed entirely in port if desired. Sturdy telescopic struts must be fitted to prevent the skylight jumping out altogether, so the design is not recommended for the foredeck.

vi. Sliding Hatches

The design shown in Fig. 36 is only one of the many ways of building a sound sliding hatch, but it follows the principles employed elsewhere in these pages, namely the construction uses principally straight pieces of wood and easily obtainable materials, it is strong and it works. There are two variations, depending on whether you want a housing or not.

A housing is more leak-resistant and looks better, but is also more costly in time and materials, and you cannot fit a look-out dome. The basic construction is to fit two parallel pairs of rails, the outer one of which steps up forward to receive the housing cover. Without the housing, only one pair of teak rails is required. In both cases, the hatch cover is similar—essentially a box with half-jointed corners—but with the housing, the corners need not be notched to receive the rail, and the design is, therefore, much stronger.

Some houseless designs have no corner jointing at all—the rail bears directly on the underside of the plywood top—but this is not recommended.

In both versions shown in Fig. 36, the bearing and sealing surfaces are teak-to-teak slides. The brass strip should not take the hatch load; its main purpose is to prevent the hatch lifting, and it also acts as a water baffle. The forward end is sealed very effectively with a rubber strip, which should come right down to trail along the deck in the houseless version. This strip also acts as a stop to prevent the hatch sliding out, and is screwed on from the inside after the hatch is in place. It can easily be unscrewed to remove the hatch, thus avoiding the ridiculous but all too common designs which make the hatch non dismountable and therefore non maintainable. Sealing the corners is rather more difficult, and one effective trick is to saw little grooves at an angle across each rail, as shown, to discourage water from creeping in.

As mentioned elsewhere in these pages, sliding things are decidedly tricky, and the gaps must be just right. Too large, and the hatch will cockle over and stick, too small, and it will swell and jam. With teak hatches, the $\frac{3}{32}$ in gaps shown are about right. In any event, everything should be measured and drawn very carefully before starting, especially as the hatch is likely to fit a curved coachwork, and if off-centre, one side will be higher than the other.

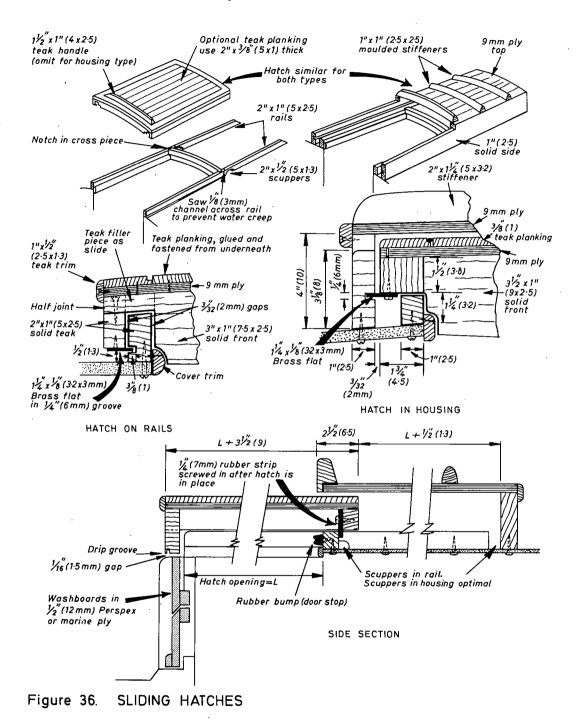

1½" x 1" (4 x 2·5)
teak handle
(omit for housing type)

Optional teak planking
use 2" x ⅜" (5 x 1) thick

Hatch similar for
both types

1" x 1" (2·5 x 2·5)
moulded stiffeners

9 mm ply
top

2" x 1" (5 x 2·5)
rails

Notch in cross piece

2" x ½" (5 x 1·3)
scuppers

1" (2·5)
solid side

Saw ⅛ (3mm)
channel across rail
to prevent water creep

2" x 1¼ (5 x 3·2)
stiffener

Teak filler
piece as
slide

Teak planking, glued and
fastened from underneath

9 mm ply

⅜ (1)
teak planking

9 mm ply

1" x ½"
(2·5 x 1·3)
teak trim

9 mm ply

3/32 (2mm) gaps

1½ (3·8)

9 mm ply

Half joint

3" x 1" (7·5 x 2·5)
solid front

3½" x 1"
(9 x 2·5)
solid
front

2" x 1" (5 x 2·5)
solid teak

1¼ (3·2)

½ (1·3)

4" (10)

3⅜ (8)

¼ (6mm)

1¼ x ⅛ (32 x 3mm)
Brass flat

1" (2·5)

1" (2·5)

1¼ x ⅛ (32 x 3mm)
Brass flat
in ¼" (6mm) groove

Cover trim

⅜ (1)

1¾
(4·5)

3/32
(2mm)

HATCH ON RAILS

HATCH IN HOUSING

L + 3½ (9)

2½ (6·5)

L + ½ (1·3)

¼" (7mm) rubber strip
screwed in after hatch is
in place

Drip groove

1/16 (1·5 mm) gap

Washboards in
½" (12 mm) Perspex
or marine ply

Hatch opening = L

Rubber bump (door stop)

Scuppers in rail.
Scuppers in housing optional

SIDE SECTION

Figure 36.   SLIDING HATCHES

vii. Washboards

There is nothing complicated about washboards, the only thing to remember being that they do not work on the sealing principle so much as on close-fitting joints that will leak slightly. The shape must, therefore, be carefully designed so that any water leaking in will automatically leak out again. An example of such a design is shown in Fig. 36.

Perspex washboards are an excellent idea (Photo 36), for in foul weather you can close the cabin without making it dark and claustrophobic.

36. Perspex washboards keep the weather out, while allowing the light in. These boards, made of 12 mm material, are reinforced top and bottom with Perspex battens glued and screwed on.

I MISCELLANEOUS DECK GEAR

i. Cleats

There is often an advantage in making your own cleats, for not only can they be cheaper than buying, but they may be better designed too. A wooden cleat is not as strong as a metal or plastic one, but it is kind to rope, and above all it can be made big. Too often, cleats are sized to make fast only one rope, and no account is taken of other ropes or halyard coils. The dimensions in Fig. 37(a) should, therefore, be regarded as a minimum, for cleats cannot be too large.

Making cleats from a solid plank is simply a matter of drilling, cutting (preferably with a bandsaw), planing or cutting the taper, and finally smoothing off. If you are making several, interlocking the shapes, as with handrails, saves wood. Suitably strong and wear-resistant woods are: afrormosia, ash, teak, makore, greenheart and possibly elm and beech.

Mounting is important to the strength and life of the cleat. The base should fit the deck closely (I have designed broad cleat bases to distribute capsizing loads) and large bolts should penetrate right through to beams or packing pieces. It is bad practice to countersink bolts, even plugged, for this weakens the wood and invites penetration of water. The cleat should be angled a few degrees away from the lead of the rope, which should be as nearly horizontal as possible; on no account should the rope pull the cleat upwards.

A hole may be drilled through the large cleats to retain the rope.

ii. Blocks

There is little advantage, in my view, in building your own blocks, but if you fancy a home-made wooden block, details are given in Fig. 37(b). Design has been simplified down to a pair of equal-sized wooden spacers, a pair of wooden cheeks and four metal strips cut from one strip. These are best in stainless steel, but may be mild steel provided that galvanising is done after cutting and drilling. The sheave itself, preferably with pin, is best purchased and the block dimensioned around it as indicated. I have found Tufnol a very reliable sheave material, and fairly readily obtainable.

The block should be glued with resorcinol or epoxy first, then cleaned up and riveted. The drawing shows the axle pin not penetrating the side straps, so that the block can be dismantled relatively easily for maintenance. In fact, riveting the axle pin right through is stronger, but take care not to squash the block.

Suitable woods are: afrormosia, ash, beech, oak, teak and makore. Or, if you are very lucky, lignum vitae.

iii. Duckboards and Gratings

Square gratings look very nautical, but they are not easy to make, and sometimes defeat their purpose by hindering drainage of water. I tend to plump for slat **duckboards**, a robust design of which is shown in Fig. 38(a). There is nothing difficult in the construction, but it will be found best to build the outer frame first, then add the slats between, else there is no stable shape to work to and you may end up with everything slightly askew. Bronze 'Gripfast' nails are ideal fastenings for this job, but every single one must be pre-drilled to avoid the teak splitting. I say teak, as that is really the only satisfactory wood for exposed duckboards and gratings.

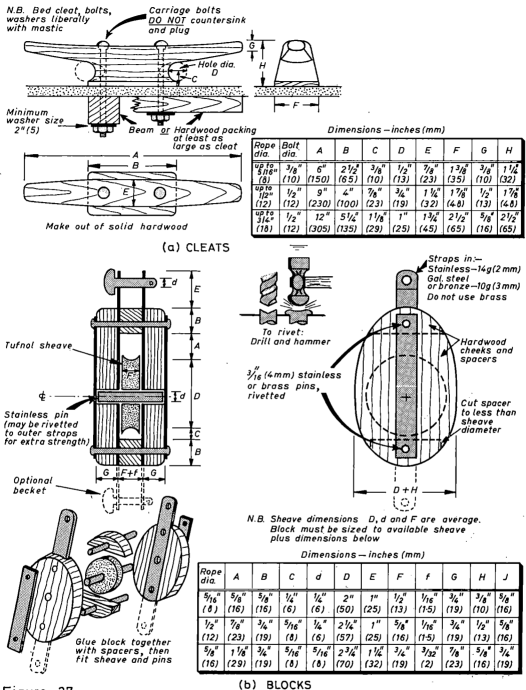

N.B. Bed cleat, bolts, washers liberally with mastic

Carriage bolts <u>DO NOT</u> countersink and plug

Hole dia. D

Minimum washer size 2"(5)

Beam _or_ Hardwood packing at least as large as cleat

Make out of solid hardwood

Dimensions — inches (mm)

Rope dia.	Bolt dia.	A	B	C	D	E	F	G	H
up to 5/16" (8)	3/8" (10)	6" (150)	2 1/2" (65)	3/8" (10)	1/2" (13)	7/8" (23)	1 3/8" (35)	3/8" (10)	1 1/4" (32)
up to 1/2" (12)	1/2" (12)	9" (230)	4" (100)	7/8" (23)	3/4" (19)	1 1/4" (32)	1 7/8" (48)	1/2" (13)	1 7/8" (48)
up to 3/4" (18)	1/2" (12)	12" (305)	5 1/4" (135)	1 1/8" (29)	1" (25)	1 3/4" (45)	2 1/2" (65)	5/8" (16)	2 1/2" (65)

(a) CLEATS

Tufnol sheave

Stainless pin (may be rivetted to outer straps for extra strength)

Optional becket

Glue block together with spacers, then fit sheave and pins

To rivet: Drill and hammer

3/16" (4mm) stainless or brass pins, rivetted

Straps in:— Stainless—14g(2 mm) Gal. steel or bronze—10g(3mm) Do not use brass

Hardwood cheeks and spacers

Cut spacer to less than sheave diameter

N.B. Sheave dimensions D, d and F are average. Block must be sized to available sheave plus dimensions below

Dimensions — inches (mm)

Rope dia.	A	B	C	d	D	E	F	f	G	H	J
5/16" (8)	5/8" (16)	5/8" (16)	1/4" (6)	1/4" (6)	2" (50)	1" (25)	1/2" (13)	1/16" (1.5)	3/4" (19)	3/8" (10)	5/8" (16)
1/2" (12)	7/8" (23)	3/4" (19)	5/16" (8)	1/4" (6)	2 1/4" (57)	1" (25)	5/8" (16)	1/16" (1.5)	3/4" (19)	1/2" (13)	5/8" (16)
5/8" (16)	1 1/8" (29)	3/4" (19)	5/16" (8)	5/16" (8)	2 3/4" (70)	1 1/4" (32)	3/4" (19)	3/32" (2)	7/8" (23)	5/8" (16)	3/4" (19)

(b) BLOCKS

Figure 37.

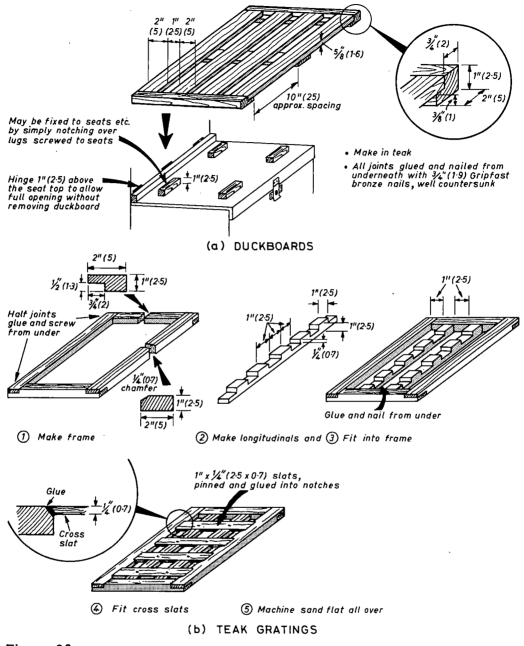

2" 1" 2"
(5) (2·5)(5)

5/8" (1·6)

10"(25)
approx. spacing

3/4" (2)

1"(2·5)

2" (5)

3/8" (1)

May be fixed to seats etc.
by simply notching over
lugs screwed to seats

Hinge 1"(2·5) above
the seat top to allow
full opening without
removing duckboard

1"(2·5)

• Make in teak
• All joints glued and nailed from
  underneath with 3/4"(1·9) Gripfast
  bronze nails, well countersunk

(a) DUCKBOARDS

2"(5)

1/2" (1·3)

1"(2·5)

3/4"(2)

Half joints
glue and screw
from under

1/4"(0·7)
chamfer

1"(2·5)

2"(5)

1"(2·5)

1"(2·5)

1"(2·5)

1/4"(0·7)

1"(2·5)

1"(2·5)

Glue and nail from under

① Make frame   ② Make longitudinals and ③ Fit into frame

Glue

1/4"(0·7)

Cross
slat

1" x 1/4"(2·5 x 0·7) slats,
pinned and glued into notches

④ Fit cross slats   ⑤ Machine sand flat all over

(b) TEAK GRATINGS

Figure 38.

Duckboards should be readily removable, especially on seats, so the latter can be cleaned and painted. A simple method of securing over lugs is illustrated. Incidentally, access for painting and cleaning (not to mention drainage) is the reason why screwing slats directly on to the seats is bad practice.

If **gratings** you must have, then Fig. 38(b) shows how. First a frame is made up of 2 × 1 in (5 × 2.5 cm) teak, one pair of sides being rebated underneath, while the other pair is slightly chamfered along the top inner edge. Longitudinals are notched, as shown, then glued and fastened into the frame 1 inch apart. Professional joiners would use slots and tenons, together with mortice and tenon frame corner joints, but this is considerably more complex. Once the longitudinals are made fast, the cross slats are cut carefully to length, and merely glued into the notches and chamfer, with perhaps brass pins in the former. It is impossible to construct the grating perfectly flat; this has to be done afterwards with a belt or orbital sander.

iv. Miscellaneous

Fig. 39(a) illustrates a stowable **cockpit table**, intended primarily for use in port. There are many variations on this theme, including a table with no legs, or stubby fixed ones, but the one illustrated at least has the advantage of few metal parts to corrode in damp cockpit lockers. Relatively few parts are involved in the design, which is self-explanatory.

Boarding ladders come in even more shapes and sizes, and if you want a simple, collapsible one, best buy a plastic ladder, or make a wooden step and rope ladder. However, when laden with groceries and boarding ship from a pitching dinghy, a solid ladder has manifold attractions, and I was particularly impressed with the sea-level boarding platform that round-the-world sailor Sven Lundin had fitted to the stern of his tiny yacht, *Bris*. Not many of us, though, are prepared to fit a permanent platform on to our boats, and the ladder illustrated in Fig. 39(b) is an alternative.

The ladder is made of hardwood sides, shaped to the profile of the hull, both for appearance and stability. The bottom step is large enough to be called a platform which attaches you, in effect, to the yacht; subsequent steps (one or two) can be tubes with through-bolts inside, held by wing nuts which can be easily removed to dismantle the steps for stowage. The toerail hooks can be wood, as shown, or alternatively in metal.

J UPHOLSTERY

In preparing this section I am indebted to Mrs. Marjorie Lloyd for supplementing my distinctly layman's knowledge of boat upholstery with professional expertise.

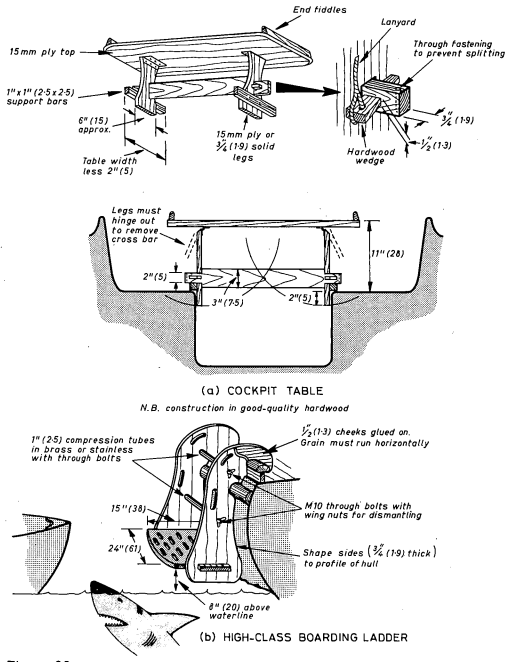

End fiddles

Lanyard

Through fastening
to prevent splitting

15mm ply top

1"x1" (2·5 x 2·5)
support bars

6" (15)
approx.

15mm ply or
¾" (1·9) solid
legs

Table width
less 2" (5)

¾" (1·9)

½" (1·3)

Hardwood
wedge

Legs must
hinge out
to remove
cross bar

11" (28)

2" (5)

3" (7·5)

2" (5)

(a) COCKPIT TABLE

N.B. construction in good-quality hardwood

1" (2·5) compression tubes
in brass or stainless
with through bolts

½" (1·3) cheeks glued on.
Grain must run horizontally

15 " (38)

24" (61)

M10 through bolts with
wing nuts for dismantling

Shape sides (¾" (1·9) thick)
to profile of hull

8" (20) above
waterline

(b) HIGH-CLASS BOARDING LADDER

Figure 39.

i. Covers

The basic technique for making nearly all covers is illustrated in Fig. 40. First the piping is made, preferably with a synthetic fibre rope core because, unlike conventional piping core, it will not rot or absorb moisture to the same extent. The panels are then cut to size, stitched together with piping to make the cover, then turned inside out and fitted over the cushion. The final seam may be either hand-stitched or embody a zip. Either way the cover will be removable.

There are a number of important points to observe. First, the measurement of the panels must be accurate, for if the cover is too tight, it will pull the cushion out of shape and wear quickly, while if it is too loose it will bag and look amateurish. A professional and neat appearance is imparted by the piping (which can be of a different colour if you want to get fancy) but that is not its only purpose; piping greatly reduces wear, and should, therefore, run around the bottom of the cushion as well as the top, if the cushion is to be reversible. Upholstery buttons (their fitting is shown in Fig. 40) also have a function other than cosmetic—they serve to hold the fabric firmly, and prevent it slipping around the foam. They make removal more difficult, of course, and it is often preferable to cover the cushion first with a cotton fabric lining. This also reduces wear.

What fabric should be used? Essentially, there are two alternatives—a vinyl material, or a washable upholstery fabric. Vinyl is practical in that it can be wiped clean and will not absorb salt, moisture, or other things which it is not nice to specify. It is, however, unpleasant to sit on, especially in warm weather, and if the cushion should become soaked it is difficult to dry. Stretch covers avoid contact with the bare vinyl, but many people who use their boat a lot prefer a hard-wearing, washable cloth. Fabrics that can be neither washed nor wiped should be totally avoided, as also should artificial velvet types through which cigarette ash burns easily.

ii. Stuffing

Stuffing is now virtually all foam plastic, which does not rot like foam rubber. Foam should be of the dense (i.e. the expensive) type if to resist bottoming, 4 inches thick for seats and 2 inches for back rests. After years of butchering foam with a carving knife, I made the happy discovery one day that a bandsaw cuts the stuff beautifully. No foam need be wasted, for it can be readily glued together with an impact glue (test a piece first to check that it doesn't dissolve).

iii. Miscellaneous

Any cushion liable to start flying about in a seaway should be fixed by some means. Velcro tacked and glued to the wood face is very handy for this purpose.

Mattresses are made in a similar way to cushions, but if they are to be used solely as mattresses, the piping can probably be omitted.

A relatively quick and easy way to make a cushion (for a joiner at any rate) is to tack the fabric onto the back of a piece of plywood, pulling it hard over the foam first.

127

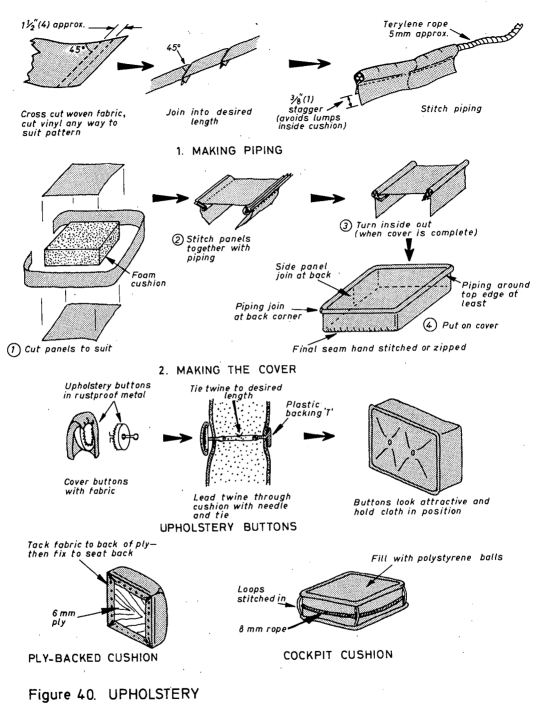

1½"(4) approx.

45°

Cross cut woven fabric,
cut vinyl any way to
suit pattern

45°

Join into desired
length

Terylene rope
5mm approx.

⅜"(1)
stagger
(avoids lumps
inside cushion)

Stitch piping

1. MAKING PIPING

② Stitch panels
together with
piping

③ Turn inside out
(when cover is complete)

Foam
cushion

Side panel
join at back

Piping join
at back corner

Piping around
top edge at
least

④ Put on cover

① Cut panels to suit

Final seam hand stitched or zipped

2. MAKING THE COVER

Upholstery buttons
in rustproof metal

Tie twine to desired
length

Plastic
backing 'T'

Cover buttons
with fabric

Lead twine through
cushion with needle
and tie

Buttons look attractive and
hold cloth in position

UPHOLSTERY BUTTONS

Tack fabric to back of ply—
then fix to seat back

Fill with polystyrene balls

6 mm
ply

Loops
stitched in

8 mm rope

PLY-BACKED CUSHION

COCKPIT CUSHION

Figure 40. UPHOLSTERY

128

This is handy for small cushions, particularly those which double as locker fronts.

Cockpit cushions are always a knotty problem, for they get repeatedly drenched. We found, some years ago, that if they were filled with polystyrene foam balls, they did not soak up water and dried quickly. They also mould themselves to your shape, and so seat you firmly in rough weather. Furthermore, they float and can be used as a rough buoyancy aid in an emergency—a cushion 15 in square and 4 in deep will have a buoyancy in the region of 20/30 lb. The design shown in Fig. 40 incorporates fabric loops, sewn into each corner, and a rope running clear around.

PART IV

Finishing

1. Shape Finishing

The finished shape of the work will, to a large extent, be part of the structure, but much is done right at the end, and it is convenient to treat this separately. The main shape finishing—as opposed to coating or covering—is fitting trim, beautifying fastenings, and certain fancy work.

A TRIM

Trim consists of mouldings and edgings fitted to corners, edges and joints. More than anything else, it adds class to a boat, particularly if professionally done in varnished wood, but its function is frequently more than cosmetic. Trim stiffens an edge, and protects corners from damage; it also protects people from sharp corners, and provides a hand grip. All plywood end grain has to be protected in some manner, and trim is the most professional way of doing it.

A variety of wood mouldings are shown in Fig. 41, none of which needs fancy moulding tools. In fact, they can be shaped relatively easily with hand tools, but the grooves and rebates are best done with a circular saw, and a routed edge will always look more professional than one done with a plane and spokeshave.

Trim is fixed by gluing and pinning with brass panel pins, countersunk with a punch. It is important when designing trim to provide as large a glue area as possible, hence the various L-shaped profiles.

A ready form of trim is wood veneer tape, backed with a hot-melt glue (see Appendix D). You literally iron it on with an iron, set to *cotton* (i.e. fairly hot), and follow up with a smoothing block, for the few moments it takes the glue to harden. Ensure that the edges are perfectly glued down, round over with sandpaper and seal the veneer with varnish. The technique finds ready application for edging plywood—table edges, locker cutouts and so on. The only problem arises inside curves, which are impossible to reach with an iron. One solution, shown in Photo 37, is to drill a short length of brass rod, about $\frac{3}{4}$ in diameter by $1\frac{1}{2}$ inches long (1.9 by 4 cm) to receive a small soldering iron; this is then used as a hot wheel inside the curves.

Iron-on tape can also be purchased in plastic, and makes a neat job of finishing the edges of plastic laminate surfaces. Alternatives are plastic or metal edge extrusions, some of which are illustrated.

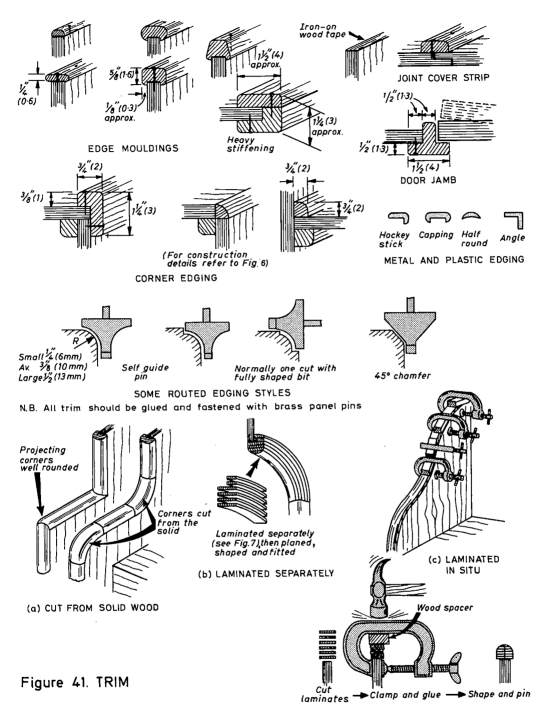

EDGE MOULDINGS

Heavy stiffening

JOINT COVER STRIP

DOOR JAMB

CORNER EDGING

(For construction details refer to Fig. 6)

Hockey stick   Capping   Half round   Angle

METAL AND PLASTIC EDGING

Small ¼″ (6mm)
Av. ⅜″ (10 mm)
Large½″ (13 mm)

Self guide pin

Normally one cut with fully shaped bit

45° chamfer

SOME ROUTED EDGING STYLES

N.B. All trim should be glued and fastened with brass panel pins

Projecting corners well rounded

Corners cut from the solid

Laminated separately (see Fig.7), then planed, shaped and fitted

(b) LAMINATED SEPARATELY

(a) CUT FROM SOLID WOOD

(c) LAMINATED IN SITU

Wood spacer

Cut laminates → Clamp and glue → Shape and pin

Figure 41. TRIM

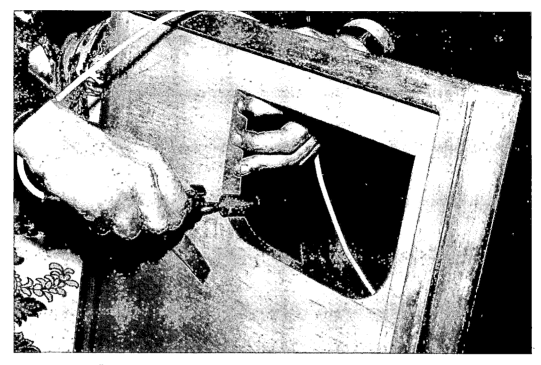

37. Ironing on hot-melt veneer tape inside curves with a brass roller
on an electric soldering iron.

The actual fitting of wooden trim to curves and corners generally takes time and a good deal of care. Essentially, there are three methods: cut the trim from the solid plank, then shape and fit each piece; take a template of the curve and laminate the trim from thin strips, normally ⅛ in (3 mm) maximum thickness; or laminate on the workpiece itself, then shape after the glue has set, removing the piece to do so. It is difficult with this last method to make a groove or rebate, so glue or drive panel pins in afterwards for safety's sake. All three methods are illustrated in Fig. 41, which is self-explanatory.

As previously mentioned, the old-fashioned technique of steam bending has not been treated because it requires a steaming chest as well as the appropriate skills. Not all woods are suitable either; ash, however, steams well and makes a nice contrast with the darker woods.

B   FASTENINGS

Heads of fastenings, if simply left standing proud, not only look ugly, but are liable to become the starting points for breakdown of paint or varnish. There are various ways of dealing with fastening heads:

i. Countersunk and Fill

If you intend to paint the work, then the best method for both screws and nails is to countersink the head slightly below the surface and fill. Screw countersinking is done with a rose bit, or Stanley bit, and nail heads are driven down with a punch; smaller screws in ply can be countersunk by punching the ply lightly before sinking the screw. Bolt heads can also be countersunk with an appropriately sized drill, but take care that the large hole does not weaken the fastening point too much.

A wide range of proprietary fillers is available, but the most satisfactory, in my experience, is a liquid epoxy glue, like Peredite, stiffened with microballoons, microspheres or cheap talc, (see Section I 7 on Adhesives). Correctly mixed, this paste will not sag in the slightest, it presses in cleanly and easily, adheres strongly to most materials, and retains a slight flexibility when set that prevents hairline cracking over the years. When set, the filler sands flush without difficulty—if a filler is too hard, the surrounding wood sands down, leaving the filler as a faint bump. The correct technique for filling is to press just the right amount of filler into the hole, with a corner of the putty knife, to fill completely and make a slight mound. Do not attempt to scrape this mound flush, for you will only make holes; sand instead, when set, with 120-grit paper. Countersunk panel pins should not be filled, if you are going to varnish or seal, since the coating will itself fill the small holes.

ii. Plugging

If you do not intend to paint, then the screwhole should be counterbored and plugged with wooden plugs. These are cut from the same wood that the original work was made from, using a plug cutter (Fig. 42) across the grain. The cutter size is specific to the size of the screw head (No. 8, No. 10, etc.), and is spun in an electric drill, which is best gripped in a drill stand to avoid the cutter gouging sideways. Plugs are cut in rows, then broken off one by one, dipped in glue and tapped lightly into the hole. Again, I have found Peredite epoxy ideal for the job, since it seals the fastening from corrosion and condensation, and is well-nigh invisible. When the glue has set, the plug is carefully chiselled or planed flush, and sanded. Properly done, with the grain running parallel to the rest of the wood, it should be visible only to the discerning eye. Or you can get fancy and make the plugs of a darker colour—never lighter.

iii. Fastenings Made Pretty

There are several reasons for not countersinking, yet wishing to improve the appearance of a bare fastening. The fastening may need to be removable, it may be too large to countersink, or the material itself may be too thin or too hard. Or you may not want to go to the bother of filling or plugging. Fig. 42 shows some of the alternatives. Plastic caps—e.g. Snapcaps from Unicap Plastics, available in several colours, or ready for painting over, make a very neat job of beautifying bolts. They come in a wide variety of sizes and different designs, so they can be used for screws as well. The

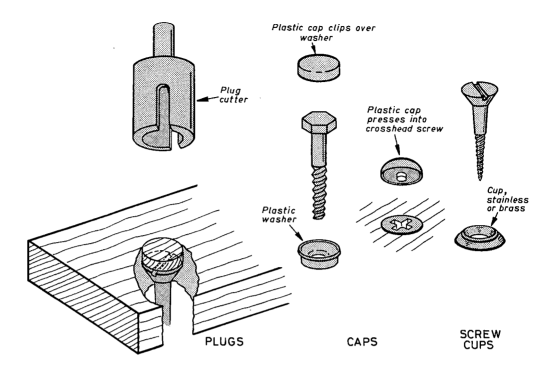

Figure 42. FASTENINGS MADE PRETTY

alternative for screws is a stainless or brass cup, which has the effect of converting a countersunk head into a flathead. The load is thus well spread, and these cup washers are particularly useful for screwing down detachable panels in galleys, electrical boxes and the like. Finally, where solid hardwood is concerned, it is not essential to use any extra device. A straight row of raised-head stainless screws, all slots in line, looks both professional and attractive. With both cup washers and straight screws, varnish should always be applied to the wood first, never over the fastening.

C FANCY WORK

Inlay and the like belong more properly to the trade of cabinet-making than to ship joinery, but for those who have the inclination, a modest degree of fancy work will add charm and individuality to your boat. It is not appropriate to go into detail in this book, but there are a few techniques that are no more difficult than joinery, yet look attractive.

Fretwork is sometimes seen on one-off yachts (Photo 38), and requires no more than careful drawing and cutting, preferably with a fretwork saw. Doors, locker

38. Door cutouts look pretty and provide ventilation.

fronts and half bulkheads are appropriate locations, and common nautical themes are anchors and square-rig profiles; other ideas are belaying pins, stars, and the bountiful variety of shapes found in the deeps and the shoals of the oceans. Fretwork also has the practical advantage of providing ventilation.

Coloured glass—or broken bottles, for that matter—set with epoxy into half bulkheads, through which light shines, can look really good if arranged in bold designs. Inlay—or just surface work using wood, seashells or turtleshell—is time consuming, but probably rewarding, as is carving. I have seen some beautifully carved bunkboards that I could not hope to emulate. Most of us would be more than content with turning shaped posts in a lathe.

2. Coating

A   COATINGS

'Not much of a handyman myself, old chap, but I'd like to lend a hand on something easy. Like painting. Just give me a brush and let me loose, ha ha!' Ha ha! I shudder every time I hear this sentiment, and I hear it all too often. Painting is a skilled business, and most of the work is done, not with a brush, but with sandpaper.

Painting comprises a surprisingly large proportion of the finished job, in terms of both cost and labour—somewhere between one tenth and one third of the total, in my estimate, depending on the size and shape of the job. The importance of coatings—and by a coating I mean any organic liquid which cures to a surface film, and also such things as preservatives—resides not only in their decorative appearance, but in their protective value. In fact, if you include gel coat, there are few boat-building materials that do not rely on some kind of paper-thin film to protect them from the aggressive marine environment, and its (normally microscopic) inhabitants. The life of the structure, whether it be of wood, steel, GRP or whatever, will often depend on the quality of the film, so it is worth putting a good deal of care and effort into the work. It follows that using poor-quality paint, though cheaper to start with, is a waste of both your hard work and your money in the long run.

Like adhesives, paints have developed into a cook-book technology of considerable complexity, but unlike adhesives, a fairly comprehensive range of products is offered by each company (or most of them, in any event) specialising in the marine field. This is fortunate, for the user can purchase the correct products from the one manufacturer who will make recommendations appropriate to the job, and, equally important, carry the can should things go wrong—indeed, the various products in a particular paint system should always hail from the one house, as the products may not be compatible with those from another source. Fortunate too for us, in that we need not delve too deeply here into the alchemy of paints, which is, in any case, carefully shrouded under brand names. We can, therefore, look at coatings under categories which are meaningful to the painter himself, namely paint systems rather than individual paints.

i. Conventional Enamel Systems

This is still the most widely used system for wood, both exposed and interior, and is generally based on air-drying alkyd paints. (The once-promising acrylics have now largely retreated in the face of various performance problems.) The system is a three-stage one of primer, undercoat, and enamel topcoat. This gives a very good finish, a reasonable all-round performance and is not difficult to repair and maintain.

(a) *Wood primer* is not only the foundation of the whole system, but more often than not, a good deal of the system itself. For wood, the primer may be grey (an aluminium/lead paint) or the so-called metallic pink (which also contains iron); my own experience indicates a slight preference for the latter, but I hasten to add that there has been no independent test, to my knowledge, proving the point one way or the other. In any event, a good primer must fulfil two functions properly—first, as an adhesive and secondly as a building paint. Some primers also have a mild anti-rot property.

With wood primer the adhesive function is achieved largely by means of penetration into the wood, and the first coat should, therefore, be thinned with 20 per cent thinners, more in cold weather. The primer should be worked into every nook and cranny, liberally applied to end grain, and you should not worry about achieving film thickness with this first coat. With oily woods, like teak, it may be necessary to sponge down first with thinners. When the first coat is dry, you will probably find a 'fur' of tiny raised fibres. Do not rub them off as they will provide a key for the next coat of primer, unthinned as its purpose is to start building the film thickness. When the second coat is dry, all the minor defects should be filled, using a epoxy filler (see Filling, p. 133) or another recommended type. Major imperfections, like screwholes, will have been dealt with before laying the first coat. When the filler is hard, the whole work should be rubbed down with 120- or 180-grit wet-and-dry paper, and another coat of primer applied. Any defects should now be difficult to see, but they can be felt by smoothing over with the fingers, and again the work should be filled, sanded and primed. This sequence should be repeated until you achieve the desired standard of finish, and at least one complete coat of primer blankets the surface. This is a very satisfactory stage, for you will have put in far more work than the tyro would ever believe possible to achieve a near-perfect surface. Wood primer is easy to apply and leaves few brush marks.

Polyurethane primer is a clear, moisture-cured polyurethane product, also sometimes called 'universal primer' because it can be used under nearly every paint system and, since it is colourless, under varnish too. This is most convenient, and there is no doubt that the primer gives excellent results. It penetrates and adheres extremely well, fills and seals effectively, and provides an immensely tough protective film. Against this, achieving a perfect surface is possibly more difficult than with conventional primer, it is a little more costly, and it needs a different kind of thinners. The biggest drawback, however, is that it must be overcoated within 24 hours, else the cure proceeds so far that nothing will adhere safely. If this happens, you will have to cut it right back with wet-and-dry paper and start again with a fresh coat of primer.

(b) Other primers. The conventional gloss-enamel system need not be restricted to wood. It performs adequately on other materials, provided the correct primer is used.

Steel primers include red-oxide base, chlorinated rubber base and moisture-cured or two-part epoxies. The essential thing with steel is that the surface must be absolutely fresh and clean, something that can be achieved completely only with shot blasting. Where this is not possible, linnish (sand smooth) and degrease thoroughly, and follow with phosphoric acid (anti-rust jelly) which provides an excellent key for any paint.

Alloy and galvanising again need thorough cleaning and degreasing, followed always by a chromatic etch primer. This, in turn, is overcoated by an oil/alkyd-based primer or by an epoxy primer, as recommended by the manufacturer.

Ferrocement primer will usually be a two-part epoxy, sometimes a chlorinated rubber. More than most primers, those for ferro will, in fact, be the main paint system and the undercoat and enamel topcoat are employed for appearance, protection of primer and ease of maintenance.

GRP primer is unlike the others in that it has a propensity to react with the polyester resin and form a chemical bond. Any wax or polish must first, of course, be removed. With the wide use nowadays of polyurethanes, highly suitable for GRP, undercoat and enamel are obsolescent, but there is no reason why the latter should not be applied over the GRP primer when convenient, e.g. in the cabin, when the employment of two-paint systems, one for wood and one for GRP, would be troublesome.

Others. Primers combining the functions of wood and metal primers (e.g. Multiprimer by International Yacht Paints Ltd.) are employed more for convenience than performance, which tends to be inferior to the single-purpose primers. Other primers are very specific in function, like primer to isolate bitumen paints which otherwise bleed through. Underwater undercoat is used sometimes as a primer, to isolate the old antifouling from the new.

(c) Undercoat is a somewhat soft, matt paint with high covering power, which adds to the system thickness and protection, but that is not its main purpose. It is designed primarily to provide opacity. Consequently, only one or two coats are normally required; just enough, in fact, to cover the primer with a perfectly even and smooth colour base. A good quality undercoat is fairly easy to lay on, does not show the brush marks, and fills any tiny scratches and imperfections on the surface. When perfectly dry it should be rubbed down lightly with dry 280/320-grit paper to remove the tiny nibs before applying the final enamel.

(d) Gloss enamel. The function of the final enamel coat in the paint *troika* is to provide a protective film over the lower coats, a film that is tough, durable and glossy enough to prevent dirt from becoming ingrained. In effect, enamel is a sort of coloured varnish and should not be expected to cover or fill where the substrate coats have failed. One coat down below and two outside will normally be found sufficient. Paints containing urethane are similar to the conventional enamels but have shorter drying times.

One question often asked is, whether good-quality household paints cannot be used instead of yacht paints. As far as I am aware, there is little reason why not; and I have often used them with good results in the cabin. Yacht paints do carry a guarantee of suitability for the job of course, but there is another difference. Most white yacht paints are paints are formulated to whiten rather than yellow in exposed conditions, but they do yellow inside, the effect being most noticeable in dark places. Conversely, most white household paints are designed to whiten inside, but sunlight has a yellowing effect. There is a case, therefore, for using yacht paints in exposed conditions and household paints in the interior.

ii. Reactive Systems

Reactive paints are those—normally two-part—where the components react to form a solid coating, polyurethanes and epoxies being the two of importance to yachts. They are very high-performance paints in terms of mechanical and chemical resistance, impermeability and adhesion. Although manufacturers may recommend primers and undercoats, these are usually variations on the basic formulation; in essence, reactive paints are a single-part system, all three functions discussed above being carried out by the one paint. Why then are they not used to the exclusion of other paint systems?

The two main reasons are that reactive paints are more difficult to use, and they are about twice as costly as conventional paints. The drawbacks are considerable. The two components must be mixed accurately, and in just the right quantity to avoid waste. Reaction begins immediately so you cannot knock off for lunch, or for a rain squall, and your brush may solidify from the roots up while painting. Special thinners are needed and these too are very costly. Ambient conditions are critical for an effective job—humidity must not be too high nor temperature too low—and if things go wrong halfway through you are in a pickle, particularly so with reactive systems, because overcoating must normally take place within 24 hours for the bond to be effective. Consequently, not only the one coat but the whole job sequence, including rubbing down between coats, must be executed to plan. So building up a quality finish is likely to be more difficult (the paints are often tough to sand, too) as are minor repairs later. Finally, hazards to health are generally more severe.

This is quite a formidable list of cons, but there are instances when a reactive paint system is preferred, and it may be that only a reactive system will do a proper job, especially in the coating of hulls.

(a) Polyurethanes are paints with exceptional resistance to exposure, high impact strength and abrasion resistance and a high gloss. Their main application is in overcoating GRP, with which they form an excellent bond. They are also used as a topcoat over epoxy, and more and more now, on wood. In fact, years ago, before polyurethane became popular, I had not one but two boats painted with the system, and found it entirely satisfactory. But, because of the difficulty of repair and relative rigidity of the film, it will pose problems if the wood tends to move.

Normally, polyurethane will be applied directly to the surface, which has been thoroughly cleaned and, if necessary, abraded. On wood the first coat can be thinned, or a clear, moisture-cured polyurethane primer applied first. Polyurethane is not, as a rule, a high-build paint, and surface imperfections will probably show through. Filling—with epoxy paste—and fairing should therefore be done *before* applying the polyurethane, and if a good film thickness is desired, it is best to use an epoxy paint underneath. This is particularly necessary if the reason for painting GRP is blistering of the gel coat. Some firms supply a polyurethane 'undercoat' with a higher solids content to give opacity if a colour change is wanted.

Polyurethane requires a different brushing technique, as the paint hardens so rapidly, once on the surface, that you cannot work it in.

(b) Epoxy paints have a great range of properties according to their formulation, but those used on boats are, like the polyurethanes, extremely tough, durable, water-proof and adhesive. Unlike polyurethanes they are high-build paints, sometimes exceptionally so, and have a matt or low-gloss finish; this finish becomes worse with time, as epoxies tend to chalk (surface only) on exposure. Many epoxies are less sensitive to damp conditions than polyurethanes, and some are designed for application to wet surfaces.

The prime use of epoxies on boats is undoubtedly on steel, where they are applied directly onto a shot-blasted surface. Properly done, two or three coats will give years of protection; the topsides should be overcoated with polyurethane or, at least, an enamel, applied before the epoxy has completely cured. Epoxy tar offers a cheaper and still highly effective protective system, but because of bleed-ing, overcoating can present a problem. Epoxy tar is, therefore, generally restricted to below the water line, to the bilges and to work boats.

Epoxies are also used on GRP boats suffering from the pox, on alloy over a self-etch primer, on ferrocement (but see p. 145) and for sheathing systems over plywood coachworks and decks. The latter application arises from the high-build, almost structural nature of the epoxy paint which, used in conjunction with fibreglass cloth (scrim), provides probably the best sheathing system of all. All fittings should first be removed, and a thinned coat of epoxy paint applied on to clean, dry wood. While the coat is still tacky, the scrim is stippled down flat and all wrinkles and air bubbles eliminated. A second coat is applied when the first has cured. When that coat is hard, all rough edges, frayed ends and the like are sanded smooth with wet-and-dry paper, and further coats applied at 24-hour intervals until the required thickness is achieved. Final overcoating with enamel, polyurethane or deck paint is advisable, and all the fittings are then bedded. It is important that there are no breaks in the sheath, which should sweep down over the edge of the deck or coach roof, and a wood trim, or the rubbing strake itself, should then be screwed down over the top. Where breaks are unavoidable at places like hatches and the junction of deck and (unsheathed) coachwork, teak trim should be carefully bedded on top to minimise the chance of delamination. Properly done, such a sheathing system should last the life of the boat.

One final point on epoxies—do not expect a top cosmetic appearance. Their high-build properties make for a lumpy finish, and they are normally so tough and abrasion-resistant that flattening down is at best hard work and at the worst a lost cause.

iii. Varnishes

It must be said at the outset that the weather-resistance of varnish is invariably inferior to an equivalent paint, and the only justification for its use is that it makes the wood look so pretty. Advances in technology have put men into space and computers into the local corner store, but so far they have not produced a varnish that will endure more than a couple of years of severe exposure. So, however carefully you do your exterior brightwork, expect it to need regular maintenance. Inside, though, varnish should last five years or more.

Like paints, varnishes are of the conventional, or two-part reactive type.

(a) Conventional varnishes can vary considerably in quality, and it is advisable to stick to a proven brand. There is a choice of appearance; a clear, high-gloss type is normally used above decks, while below the final coat in matt or a pearly type (termed 'eggshell') is attractive. Unlike paints, conventional varnish is applied as a single-product system. After sanding the wood perfectly smooth, two coats are applied, the first thinned 20 to 30 per cent, the second 10 per cent. The surface is then rubbed down with 280 wet-and-dry and an unthinned coat applied. This in turn may be lightly rubbed down with 320-grit dry only a final coat applied. For maximum protection and lustre a further two coats, making six in all, should be applied. Oily woods, like teak, are best scrubbed down first with detergent and/or solvent, and special teak varnishes containing detergent are available. But varnishing teak is tricky and, to my mind, needless.

An alternative system is to use the clear moisture-cured polyurethane primer, mentioned above, for the first coat overall and the first two coats for end grain. This seals better than thinned varnish, provides a tough substrate, and one is often able to eliminate one coat of varnish and still achieve the same result. But, you must overcoat within 24 hours. A further variation to the conventional system is to use a one-part polyurethane varnish in lieu of the conventional varnish, but this offers little advantage except, perhaps, shorter drying times.

The enemies of quality brightwork are humidity and dust. In allegedly temperate climes, like Britain, you should never varnish after 4 p.m., and shipwrights were wont to maintain that you should not varnish at all between October and March. This is pushing the point, perhaps, but it is true that quality brightwork is impossible in damp conditions.

Dust trapped in the varnish shows up very clearly, so try and varnish in windless conditions, and in clothes that do not shed dust and fibres. A completely dust-free atmosphere, however, is virtually impossible outside an air-conditioned environment, and even with the greatest care, minute spots in the final coat will be revealed to the touch. The perfectionist then resorts to rubbing down the final coat on interior work with fine brass wool and furniture wax, a technique that imparts a pearly lustre to the work.

(b) Reactive varnishes. The pros and cons of reactive paints apply also to the two-part polyurethane varnishes. But, like all varnishes exposed to the sunlight, polyurethanes are subject to penetration by ultraviolet light, and the experience of their performances by many yachting folk has not been particularly favourable. This may be, as manufacturers claim, because of incorrect application, but touching up is more difficult, and I personally would hesitate to use the more costly, two-part varnish. Down below, the system has its uses, especially on work surfaces, for it is both strongly heat-resistant and hard wearing.

Other reactive lacquers—there is quite a variety—include urea formaldehydes and melamine. Melamine is the only one used to any significant extent on boats, normally by spraying in production yachts. Durability and appearance are both good.

iv. Oils and Sealers

Natural wood, freshly sanded, is more attractive to the eye, pleasant to the touch and comforting to the nose than any paint or varnish. Unfortunately, it does not stay that way for long; depending on the wood and the conditions it is exposed to, time will turn the grain to dull grey and the wood may also start to warp, crack or fur.

The alternative to varnish is some kind of oil, wax or sealer (halfway between oil and varnish). There are many products available, but I am bound to say that I have not yet discovered one which is as resistant to exposure as a good varnish. Deks Olje, a popular Norwegian product, is available in two forms; No. 1, applied as twenty or more coats in rapid succession, is a highly thinned sealer, and No. 2 is virtually a varnish. Other examples are Benan Oil, Ronseal Sealer, furniture wax, linseed oil and Teak Oil, which is not extracted from teak at all but is basically tung oil; the latter should not be applied too thickly as it tends to remain sticky. These products will give good service down below, but will need regular renewal in exposed conditions. An exception may be those products made by Sadolin specifically for protection of building timbers exposed to high-latitude weather. The Sadolin treatment I have seen hitherto does, however, give the grain a lifeless appearance.

Because of these problems of maintaining a protective coat on exposed woodwork, teak is the indicated wood for above deck. It is resistant to cracking, warping and so on, but it does dull with time. Various costly conditioners are marketed to restore the appearance, but I have found that either wire wool or a stiff scrubbing brush with a strong detergent is perfectly satisfactory.

v. Special Applications

(a) Emulsion paint. Vinyl emulsion is not generally thought of as a marine paint, but is used quite widely. The main application is in the form of multi-colour

speckle paints, sprayed on to the interior of hulls which are rough in texture, notably GRP and ferrocement. The speckle has the effect of throwing the eye off the roughness as well as off fastenings and fittings, and the paint has proved to be both durable and hard wearing. Emulsion is also the correct paint to use over expanded polystyrene, and it has been suggested, furthermore, that it is more resistant to fungoid growth inside lockers and the like than conventional paint. But vinyl emulsion is not in any way waterproof; it will not insulate the substrate from moisture absorption, and steel fastenings will bleed rust through.

(b) Condensation is a problem best solved by techniques of proper ventilation, lining with insulation, and using a stove with a flue. But thermal paint containing cork is marketed and this can be quite effective under the deckhead and against the hull. An alternative, used in small naval ships during the war (so-called 'sweat cans') was to press a board full of granulated cork on to wet paint.

(c) Decks and bilges. Most marine paint firms sell non-slip deck paints, and these are generally chlorinated rubber-based with little or no grit content. Others contain grit, or you can add your own to conventional paint; I have also used finely sifted sawdust sprinkled on when the paint is wet, and lightly sanded before overcoating. This is kinder to the seat of the pants than sand.

Again, most firms sell bilge paints, rugged formulations—usually alkyd-based—designed for protection and durability rather than appearance. Epoxy tar or any tough paint will do just as well, and for GRP I suggest a two-pack polyurethane. In one's anxiety about protecting the outside of the hull from osmotic blistering, it is easy to forget that the bilges are wet, oily, inaccessible and not protected by gel coat; in short, they may well be the route for any water absorption that takes place in the laminate.

(d) Tanks and mechanicals. The exterior of tanks should be treated as for bilges, but with the primer appropriate to the material. Monel and stainless tanks do not need painting, but there is no harm in using belt and braces. The interior of water tanks is best lined, after priming, with several coats of an innocuous and tasteless bitumen paint, sold for the purpose. The interior of fuel tanks should on no account be painted.

Engines and other mechanical equipment are difficult to paint effectively, not least because their intricate shape precludes thorough cleaning. Copper and its alloys are inclined to shed any sort of paint. The best solution is probably to spray with any heat-resistant paint, recommended for engines, that is readily available, and keep touching up as needed.

vi. Problem Areas

(a) Overcoating and compatibility of systems. The foregoing discussion on coating has tacitly assumed that you are starting with virgin material, but frequently, of course, you will have to re-paint an ageing surface. If the old paint is basically in

143

good condition, then all you have to do is cut back to sound surface with wet-and-dry paper. I say 'only', but this is usually the major part of the whole job, and one that cannot be skimped. The surface must be truly sound or the entire repaint is a waste of time. Whether the first new coat is primer or undercoat depends on how far back you have cut. Do not lay on too many coats, though, because a paint system that is excessively thick is just as liable to peel as one that is too thin.

If the old coating is separating here and there from the surface, then it is best to have the whole lot off and start anew, as described under Preparation, below. *(b) Wood* presents a special problem as it moves with change in moisture content, a point that has received more than passing comment in this book. The result may well be the failure of the coating. The effect is especially noticeable at joints, where any movement will probably crack the coating slightly. Moisture enters, and wicks in rapidly through the end grain. When the temperature rises, the vapour cannot escape at the same rate and the vapour pressure inside the wood rises too. It is rather like a man in an overcoat, who gets soaked by rain seeping in around his collar; when the sun comes out, the poor fellow starts steaming within. With varnish, the result is coat separation followed by blackening of the wood, usually spreading out from the joints, untreated end grain and the like.

The traditional view is that wood must 'breathe', i.e. if you coated one side with an impermeable paint, the other ought to have only a light coating of, say, primer. The current view is that the wood ought to be sealed completely, certainly quite possible with the quality of modern coatings, and especially products like clear polyurethane primer. Having witnessed too many failures under the old system, I am now inclined to the modern view, but there are several *caveats*. First, the wood must have a reasonably low moisture content, no more than 15 per cent equivalent to 65 per cent relative humidity, to start with. Considering the climate enjoyed (sic) in Britain, this is not easy. Secondly, and more difficult, every square millimetre of surface must be properly coated. Take a simple grabrail, for instance. This must first be fitted, then removed and varnished all over, then bedded down for good, then the screwholes plugged and finally those varnished. The more intricate the joinery, the more complex the coating procedures have to be. With cabin furniture, where you simply cannot reach every part after completion, it is necessary to complete and assemble the work temporarily, then dismantle and paint each part separately, leaving glue lines clear, then re-assemble finally, and finish coating all the accessible surfaces. Dismantled parts of a chart table unit are shown being painted in Photo 39.

The final *caveat* is that if any part of your sealed system fails, perhaps through mechanical damage or ultraviolet degradation, you may be worse off than with a breathing system. We are back to our man with his faulty overcoat, which he now

144

39. A navigation area has been dismembered prior to final assembly, and taken
out of the boat so each piece can be painted thoroughly all over. These are a few of
the 37 separate pieces involved.

cannot get off. If the coating is impermeable to vapour, as for instance with
polyurethane varnish, then the vapour pressure at higher temperatures is apt to
blow the whole coat off. One must conclude that the sealed system is superior, but
it needs care and extra work, and must be maintained in good condition.

Another facet of wood coating is protection against rot and worm. A sealed
system will offer protection against the former, but it is only prudent to treat the
wood with preservative before coating. Use a clear-type—normally pento-
chlorophenyl base—brushed on and allowed to dry completely. The green-
coloured copper naphthenate is also effective but may bleed through the coating.

The final question is whether to stain or not to stain, and my advice is not. Stain
is absorbed preferentially by certain grain and by scratches, and the results are
nearly always disappointing.

(c) Ferrocement. There are two recommended systems for painting ferro—chlorinated rubber and epoxy. All the pros and cons presented already for conventional
versus reactive systems apply in especial measure to these two, particularly as
chlorinated rubber is a completely non-hardening system, i.e. the solvent softens
the paint, whatever its age, so that overcoating and repairs can be effected with the

greatest of ease. Also, it is compatible with TBT antifoulings. There is not a great deal to choose between the exposure resistance of the two, but the mechanical strength of chlorinated rubber is much inferior to epoxy. The choice, in short, is between playing safe (and cheap) with a low-performance system, and risking a high-performance one.

Whichever paint is used, it should be adhered to throughout, including fillers. Surface preparation should be that shown in Appendix C for adhesives. And do not be in a hurry to paint; the longer ferro cures, and the more completely the alkalis leach out, the less chance of the paint blowing off later.

(d) Safety. As with adhesives, the higher performance of modern paints and their thinners has meant greater health hazards. Reactive paints may cause dermatitis, and the thinners are likely to be aggressive to eyes, lungs and skin. All the commonsense precautions regarding ventilation, skin contact and fire hazard should be observed, as well as any specific advice given by the manufacturer.

B   TOOLS AND TECHNIQUES

i. Preparation

It is a dreary but inescapable fact that sound preparation is the *sine qua non* of good paintwork. New wood, planed smooth, presents no problem; simply sand with 120-grit paper, followed by 220 for a quality varnished finish. Large imperfections are easiest to eliminate with a belt sander, or an orbital sander, followed by hand sanding to eliminate the tiny whorls left by the latter machine. Never use a disc sander, and never sand across the grain—both leave scratches which are hard to erase. Even if the surface is relatively tough, it is not worth using anything coarser than 120-grit, for coarse paper scratches and sands no faster. Sanded wood dulls within hours, so if you are going to varnish, apply a coat of something as soon as possible. Even a preservative will do.

Preparing old paintwork usually involves much more work, and reactive systems in particular are a menace. If the old system is intact, then cutting back to a sound surface is all that is needed. But if the whole lot needs removing, then you have the choice of hand scraping or planing, power stripping, burning and scraping (not to be tackled lightly, and only with protective gear for eyes and lungs), and chemical stripping. The last is the best, I feel, but make sure that the stripper does not attack GRP, if that is the substrate. Whatever the material, always try a water-washable stripper first; it is easier to use, and there is less chance of leaving residual stripper in the surface to lift off the new paint. Power stripping with a sander, or a spring-loaded finger-type stripper on a drill is also effective, and often preferable for large areas.

Preparation of other materials has been touched on in this section on coatings and elsewhere, so only a brief summary need be given here.

GRP. If the gel coat is intact, degrease and/or rub with a recommended abrasive cleaner. If the gel coat is damaged, cut back with abrasive paper, or grit blast. Inside, merely degrease and abrade slightly.

Steel. Shot blast for preference. Otherwise, degrease, sand, wire brush, and treat with phosphoric acid (anti-rust jelly).

Aluminium/Zinc. Thoroughly degrease and clean. Corroded metal is very difficult to clean, but a final treatment with phosphoric acid helps.

Ferrocement. Scrub clean and rub with carborundum stone or coarse wet-and-dry paper. If there is any sign of alkali bleeding, acid wash as recommended in Appendix C.

Stainless steel and copper alloys take poorly to paint. Degrease and either shot blast or abrade to provide a mechanical key.

ii. Application

The quantity of paint needed depends on type and film thickness, but will usually lie between 7 and 13 m², with an average of 10 m² per litre per coat (roughly 8, 15 and 12 square yards per quart respectively). Paint can be applied in one of four ways: brush, roller, pad or spray.

(a) Brush. Professional painters have a whole ethic of brushes and brushwork, which is revealed to us simple mortals only through the harsh lessons of practical mistakes. You cannot, for instance, get away with a cheap brush. The brush should be made of long, fine bristle that does not come out; it should be fairly thick, and preferably shaped to a slight taper; painters will often trim their brushes to shape. A brush should be used for one duty and no other, i.e. a varnish brush, one for wood primer, another for white undercoat/enamel and so on. After use, brushes ought to be cleaned of the bulk of the paint and stored with a rubber band around the bristles to prevent splaying, and with the last half inch (12 mm) of bristle dipped in thinners. A glass jar makes a convenient holder, as illustrated in Photo 40; a matchstick through a hole in the handle keeps the bristles suspended, for they would otherwise be ruined by resting on the bottom of the jar.

40. A jam jar serves well as a paintbrush holder. The bristles dip into the thinners and a matchstick or wire through the handle keeps them off the bottom.

Brushes can be cleaned with a relatively small quantity of thinners, in the following manner: holding the brush upright, tip a few teaspoonfuls of thinners into the bristles, then invert and work the brush into a newspaper laid on the floor, with preferably a slight hollow; when thoroughly worked, flick the brush vigorously clear of liquid and wipe on clean newspaper. Repeat the process until no colour is visible.

Painting is best done by laying the paint in vertical strokes, spreading it horizontally, then finishing off with light vertical strokes. If laid on too thickly, runs may develop, so it is generally better to apply several thin coats rather than a few thick ones. This may not apply to high-build epoxy paints, and the brushing out technique may also have to be modified if the paint dries so quickly that it 'grabs' the bristles—polyurethanes and chlorinated rubbers are likely to do this. Getting the paint from the can to the work face frequently marks out the amateur, who probably plunges the brush in to the hilt, and wipes it off on the side of the can. The correct technique is to dip only a quarter of the bristle length (less, if painting upside down), then neatly invert the brush to prevent it dripping, and apply straight to the surface.

The size of the brush will depend on the area to be covered and the viscosity of the paint. Do not use a brush larger than can be easily worked, for it will only slow up the job. $2\frac{1}{2}$ inches (6.5 cm) is about the largest that is convenient, and other handy sizes are 2 in (5 cm), $1\frac{1}{2}$ in (4 cm), 1 in (2.5 cm) and $\frac{3}{4}$ in (2 cm).

(b) Rollers are fast, but since they soak up so much paint and are difficult to clean, they can be justified only for large jobs. And here they are well worth it. I once owned a horrible old fishing trawler, and anti-fouling this huge stranded, hog-backed whale of a boat would take my wife and me hours, if not days, crawling in the mud between tides. Until one day someone took pity on us and suggested I tie a roller to a broomstick handle. I took his advice and, running around the old tub like an unhorsed jouster, managed to paint her in an hour.

Rollers can give a fair quality finish, provided that pure mohair, of the correct length for the type of paint, is used.

(c) Pads come somewhere between brushes and rollers in speed of application and nuisance value when cleaning. But a high-quality mohair pad (expensive again) will give a superb finish, and it is surprising that pads have not been more widely used. They come in a range of sizes and the smallest one—around one inch square—will reach nearly every spot that a brush can. A different technique must be developed for pads; you are wiping the paint over the surface rather than laying it on, so a light touch is needed. The paint has to be well thinned, hence film thickness will be less and more coats may be needed. The whole job is, nevertheless, much speedier than with a brush, and for anyone seeking a high-quality finish over a large area, like the topsides, a pad is well worth consideration. It bears

repeating though, that the quality of the bristles and backing must be high, and the handle must be a proper one, firmly attached to withstand the considerable twisting strains imposed.

(d) Spray offers the ultimate in speed and quality of finish (provided you have mastered the techniques) and conversely, is by far the most troublesome to use for the odd job. Both the equipment and its choice are complex, and health hazards are high. Spraying is unlikely to be of value, therefore, except in production work, or in certain special cases. These might include painting a large hull prior to fitting out, and applying the emulsion speckle paint, mentioned above. Paint spray drifts everywhere, so everything which is not to be painted must be completely masked (Photo 41).

41. An extreme case of masking, but very necessary for spray painting. But even for brush painting, masking is necessary for a clean line between, say, paint and varnish.

iii. Techniques

Before concluding this section on coatings, it is worth mentioning the planning and techniques of a paint job. Supposing it is a new section of interior joinery, demanding a mixture of varnish and paint. It is best, as already described, to plan the whole joinery so that most of it can be dismantled for painting after construction. This not only means that every item can be coated all over, but the job can be done in conditions of good light and ventilation, with the work laid flat, which is always a help. An example of such a job has been shown in Photo 39. The sequence of operations will be, therefore: sanding; coating with preservative; varnishing; taping the varnish with masking tape, as it is impossible to achieve a really professional-looking job painting the lines by eye—Photo 41 has illustrated an extreme example of masking; painting; removing the tape and reassembling the work for good, and doing the final joinery which may be needed to complete the job; filling, sanding, varnishing, masking and painting the final assembly. Not a trivial task, you will agree, and little wonder that production yards avoid paintwork in favour of a couple of coats of sealer wiped over the ubiquitous teak veneer.

3. Veneers and Linings

A VENEERS

There are both cosmetic and protective reasons for wishing to veneer—I use the word in its widest sense, of gluing any type of covering hard on to a substrate. As most boats nowadays are of seamless construction, the hull interior itself can be veneered, if fancy seizes, and veneers need not be restricted to a chandler's supplies. A wide variety of modern materials, adequately durable is available from builders' merchants. The following is a selection.

i. Wood Veneers

Traditional veneer comes in strips up to 8 feet (2.4 m) along the grain and 1 foot (30 cm) across, and a thickness of normally less than $\frac{1}{32}$ inch (about 0.6 to 0.8 mm). As such, it affords slim protective value, and is nearly always chosen for decorative reasons. Outside factory conditions, where presses can be used, veneer must be stuck down with an impact glue, and great care is needed to ensure contact over the entire surface. Any air bubbles will certainly cause wrinkling and perhaps rupture of the veneer. Iron-on types, ready backed with a hot-melt glue, have been mentioned already as a veneer which is highly convenient to apply.

Fancy wood mouldings are not strictly veneer, but they are used as cladding for decorative purposes, with good effect, as Fig. 43 illustrates. And they have the virtue of being more robust than veneer. Cladding should be pinned and glued to bulkheads as for edge moulding.

ii. Plastic Laminate

Laminate, like Formica, is widely used in galleys and heads as a hard-wearing and easily cleaned surface. Like wood veneer, laminate must be affixed with a contact glue, and to ensure good adhesion, maximum pressure has to be applied by beating with a rubber hammer or, better still, clamping momentarily in a vice. This can often be done in bites along the edge, and with laminate it is the edge rather than the centre

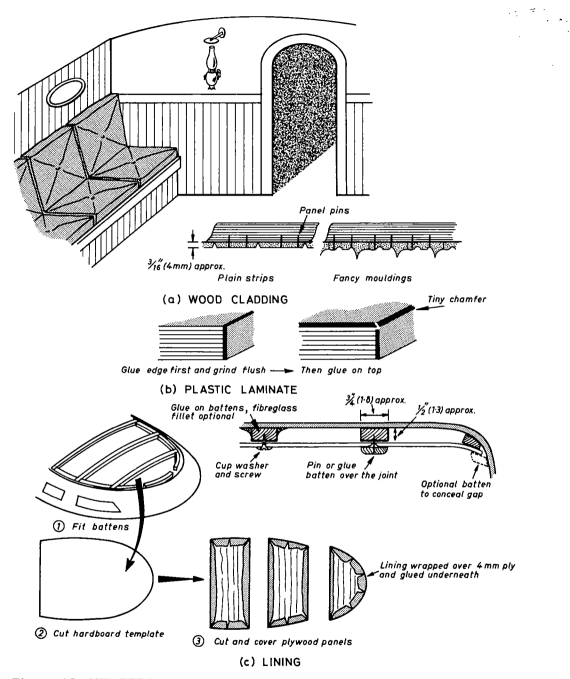

Panel pins

$\frac{3}{16}$" (4mm) approx.

Plain strips   Fancy mouldings

(a) WOOD CLADDING

Tiny chamfer

Glue edge first and grind flush → Then glue on top

(b) PLASTIC LAMINATE

Glue on battens, fibreglass fillet optional

$\frac{3}{4}$" (1·8) approx.

$\frac{1}{2}$" (1·3) approx.

Cup washer and screw

Pin or glue batten over the joint

Optional batten to conceal gap

① Fit battens

Lining wrapped over 4 mm ply and glued underneath

② Cut hardboard template

③ Cut and cover plywood panels

(c) LINING

Figure 43. VENEERS AND LAMINATES

that must be perfectly glued, as there is no varnish to seal it. Edges should always be done first, then sanded flush before gluing down the top. The vertical joint will then be protected, as shown in Fig. 43b. Plastic laminate can be readily cut, incidentally, by scoring the surface heavily with a sharp instrument, and breaking.

iii. The Cabin Sole

If cabin soles are not solid wood (which is certainly the most pleasant underfoot), then the planking is frequently simulated, usually with purpose-veneered ply. This tends to be costly, and rather slippery too. A home-made alternative is to lay on 2 in (5 cm) wide, iron-on veneer strips, leaving gaps between of about $\frac{1}{16}$ in (1.5 mm); these gaps are blackened with a felt-tip pen to simulate caulking, and they also provide some degree of grip. They furthermore serve an important function in allowing for expansion of the veneer, which is considerable across the grain. The whole surface must be well sealed afterwards. The result can be judged in Photo 42.

Cork tiles are also pleasant underfoot, but they too must be well sealed with floor varnish to prevent water absorption and consequent lifting. Even so, they are susceptible to mechanical damage. This is not the case with plastic vinyl tiles, but these, in my view, are too slippery for safety when wet and oily.

Another floor covering that is both hard-wearing and non-slip is the close pile of nylon carpet tile, of the type often used in public foyers. The trouble with these is that they become wet and dirty, and should be used only where the sole can be lifted out and taken outside for scrubbing. The best all-round sole in my experience has been wood planking, real or simulated, partly covered with judiciously placed rugs which can be readily stowed when the going gets rough.

iv. Miscellaneous

It is often desirable to cover the inside of the hull against condensation, or merely to look nice. The proper way to do this is by lining it, as discussed in the following section, but there are a couple of quickies that pass muster. **Foam-backed vinyl** lining can be glued directly on to the hull; the faintly botched appearance that generally results can be mitigated by using thick foam, say $\frac{1}{2}$ in (1.3 cm). More individual is to stick on **carpeting**, especially in the way of bunks, where a long pile is comforting to lie against. Do not stick it too well, because it will probably need replacing every few years.

Inside lockers, $\frac{1}{2}$ in (1.3 cm) thick **expanded polystyrene** is efficient in keeping condensation at bay. It is available in tiles or sheets, which can be battened down or glued against the hull and overcoated with an emulsion paint. Highly flammable of course, but then so are many of the foams and fabrics used aboard nowadays.

Ceramic tiles have been used in boats for centuries; in the galley and around the heating stove they provide a delightful touch of homely efficiency. In order to make a lasting job of fixing rigid tiles to a slightly flexible plywood panel, each tile should be affixed with epoxy adhesive over the central area, leaving the edges free. Pointing is

42. Iron-on cabin sole. These veneer strips, backed with hot-melt glue, are sycamore, the 'caulking' between— felt-tip pen.

then carried out with a flexible sealant—silicone rubber is excellent for the purpose, as it withstands high temperatures. I have seen **mirror tiles** used to expand and lighten the cabin. Effective certainly, and if you fix rose-tinted ones under the deckhead, you could, no doubt, use the boat to diversify business activities.

Finally, at the least yachty end of the spectrum, we find on board such things as **wallpaper**. Do not snigger. Our indefatigable commercial scientists, ever concerned with upgrading the consumable minutiae of daily life, have produced a vinyl wallpaper that is waterproof. It can, in fact, be peeled off when dirty, tossed into a washing machine, afterwards flattened to its original smoothness by the simple means of allowing it to dry, and stuck back on the wall—or rather bulkhead. Which returns us to the point made at the beginning of this section—namely, that a great variety of products is available nowadays from the building and do-it-yourself trade that can be applied imaginatively to yachts.

B LININGS

Linings are different from veneers only in that they are fitted over, rather than glued onto the substrate; there is normally a gap between the two, and linings are usually made as a separate and detachable unit. This means that cables can be conveniently concealed, and these should always be installed first.

The method of fitting conventional foam-backed vinyl lining is as follows: First the supports must be installed. These are wooden battens, about $\frac{3}{4}$ in wide by $\frac{1}{2}$ in deep (1.9×1.3 cm)—less if there is considerable curvature. If the boat is wood, or if you are fitting the lining between bulkheads, then these battens may be screwed, but more often than not you will be lining a hull or deckhead which should not be drilled. The only possibility then is to fix the batten with a contact glue, and follow up with a fibreglass filleting if you are concerned about the strength of the attachment. Much will depend on the way the batten is sprung into position, the area of lining and the bondability of the substrate.

The next step is to make a template. For a small area, especially a vertical one, use heavy brown paper, marking the shape by running an instrument around the edge. For larger areas, and the more difficult curved ones, a hardboard template must be fashioned, for the precision required is too high to risk cutting the lining plywood directly. Small edge gaps, which would be screened on a bulkhead by the glassing-in, say, will show only too clearly on a lining.

The 4 mm supporting plywood is then cut accurately into panels of a size and shape indicated by the fixing and accessibility. Foam-backed vinyl is glued on to the face with contact adhesive, a neater appearance generally being obtained by wrapping the material right over the edge, as was shown in Fig. 43. Before screwing the panels on, with trim battens over the joints, it is prudent to dress the back with at least one coat of preservative and one of wood primer.

While there are a number of variations on lining, the technique described above is basically the same. Thick, foam-backed vinyl interspersed with buttons gives the cabin an air of opulence, or foamless material with an embossed pattern can be used. Pine or cedar strips, like those described above for veneers, look ship-like, and no templates need be cut. To improve insulation and reduce condensation, polystyrene tiles can be attached to the deckhead first; never use mineral wool, for it is apt to shed fibre particles, a drizzle that is both distressing and dangerous.

PART V

Other Materials

As pointed out in the Introduction, fitting out nowadays is largely a matter of fitting wood to other materials. The working properties of the latter are, therefore, of interest to the yacht fitter, both for the fixing of wood and, in a broader sense, for making small items in a different material. An outline of the important properties and techniques is given in this section, except for bonding, which has already been treated in the section on Adhesives (I 7). A comparison of the more important material properties is given in Appendix E.

1. Plastics

A   GRP

Glass-Reinforced Plastic—to give it its full name—is a composite of glass fibres bonded with an unsaturated polyester resin into a rigid mass. The resulting material has a rather poor flexural strength, but compares favourably in many other ways with competitive construction materials. Recently, increasing use has been made of different reinforcing fibres, and occasionally different resins—carbon fibre and Kevlar are examples—to improve rigidity, tensile strength and impact strength, but essentially the material remains one that can be worked with the usual woodworking and metal craft tools. Drilling is carried out with normal twist bits at high speed, and cutting with a metal working saw. Shaping and smoothing are best done by grinding or sanding, though thin material can be edge-planed with a sharp plane; but most, if not all, shaping is done, of course, by moulding.

In short, GRP is not a difficult material to operate on, but there are a number of problems. First, even with sharp tools (and the glass does blunt tools), the fibres tend to tear free of the resin, and a frayed edge results. This has to be ground smooth, and one of the most unpleasant aspects of working GRP is that the detritus contains minute lengths of glass fibre which can damage the lungs, and which lodge in the pores of the skin and itch, sometimes so severely that inflammation results. Precautions must be taken, especially with a big grinding job, to keep these fibres away from the skin and the eyes, and a face mask is essential; and clothes must be washed well, for the fibres nestle in the cloth and continue to attack you long after the job is complete.

Another problem is the gel coat, which may craze or spall. To avoid this, holes

155

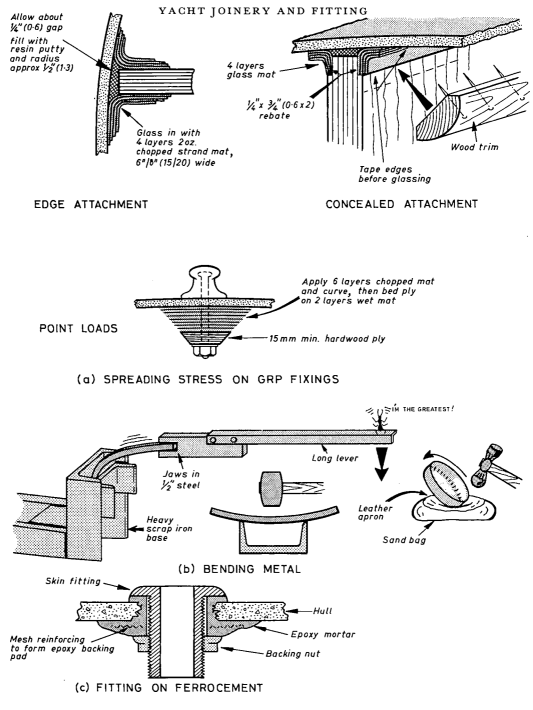

Allow about ¼" (0·6) gap

fill with resin putty and radius approx ½" (1·3)

Glass in with 4 layers 2oz. chopped strand mat, 6"/8" (15/20) wide

4 layers glass mat

¼" x ¾" (0·6 x 2) rebate

Tape edges before glassing

Wood trim

EDGE ATTACHMENT

CONCEALED ATTACHMENT

POINT LOADS

Apply 6 layers chopped mat and curve, then bed ply on 2 layers wet mat

15 mm min. hardwood ply

(a) SPREADING STRESS ON GRP FIXINGS

ĪM THE GREATEST!

Long lever

Jaws in ½" steel

Heavy scrap iron base

Leather apron

Sand bag

(b) BENDING METAL

Skin fitting

Hull

Mesh reinforcing to form epoxy backing pad

Epoxy mortar

Backing nut

(c) FITTING ON FERROCEMENT

Figure 44. WORKING OTHER MATERIALS

should be drilled from the outside, (i.e. through the gel coat first) or, if this is not possible, a pilot hole should be bored. Along a cut, the gel coat should first be scored with a sharp instrument. Cut ends must be sealed with gel coat, epoxy or sealing compound, to avoid water absorption into the laminate, particularly important with skin fittings and other openings below the water line. One advantage of GRP, when cutting skin holes, is that the latter can be accurately located by shining a light through the desired spot from inside.

Fixing wood to GRP is commonly done with a fillet, built up of chopped strand mat and finished with woven tape if appearance is critical. With lightly laid up hulls, the danger is that such an attachment will form a 'hard spot' if the contact area is too concentrated. The line of bulkheads, for instance, will be visible from outside, and it is advisable to spread the load in some manner. One technique is to position the bulkhead with a few small wedges, to allow a gap of roughly $\frac{1}{4}$ in (6 mm); fill with resin putty and radius, as shown in Fig. 44, then glass in. If the glassing in will be visible later, it is necessary to rebate the ply to receive the tape, masking the veneer itself. This technique is necessary, anyway, with teak-faced ply, as resin adheres badly to teak. The result is poor from a load-spreading view, but avoids that unsightly border of fibreglass around an oiled veneer bulkhead (Fig. 44).

GRP is particularly vulnerable to stress concentrations in the way of fastenings and heavily loaded metal contacts, a fact that was once illustrated to me in a spectacular fashion. Sitting in my office one lunch-time, munching sandwiches and gazing vacantly out of the window, I suddenly beheld a wall of water plunge over the edge of the roof of the nine-storey hotel opposite, taking the parapet wall with it. Falling in a nearly solid lump, the water totally flattened two cars parked below. Fortunately, the drivers were propping up the hotel bar, and no-one was injured. The remarkable cascade was occasioned by the shattering of a 10,000-gallon water storage tank, and investigations, in due course, elicited the root cause. The tank was constructed of GRP panels, bolted together through upturned flanges around their perimeter. Slight flexing during some four years' use resulted in stress cracks radiating from bolt holes; one of these had failed, putting the strain on its two neighbours, which in turn failed and overloaded the adjoining bolts. The ensuing chain reaction was literally shattering. This tale is not intended to be alarmist, but it does underline the need to spread metal/GRP contact stresses. On good production mouldings, including those for home completion, critical areas, like chain plates, stanchion bases, winch pads and sheet anchors will have been beefed up already, and large washers bedded on resin putty to avoid point contact is all that is necessary. In other cases, you will have to fit your own backing pads along the lines indicated in Fig. 44.

The foregoing applies generally to foam-sandwich and balsa-core construction too. Hard spots, of course, cannot occur, but allowable compression loadings are lower than for GRP, and side-thrust of fastenings is little different. Spreading stress is, therefore, important.

GRP applications. Apart from glassing-in, there are a number of applications for GRP in yacht work—hatches, bathtubs and washbasins, cockpit floors (Photo 43), drip trays, lining and sheathing are some examples. Its usefulness to the yacht fitter derives mainly from its adaptability to complex shapes, from its watertight properties and, to a lesser extent, from its translucency. It offers an attractive solution to many problems, to someone short of the skills or equipment to do the job in another material. But beware! Without the appropriate skills and gear, your simple basin will look like a nursery-school exercise. You need the right rollers, gel coat, measures, gloves, brushes, and so on, all of which are obtainable from GRP suppliers (e.g. Strand Glassfibre), together with instructions on their use. Above all, you need a good mould, and since this is usually a female mould, it is difficult to finish to perfection. The usual technique of making a male plug and then taking a mould off that is seldom worth it for a production run of one. I have had moderate success with resin putty fillets to round the inside corners of hardboard moulds, which are then lined carefully with thin polythene. But, wherever possible, I prefer

43. A cockpit sole in translucent GRP lets light into the dark corners of engine compartment and stowage area.

158

to make sheets of GRP and use them much as you would use plywood, except that the joints are glassed together instead of fastened. Good-quality GRP sheets are easily made by laying up on glass or polythene film.

Sheathing and lining wood relies on a permanent bond for long-term success, and failures are not uncommon. The answer to poor adhesion is to sponge the wood thoroughly, (clean and dry, of course) with styrene and allow to dry before glassing. As with other strong solvents, due precautions must be observed against breathing or touching excessive quantities, and against fire.

B PERSPEX AND MAKROLON

Perspex (also called Perloid, Superloid and Plexiglass) is an acrylic plastic, used on boats mainly in the form of clear, tinted or frosted sheet, for window panes, hatches and locker fronts. Common thicknesses are 6, 9, 12 and 18 mm; 6 mm is adequate for lockers and internal work, 9 mm for small windows and 12 mm for hatches and the like. Only the heaviest work requires 18 mm. Characteristics are good strength and impact resistance, good weathering properties, and good resistance to oils, though strong solvents, including petrol, attack it. The latter, and long exposure, may cause surface crazing, and Perspex scratches easily, its main disadvantage. Crazing and scratching, fortunately, can be removed with 400/600-grit wet-and-dry, followed by rubbing compound and finished off with a metal polish. A lot of elbow grease is involved in restoring the surface to its original pristine condition, but it can be done.

Like GRP, Perspex is readily worked with metalworking tools and woodworking power tools. Drilling is done with high-speed twist drills, and cutting with a hacksaw-type blade. Perspex shows a nasty tendency to chip at the edges, and the answer is to keep the tools razor sharp. The best way to cut it is with a tungsten-tipped saw or, failing that, a bandsaw. Watch also for overheating, which melts the swarf and spoils the edge. Edges are smoothed with files or sandpaper, and corners should always be rounded.

Perspex is rigid up to 85° C (185° F). Above this temperature it begins to soften, and can be formed into shapes at 150° C (302° F), best achieved by placing the sheet in an oven. This property, together with the relative ease of gluing, opens up a variety of possible constructions for the experimentally minded. A point to watch is that after heating and then cooling again for the first time only, the sheet will become smaller but marginally thicker. Like all plastics, the thermal expansion of Perspex is relatively high (about seven times that of steel) so allowance must be made when fitting the material into frames, and holes should always be well over-size—refer to Fig. 33, p. 113.

Makrolon, a polycarbonate, is similar to Perspex in that it works and forms in the same manner, has similar weathering properties, and scratches the same, but there are two important differences. First, it is so tough that the manufacturer guarantees

159

that it is unbreakable, and consequently, thickness required is half that of Perspex. Secondly, it is much more expensive. Nonetheless, it is now widely used in the manufacture of hatches and windows, the usual thickness being 6 mm.

C OTHER PLASTICS

Of the many types of plastic used on boats nowadays, only a few are likely to be of interest to the yacht fitter.

Tufnol is a composite material of fibres and resin, with appearance and properties rather like an extremely tough and stable wood. It is used for sheaves, fairleads and engineering components (for instance, on self-steering gears) and can be worked accurately with metalworking tools.

Nylon is the name of a family of plastics with common characteristics of great toughness, low friction, high abrasion-resistance and fairly high temperature resistance. It can be used for small engineering components, including screws, but has a propensity to absorb water, with subsequent swelling and distortion, and is also subject to gradual embrittlement in strong sunlight. Consequently, it must never be used for rudder pintle-bushes, or in any exposed situation where dimensional stability is important (e.g. free-running sheaves). These jobs are better done by Delrin.

Delrin (also Kematal) is a polyacetal plastic, with somewhat similar properties to nylon. But it is stable in water and is, therefore, the indicated material for such jobs as rudder bearings and bow rollers. It machines well with ordinary tools, but cannot be heat-formed without factory equipment, and cannot be glued. There is no problem, however, in bolting, tapping, or even using self-tapping screws. It is available in white and black, but due to a slight chalking in prolonged sunlight, the latter is preferable outside.

P.T.F.E. (also Teflon and Fluon) is a plastic with distinctly 'way-out' properties. It is inert to attack by practically anything you care to name, is indifferent to sunlight, impervious to water, has the greatest temperature-operating range of any plastic, and the lowest frictional coefficient of any solid. It would seem to be ideally suited to bearings (in small quantities, since P.T.F.E. is also very costly) but it is weak, gradually flowing under relatively low stresses. It must only be used in places where pressures are low and/or contact areas are large. Since it deflects under the pressure of a tool, machining needs care, and it can be cut with a knife.

2. Metals

As with plastics, the working of metals is a vast subject that could quite easily fill several books on its own. We can only touch in the briefest way on the few points that directly concern the yacht fitter; namely, drilling, cutting and grinding and, to a lesser extent, bending, welding and casting.

A DRILLING

Drilling most metals with a handyman-type drill is hard work, but perfectly straight-forward, provided that a few basic rules are observed. Always pop the centre first with a centre punch to prevent the bit skating around. Always bore a pilot hole first, because it is the centre area of the hole, where cutting speeds approach zero, that offers the greatest resistance to a large bit. The cutting pressure of a small drill is very much higher—the amount of metal removed is proportional to the square of the diameter—so use the smallest bit that will not break, and increase the size in steps; say, $\frac{1}{8}$ in, $\frac{3}{16}$ in, $\frac{3}{8}$ in and $\frac{1}{2}$ in (3, 5, 9, and 12 mm) for a $\frac{1}{2}$ in hole in steel. Whenever possible, put your drill into a drill press, which enables you to exert higher pressures and gives a better control, especially in the final stage of drilling when the rags are liable to catch the bit and wrench your wrist.

Cutting speeds tend to be too high with handyman drills, but this depends on the size of the hole and the type of metal. For a $\frac{1}{4}$ in (6 mm) High Speed Steel twist bit, appropriate speeds are: mild steel, 1500 r.p.m.; carbon and stainless steel, 750 r.p.m.; aluminium, 3500 r.p.m., (less for the harder alloys); and brass, 1000 to 2300 r.p.m. depending on hardness. Optimum speeds are inversely proportional to bit size, i.e. a $\frac{1}{2}$ in bit (12 mm) should rotate at half the above speeds.

Formal cooling with emulsified cutting oil is neither practicable nor generally necessary on the average boat-fitting job, provided that drills are kept sharp. On deep holes it helps to use some form of handy cooling—light oil or paraffin (kerosene) for steel, paraffin for aluminium, water for stainless, but nothing at all for cast iron or brass.

Some metals present particular problems. Stainless steel is exceedingly tough, and it work-hardens. That means bending increases its strength, and repeated flexing, such as might occur in some circumstances in the region of a cutting edge, renders it well-nigh impenetrable. The answer is to drill straight through with a constant high pressure, and not to stop. In this way, fresh, unworked metal is continuously exposed to the cutting edge. Drills must be very sharp, pilot holes small, and size step-ups moderate.

Aluminium is soft, and in thick sections hot metal can fuse and grab the drill. Or it can plant a little cap on the end of the bit, that blinds cutting. Cooling and frequent cleaning are the solution. Lead grabs very badly, and extreme caution is needed when drilling.

B CUTTING AND GRINDING

Hand cutting of heavier gauges is done with hacksaw, file and cold chisel. Hacksaw blades come in three broad types—*flexible*, which blunts rapidly, but seldom breaks; *all hard*, where both blade and teeth are hardened, and which breaks more easily; and *high-speed steel* for very tough work, but which is brittle. Tooth pitch is obtainable from about 14 to 32 teeth per inch. 18 or 20 is average, 24 for stainless steel and thin material, since a minimum of 3 teeth must be in contact with the material to avoid chattering. It is pointless to describe the full range of available files here, since even a nodding acquaintance with the tool will indicate what is appropriate. An example of a general-purpose file is a half-round, 10 in (25 cm) double cut, i.e. two sets of teeth crisscross the file. Single cuts are used for softer metals, and with aluminium one can even use a rasp. Aluminium can, in fact, be worked with many woodworking tools. Rubbing files with chalk prevents clogging.

Chisels are used principally for cutting out internal shapes, e.g. a rectangle whose edges are first pierced with a chain of holes. In the lighter metal gauges, the appropriate cutting tool is a pair of snips. The universal type, with the thick, half-round blades, is the best all-rounder, as it will cut both internal and external curves and is suitable for heavy work.

If you plan to do a considerable amount of work in thick material, like chain plates and stemhead fittings, then an angle grinder is a must, not only for grinding and shaping but also for cutting with the appropriate disc. A 6 in (15 cm) size is neat and handy, and adequate for the general run of small jobs. Few yacht fitters will have cause to go as far as buying an oxy-acetylene cutter, though this, of course, is the professional's tool for heavy cutting. It should never, though, be used on stainless steel, as it makes a mess and reduces the resistance to corrosion.

C   WELDING AND RIVETING

A welded joint *can* approach 100 per cent of the strength of the original material, though for most amateurs it will be much less. Nonetheless, welding is the strongest and most durable method of joining metals, and if you intend to do your own mild steel fabrication, an arc welder (the best you can afford and the largest that can be plugged into the domestic mains supply) is essential. For a newcomer, possibly the best way of learning the art and unravelling the intricacies of welding-rod types and sizes, currents, and so on, is to attend a short welding course. These are organised regularly by local Colleges of Further Education and suppliers of welding materials.

Unfortunately, arc welding is suitable in the main only for mild steel. Stainless steel and aluminium demand argon arc equipment, which is well beyond the financial scope of the average yacht fitter. Stainless can be brazed, i.e. welded with brass using a gas torch; brazing is relatively weak and there is the danger of electrolytic corrosion, but it is one way out for minor jobs, like cooker fiddles. For aluminium and aluminium/stainless jobs, the common jointing method is pop riveting. All that is required is a drill and a pop riveter, available in several sizes according to duty. One great advantage with pop riveting is that it can be done from outside, so that fixing pads to an alloy mast, for instance, presents no problem. To minimise corrosion, sealant should be used between all joints and in each rivet.

Alternatively use an epoxy adhesive which will also greatly strengthen the joint.

Conventional hammered rivets are hardly used nowadays, but they have got me out of several scrapes, and I always carry a handful of copper, aluminium and soft-iron rivets on board.

D SHAPING AND CASTING

Most shaping is best done by fabrication, i.e. by welding the appropriate shapes together, but bending the metal is sometimes called for. Mild steel, aluminium and other malleable metals are not difficult to bend cold, provided that your vice or anvil is man enough and your hammer heavy enough. The main thing is to find a base sturdy enough to grip or support the work, and a great deal can be done if you have access to heavy scrap from lorries, agricultural machinery and so on (Fig. 44, p. 156). I do not aspire to the heights reached by a man I know who constructed a 70 ft yacht using the forked trunk of a large tree as his only 'clamp', but I have shaped $\frac{3}{8} \times 5$ in (1×12 cm) chain plates to the curve of a hull without too much difficulty. The sandbag technique shown in Fig. 44 is an accepted means of dishing light gauges. Working steel red-hot greatly extends the scope of possibilities and is less difficult than might appear, but you do, of course, need a forge.

Several metals cannot be bent successfully beyond a certain point. Stainless steel work-hardens, and is apt to crack if bent too sharply. A right-angle bend is safer in stainless if welded. Many brasses also crack, but they can often be annealed to a more ductile state. The method, which also applies to copper, is to heat to red heat, allow to cool until the red disappears, then quench in water. Annealing steel that is too highly tempered is the reverse process; it is heated and allowed to cool as gradually as possible. Aluminium is rubbed with soap, heated gently until the soap turns black and then cooled in water.

Casting was once a common method of making special yacht fittings, but the cost of foundry work for one-off jobs, and the availability of mass-produced items has made it uneconomical. But if you need such things as heavy bronze rudder hangings, that cannot be bought off the shelf, then casting may be the proper solution. You make your own patterns in a stable hardwood, sanded and varnished all over, but before commencing, get details from the foundry on where the split line must be, how much the pattern must taper to allow it to be withdrawn from the mould and how much shrink to allow for; the casting will always be smaller than the pattern.

3. Ferrocement

Unlike plastics and metals, little has been published about the working of ferro-cement after it has set. It is not a co-operative material, for it cannot be cut at all. It can only be abraded. It is also a composite material, with a wide difference in the working properties of the two components, steel and cement. Nevertheless, suitable techniques enable all necessary fitting-out operations to be carried out, as discussed below.

A DRILLING

Holes are drilled in ferro with tungsten-tipped masonry bits, rotating at about the same speed as for steel (p. 161). Boring through the mortar is fairly rapid, but the steel, especially high-tensile steel, is difficult to penetrate with a masonry bit, and a steel twist-drill cannot be used, as the slightest trace of mortar powder will blunten it immediately. Some people use hammer drills, but this has no effect on steel and may endanger the whole area by setting up vibration in the reinforcing; the hammer action certainly causes the mortar to spall badly on exit. In fact, there is little difficulty in getting through ferro if, as with steel, certain basic rules are followed. First, bits should be kept razor-sharp, and for this you will need a special stone for tungsten carbide (colour code green-grit in Britain), which can be fitted to your drill in the usual way. Bits should also be of the best quality, for cheaper bits will untwist, or lose their tungsten tips on the reinforcing, and cost more in the long run. Secondly, a pilot hole should always be bored; $\frac{1}{4}$ in (6 mm) is about the right size, and one intermediate step at $\frac{3}{8}$ in (9 mm) is a good idea when drilling up to $\frac{1}{2}$ in (12 mm). If you hit a large piece of steel, reduce the pilot size to about $\frac{3}{16}$ in (5 mm) and make sure the drill is freshly sharpened. Thirdly, great pressure is needed, so you must brace yourself somehow against a solid backing. Photo 44 illustrates a rope arrangement for drilling from the outside of the hull.

The biggest problem with drilling ferro is that the bit will not bore straight. It strikes a reinforcing bar and attempts to slide around it. The result is frequently a crooked hole that has probably shifted position as well, with the result that your carefully marked fitting will not fit. Holes must always, therefore, be bored oversize (about 1 mm) to allow for displacement, and if the bolt load is a high one, back-filled with epoxy or mortar when the bolt is being placed. The other trick is to use the fitting itself as a guide, by clamping it on first. I have done this successfully by gluing steel fittings on first with epoxy, which eliminates the need to re-bed. A wooden piece, such as a plywood bulkhead or a rubbing strake, will also act as a perfectly sound drill guide if secured by a couple of bolts first.

Ferrocement has a relatively high compressive strength, so bolts should not crush it easily; but, like GRP (or wood, for that matter) loads must be spread with backing plates and large washers. Steel provides the most suitable kind of backing, in my opinion, since it moves thermally exactly like ferro; backing pads should be bedded on epoxy mortar or at least polyester resin putty to avoid point contact, and to prevent corrosion behind the steel. The fittings outside should be bedded down firmly for the same reason. Wood is less suitable for backing as it moves differently to ferro, and its compressive strength is likely to be markedly lower. It is more shock

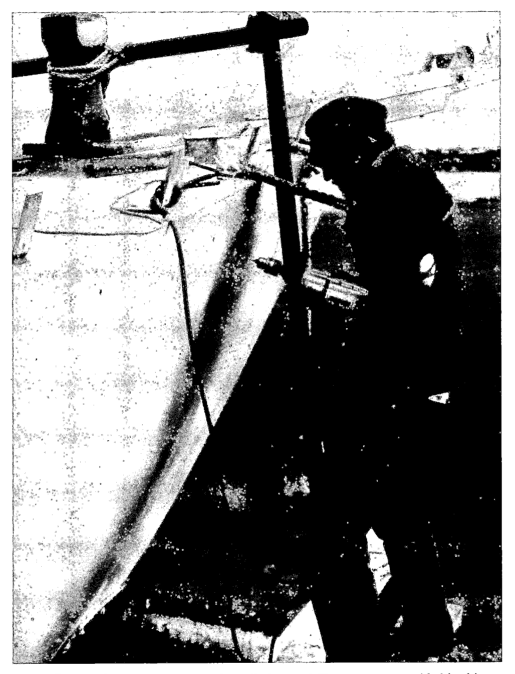

44. Drilling ferro or steel demands really heavy drill pressure—provided in this case by a rope sling. But should the rope break, the cradle will fall and down . . .

absorbent, but if the fitting demands a slightly resilient backing, then a steel pad bedded on neoprene insertion, or silicone rubber compound, is probably more reliable. Wooden components should be bedded on mastic.

B   CUTTING AND SHAPING

All major openings should be built into a ferro boat by inserting polythene-covered wooden blanks into the steel armature before plastering and knocking them out when the mortar has set.

However, ferro can be cut afterwards, though it is not easy, for as already mentioned, ferro cannot be cut in the true sense of shearing; it can only be ground or chipped away. Slicing cleanly through the material along a straight line is accomplished with a powerful 7 in or 9 in angle grinder (18 or 23 cm), fitted with a masonry cutting disc. This flings out a stream of dust and sparks, making goggles and face mask obligatory. The high-tensile steel wears the masonry disc fairly rapidly, but there is no help for it, as a steel cutter fails on the mortar.

Circles and small shapes are cut out by drilling a chain of holes around the perimeter, and cutting between them. Saws with tungsten-carbide-chip teeth are available (hand or jigsaw) and moderately effective. They are prone to lose their teeth on the steel, however, and usually have to be supplemented with a hacksaw. The alternative is to chisel through the material, effective until you hit a reinforcing rod. Never attempt to chisel through a large, high tensile rod; at best it will spall off the surrounding mortar, at worst, it will transmit vibrations, rather like a tuning fork, into the ferro, and may part the mortar-to-steel bond from which the ferro derives its whole strength. Chisel and hacksaw must, therefore, be used together. But, however carefully the work is done, the edges will be ragged and must either be ground back or built up.

Shaping ferro by grinding is seldom more than partially successful. The mortar is too hard, and even with a powerful angle grinder, the work is painfully slow. Grinding, therefore, has to be restricted to small areas, like rounding over edges and enlarging skin fitting holes. In the latter kind of work, I have found a mason's stone, spindle-mounted for fitting in a $\frac{1}{2}$ in (1.2 cm) power drill, very useful, if a trifle wild to use. The stones come in various shapes, measuring in the region of $1\frac{1}{2}$ inches diameter by 3 inches long (4 × 7.5 cm) and usually run wet, though this is too dangerous with an electric drill. One can also buy files surfaced with tungsten-carbide chips, but these are of limited use. A hand-held rubbing stone is the best tool for smoothing rough-finished plaster.

For larger shaping jobs, and certainly those that demand good quality and accurate finish, the only practicable solution is to build up rather than cut down. An epoxy resin, stiffened, if necessary, with pure cement as a filler, is suitable for small jobs. A skin fitting, for instance, is bedded as follows. First wrap the fitting in thin polythene, 'Clingfilm', and fit with backing nut, as shown in Fig. 44 (p. 156), on the epoxy filling. If the hole is particularly oversize or jagged, then it is advisable to expose some reinforcing wire for the epoxy to lock on to. When the epoxy has set, remove the fitting and backfill the small voids that inevitably will have formed under the fitting. Then, re-bed with mastic. The result is a perfect fit and one, moreover, that isolates the fitting from any electrolytic reaction with the reinforcing armature. A similar technique for achieving a perfect fit of wood on ferro has been shown in Photo 7 (p. 31).

For larger jobs, use yacht mortar, bonded on and preferably reinforced with a water-miscible epoxy, like Peredite. When mixed with water and then mortar in the proportion of between 5 per cent and 10 per cent by weight epoxy to pure cement, the final tensile strength of the mortar is increased by a factor of up to 10. Reinforcing wire will add greatly to the strength, and wherever possible the work should be locked on to the main armature. The mix is rather sticky to work but does not slump. I have had good results with many jobs, an example being the transducer fairing shown in Photo 45.

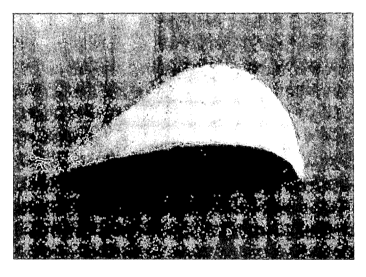

45. Ferrocement is better built up than cut down to shape. Here, a transducer fairing has been cast *in situ* from epoxy and cement mortar; internal wire reinforcing is fastened to the hull armature.

Appendix A

Wood Properties and Usage

(See Notes on pp. 174–5)

Name(s)	Appearance	Working Qualities	Cracking	Warping	Screw Holding	Durability
Abura	Brownish, fine grain, plain appearance.	Fair. Blunts tools. Very stable.	V. little	V. little	Good	Low
*Afrormosia	Light brown, fine grained, rather bland.	Good. Slight tendency to reverse grain & splitting.	V. little	V. little	Excellent	Excellent
*Agba	Pinkish brown, fine grained, bland.	Good. Planing sometimes trouble-some. Slight gum exudation.	Little	Little	Good	Good
*Ash	Straw/light brown, strongly marked, medium grain.	V. good	Little	V. little	Fair	Low
*Beech, European	Light yellow, dense tiny flecked grain.	Good. Hard but stable.	V. little	V. little	Excellent	Poor
*Cedar, Western Red	Red/brown to orange. Light markings, medium to coarse grain.	V. easy. Soft, so marks easily.	Little	V. little	Fair to poor	V. good
Cedar, Port Orford	Light brown, coarse grain, even texture.	Easy, but may split.	Some	V. little	Fair	V. good
Cedar, Yellow (Alaskan)	Bright yellowish, straight clear grain.	Easy	Little	V. little	Good	V. good
*Cedar, Central & S. American (Cigar-box cedar)	Pale pinkish brown to dark reddish brown. Open, bland grain.	V. easy. Rather soft.	Little	V. little	Fair to poor	Good
Cherry	Light red to darkish brown, attractive grain.	Easy, though wood is hard.	Some	Little	Good	Moderate
Danta	Dull reddish, fine even grain.	Fair. Some reverse grain.	Little	Some	Good	Moderate
*Douglas Fir (Oregon & Columbian Pine)	Straw with darker reddish straight markings. Coarse grain. Varies from soft to hard surface.	Easy, but prone to split at fastenings. Blackens under varnish.	Some	Little	Fair	Moderate

168

Usage	Physical Data					
	Density at 15% moisture content lb/ft³ (kg/m³)	Bending Strength	Stiffness	Shock Resistance	Crushing Strength	Moisture Movement
Generally limited. Interior joinery.	35 (560)	D	D	D	C	B
First alternative to teak. Exterior & interior joinery, decks & planking.	43 (690)	B	C	C	B	B
Planking, coamings.	32 (513)	D	E	D	C	B
Tillers, small boat frames, oars etc. Good strength but rots in unventilated space.	43 (690)	C	C	C	C	D
Joinery, but highly susceptible to rot. Use in exposed position & treat.	45 (722)	C	C	C	C	C
Joinery not exposed to heavy use. Ideal cladding in strip form.	23 (369)	D	E	E	D	A
Light planking & decking. Joinery.	31 (496)	D	E	–	D	A–B
Strongest & hardest of softwood cedars. Long lengths, hence planking.	32 (513)	C	D	–	C	A–B
A hardwood but too delicate for most work. Light joinery only & veneer.	30 avg. (480)	D	E	E	C	B
Internal joinery.	43 (690)	–	–	–	–	C
Structural & supporting pieces not exposed.	46 (738)	C	D	C	C	C
Supporting joinery. Long lengths hence planking & rubbing strakes. Spars. Beams.	33 (530)	C	C	C–D	C	C

Name(s)	Appearance	Working Qualities	Cracking	Warping	Screw Holding	Durability
*Elm, Rock	Pale brown to yellow.	Can be hard to plane. V. hard.	V. little	V. little	Excellent	Moderate to poor
Elm, Wych	As above but highly varied markings.	As for rock elm.	Some	Some	Excellent	Poor
Greenheart	Olive. Even grain.	V. difficult. May need steel-working tools.	Some	Little	Excellent	Excellent
*Guarea	Reddish brown, even texture.	Moderate	Some	Little	Good	Good
*Hemlock	Light yellow/brown. Uniform colour & texture.	Moderate to good	Little	Little	Fair	Moderate to poor
*Idigbo	Yellowish, fine markings.	Moderate	Some	V. little	Good	V. good
Imbuia (Brazilian walnut)	Rich brown/dark brown markings.	Moderate	Some	Little	Good	Good
*Iroko (Mvule)	Yellow to rich, varied brown. Darkens with age.	Moderate to difficult. Reverse grain & moves badly. May contain silica which blunts tools.	Some, worsening with age	Frequent	Excellent	Excellent
*Jarrah	Dark red, dense, well marked grain can be pretty.	Difficult. Hard and prone to split.	Some	Little	Excellent	Excellent
Karri	Red/brown, medium grain.	As for Jarrah. Both are eucalyptus.	Some	Little	Excellent	Good
*Keruing (Apitong, Gurjun Yang)	Pinkish. Coarse blend, straight grain.	Difficult. Hard & gummy.	Little	V. little	V. good	Moderate
Larch	Light brown & orange. Medium grain.	Moderate. Soapy to plane.	Some	V. little	Fair	Moderate
*Lauan (Philippine Mahogany, Meranti, Seraya)– *Yellow, Light red & Dark red	Light red, coarse flecked grain. Light & dark varieties.	Easy	V. little	Little	Good	Good

Usage	Physical Data					
	Density at 15% moisture content lb/ft³ (kg/m³)	Bending Strength	Stiffness	Shock Resistance	Crushing Strength	Moisture Movement
Bent timbers, rubbing strakes.	47 avg. (754)	C	C	A	B	C
Surface joinery. Occasionally structural work.	42 (675)	C	D	C	C	C
Extremely heavy & tough. Keels, engine beds, etc.	64 (1025)	–	–	A	A	C
Hard & stable. Sole covering, joinery.	34 (545)	C	D–E	D	C	C
Similar to ash but can be be used for spars.	30 (481)	D	D	D	C	B
Joinery & beams. V. stable. Stains yellow with water	34 (545)	–	–	–	–	A–B
Attractive joinery. Veneers.	42 (675)	–	–	–	–	–
Beams & exterior joinery, hatches, coamings, etc., all preferably laminated. Makes tough planking.	43 (690)	C	D	E	B	A–B
Heavy & tough. Keels, deadwood, etc. Suitable exterior, e.g. samson posts, but high moisture movement.	50 (800)	–	–	–	–	D
As for Jarrah	55 (880)	–	–	–	–	E
Limited use in interior, heavy structural work. Unattractive. Exudes gum.	47 avg. (754)	C	B	C	B	C–D
As for Douglas Fir but more difficult to work.	35 (560)	C	D	D	C	C
Long, clean lengths, hence planking, stringers, rubbing strakes; general joinery but poor appearance. Plywood. Dark red type is heavier, stronger & more durable.	Light red 33 (530)	D	E	E	C	C
	Dark red 43 (690)	C	D	D	C	C

Name(s)	Appearance	Working Qualities	Cracking	Warping	Screw Holding	Durability
*Mahogany, African (Khaya)	Salmon to red/brown, darkening with age. Close grain, attractive & varied.	Easy to moderate. Tendency to reverse grain.	Little. May have thunder-cracks	Some	V. good	Moderate
*Mahogany, Central & S. American	As for African, but lighter red & even blander grain.	Easy. Slight tendency to reverse grain.	Little	Little	V. good	Good
*Makore	Red. Very dense even grain.	Hard to plane & tough on tools.	V. little	V. little	Excellent	Excellent
*Oak, European	Light brown to straw. Coarse, well marked grain.	Moderate, though wood hard, may splinter.	Frequent	Some	V. good but attacks steel	Moderate to poor
Oak, American White	Similar to European though less white.	Moderate	Some	Little	As for European	Good to moderate
*Obeche (Wawa, Samba)	Lightish yellow with flecked grain.	Easy	Little	Little	Moderate to poor	Poor
Opepe	Yellow to orange/brown. Grain medium to fine & slightly speckled.	Fair, though wood is heavy & hard.	Little	Little	Excellent	Excellent
Pine, Pitch (American long-leaf yellow is similar)	Pinkish brown. Coarse grain.	Moderate. Exudes resin.	Little	V. little	Good	Moderate to good
Pine, Parana	Light brown. Attractive variations.	Easy, though may be knotty.	Some	Little	Poor	Poor
*Pine, Scots (European redwood, Red or Yellow Deal).	Pale with yellowish lines. Coarse grain.	Easy	Some	Little	V. poor	V. poor
Also *European Spruce & Whitewood, Russian & Finnish Spruce, White Deal etc. Yellow Pine (White Pine in U.S.)	Pale straw, creamy, soft uniform grain.					

Usage	Physical Data					
	Density at 15% moisture content lb/ft^3 (kg/m^3)	Bending Strength	Stiffness	Shock Resistance	Crushing Strength	Moisture Movement
Joinery. Very attractive brightwork. Plywood & veneer. Quality variable.	33 avg. (530)	D	E	E	C	B–C
General use, planking, joinery, etc. May be used exposed. Not as attractive as African.	34 (545)	D	E	E	C	B
Very tough, durable wood but bland appearance. Use as for Jarrah. Also high-grade ply.	39 (625)	C	D	D	C	C
Frames & stringers. Occas. planks. Not much used now.	45 (722)	C	D	D	C	D
Frames, stringers & planks. Superior to European oak.	40 (640)	C	D	D	C	D
Wood is soft & nondurable. Hence light usage in interior joinery.	24 (385)	D	E	E	D	B
Keels, deadwood & all heavy & stable work.	46 (737)	C	C	D	B	B–C
Planking & stringers, structural sole-bearers, etc. V. tough & shock-resistant. Bleeds resin. Long, clean lengths.	43 (690)	C	C	C	C	D
Poor boat-wood. Internal support joinery only.	34 (545)	D	E	E	C	C–D
Not recommended for boat use unless well treated against rot. Hidden joinery & sometimes decking etc. in cheap boats.	24–32 (385–515)	D	D	E	D	C

Name(s)	Appearance	Working Qualities	Cracking	Warping	Screw Holding	Durability
Ramin	Pale, fine non-descript grain.	Easy. Occasional splintering. Easily machined.	Little	Little	Good	Poor
*Sapele (Aboudikro)	Similar to African Mahogany but with blander markings; sometimes thin stripes.	Good. Slight tendency to reverse grain.	Some	Little	V. good	Moderate
Sitka Spruce	White to yellow or pinkish. Coarse grain.	Easy. Wood is v. soft.	Little	V. little	V. poor	Poor
*Sycamore	White to faint pink. Fine grain, attractive stripes.	Easy	Little	Little	Moderate	Poor
*Teak	Tan to medium brown. Close to moderate grain varying from bland to variegated.	Easy. Wood not hard & takes excellent surface with oily texture.	Virtually none	V. little	Excellent	Excellent
*Utile (Sipo)	Rich red with beautiful markings & fine grain.	Moderate. Takes good surface but occasional reverse grain.	Little	Little	Excellent	V. good

NOTES

1. *Names & properties.* Properties can vary widely around the averages given, especially when a common name covers several species.
2. *Durability.*   Excellent   25+ years
   (in harsh   V. good 20–25 years
   conditions)   Good   15–20 years
                 Moderate 10–15 years
                 Poor   5–10 years
                 V. poor under 5 years
3. I am indebted to the Forest Products Research Laboratory, Princes Risborough, for the durability and physical data.

* Asterisked woods are featured on the plate between pp. 16 and 17.

Usage	Physical Data					
	Density at 15% moisture content lb/ft³ (kg/m³)	Bending Strength	Stiffness	Shock Resistance	Crushing Strength	Moisture Movement
Limited usage in cabins. Must be treated against decay.	41 (660)	B	C	C	B	D
As for mahogany though slightly more durable. Much used in veneer & cold moulding.	39 (625)	D	D	E	B	C
High strength-to-weight ratio for spars, oars, dinghy stringers.	27 (435)	D	D	D	C	B
Decorative veneer, treated with anti-rot	38 (610)	C	D	D	C	D
All boat work but especially outside joinery. High stability & v. weather-resistant.	40 (640)	C	C	D	B	B
High quality for internal & external joinery. Takes lovely varnish finish, veneers.	41 (660)	C	D	D	B	C

	Max. p.s.i.	p.s.i.		Max. p.s.i.	% across grain from 60% to 90% humidity
A	>25,000	>2.8 × 10⁶	>65	>12,000	<1
B	17,500 – 25,000	2.2 – 2.8	50 – 65	8,000 – 12,000	1 – 1.5
C	12,500 – 17,500	1.75 – 2.2	35 – 50	5,000 – 8,000	1.5 – 2.5
D	7,500 – 12,500	1.4 – 1.25	25 – 35	3,000 – 5,000	2.5 – 3.5
E	<7,500	<1.4	<25	> 3,000	<3.5
			Max. drop in inches of 50 lb hammer.		

Appendix B

Weights of Average Hardwood Ply
@ 36 lbs/ft³ (594 kg/m³)

| Thickness | | lb (kg) | | |
mm	inch equivalent	per sq ft	per sq metre	per standard sheet 8 ft × 4 ft
4	$\frac{3}{16}$	0.49 (0.22)	5.23 (2.37)	15.5 (7)
5		0.60 (0.27)	6.52 (2.96)	19.5 (9)
6	$\frac{1}{4}$	0.73 (0.33)	7.85 (3.56)	23.5 (10.5)
9	$\frac{3}{8}$	1.10 (0.49)	11.80 (5.35)	35 (16)
12	$\frac{1}{2}$	1.46 (0.69)	15.7 (7.12)	46.5 (21)
15	$\frac{5}{8}$	1.82 (0.83)	19.6 (8.9)	58 (26.5)
18	$\frac{3}{4}$	2.19 (0.99)	23.6 (10.7)	70 (32)
22	$\frac{7}{8}$	2.68 (1.22)	28.9 (13.1)	86 (39)
25	1	3.03 (1.37)	32.6 (14.8)	97 (44)

Appendix C

Cleaning Schedules for Gluing

Adherend	Method
Wood	Freshly cut surface. If planing work-hardens surface, sand with 100-grit paper.
GRP	Clean and degrease with detergent or acetone; abrade with 180-grit paper; degrease with acetone.
Metals	1. Expose fresh surface by cutting or filing or heavy abrading; degrease by wiping with trichlorethylene or acetone till cloth is clean; abrade with 150-grit; degrease again. Glue immediately. 2. Degrease with any solvent and dry; shot blast. Glue immediately. 3. For quality bonds with aluminium and zinc. Degrease as in 1; pickle in a warm solution of about 25 per cent concentrated sulphuric acid mixed with 5 per cent by weight chromic acid (chromium trioxide) or 7.5 per cent by weight sodium bichromate for 30 minutes; flush with water and air-dry. Glue immediately.
Ferro	1. Scrub clean with a little detergent and water-flush; allow to dry. 2. If newly cured and shows signs of white alkali bleeding, treat as for 1; brush on about 10 per cent hydrochloric acid; flush with water; brush on about 5 per cent bicarbonate of soda solution; flush with water; allow to dry.
Rubber	Scrub with little detergent then water-flush and dry; degrease with meths; abrade heavily with 100-grit paper; wipe clean with meths (or methyl alcohol). N.B. For the highest-quality bonds, xylene should be used instead of meths.
Plastics	1. Degrease with little detergent and water-flush or better with trichlorethylene or acetone; abrade with 120-grit paper; degrease with trichlorethylene or acetone. 2. For polythene and polypropylene only (note 3 below): Degrease with little detergent and water-flush then dry; carefully wave in oxidising (blue) flame until surface is shiny.
Notes	(1) All treatments assume the surface is passably clean (no scale, rust flakes, barnacles etc.) to start with. (2) Acetone is the cleaning solvent used in GRP lay up. It is also nail-varnish remover. Trichlorethylene is obtainable from chemists. Alternatives are chloroform, carbon tetrachloride or methyl ethyl ketone (MEK). (3) It is not possible to bond these plastics really well, regardless of treatment.

Appendix D
Adhesives and Sealants

(See Notes overleaf)

Type	Description	Colour	Gap filling thous. in (mm)	Strength	Flexibility	Durability
Resorcinol-Formaldehyde	2-part viscous liquid. Reasonable fitting joints, firm clamping.	Dark red/brown	20 (0.5) opt. 50 (1.25) max.	A	B	A
Urea-Formaldehyde	2-part applied separately or ready mixed, close-fitting joints, high clamping.	Clear or white	10 (0.25)	B	C	B
Epoxies	2- (occas. 3-) part liquids, syrups or putties. Needs no pressure clamping. May be dermatitic.	Variable, clear to black	Unlimited but ¼in for most purposes	A	Variable B average	B average
Reactive acrylics	2-part usually applied separately. Viscous v. stringy liquid. Needs slight clamping. Strong odour.	Clear to slight yellow	20 (0.5) but can be larger if 2 parts premixed	A	A	C
Cyanacrylates	1-part, sets in seconds on contact with surface. Surfaces mate v. closely. Bonds flesh.	Clear	Usually less than 5 (0.12)	B	C	D
Anaerobics	1-part, sets in minutes, in absence of oxygen, i.e. small gaps.	Bright red, blue, or green	Usually 5 (0.12) occas. 15 (0.35)	B	C	B

178

Cleaning off	Main Applications	Commercial Examples
Water	High-strength exposed wood joints, esp. laminated work.	Aerodux 500 liquid/liquid 1:1 mix. 3 different setting-timed hardeners. Aerodux 185. As above but powder hardener. Cascaphen. Liquid/powder.
Water	Loaded wood joints immersed in water, moderately exposed.	Aerolite 306 powder (or 300 ready-mixed with water). Separately applied watery hardener. Cascamite. Powder mixed with water when ready to use. 'Beetle' cements—range of ureas of both above types.
Mainly solvents, occas. water	Wide gap joints & bonding dissimilar materials. High strength applications.	Araldite range. AU100/HU100 is general purpose. Permabond range. EO4, E15, E31 are toughened epoxies esp. suited to GRP. EO3 bonds & sets under water. Eccobond range. No 45 flexibility adjusted by varying catalyst ratio. No 32 cures at freezing point & wet surfaces. Epoxy pitch adhesive—low-cost type. Bostik 2024 is an epoxy polysulphide. Devcon range of epoxies esp. metal-filled types for engineering work. West. Thin, clear liquid for bonding & coating wood. Also fillers. Peredite 429/H1139 general-purpose glue, amber liquids, 1:1 mix. Mixed with water upgrades cement & bonds new to old mortar. Water washable. Fillers
Solvent	Rapid setting, hence quick, small jobs. Bonds well to GRP, plastics & metals. Tolerant to surface grease.	Permabond-Flexibond 241. Toughened acrylic, two parts separately. Bostik, 8/90 as above.
Solvent, soap & water on skin	Excellent for rubber strip to GRP, metal hatches etc. Rubber to rubber. Tiny repairs e.g. instruments.	Locktite. I.S. range with different viscosities & strengths. Permabond. 'C' range as above.
Solvent (but does not set in open)	Machined parts, e.g. locking nuts, fixing bearings, repair of pin-holes in welds. Pipe joints & machine gaskets.	Locktite, 'Superfast' range covers all applications. Permabond, 'A' range.

179

Type	Description	Colour	Gap filling thous. in (mm)	Strength	Flexibility	Durability
P.V.A.	1-part, water-based emulsion. Needs medium clamping.	Sets clear but white under varnish	10 (0.25) for strength, will bridge more	C	A	D
Contact	Stringy goo or paste applied to both surfaces & allowed to dry. Instant bond under pressure.	Variable, clear to black	Less than 5 (0.12) for strength	C or B	A+	C
Hot melt (or veneer)	Backed veneer ready for ironing on.	Opaque yellow	Variable	C	A	C
Butyl rubber	1-part, solvent evaporation. Never sets completely. Highly moisture impermeable.	Variable opaque	¼ in (6 mm) max.	–	–	B
Polysulphide rubber	2-part mixed. Also Also 1-part moisture-cured, lower performance. Up to 7 days curing.	Variable opaque	Unlimited. Depends on gap shape	C	–	C
Silicon rubber	1-part moisture-cured. Occas. 2-part. Cures in hours.	Clear to opaque	Unlimited	–	–	B

A   High performance structural — High — Excellent; withstands extreme exposure & water for many years.

B   Good performance structural — Moderate — Good; withstands exposure & water for several years.

C   Good performance non-structural — Brittle — Moderate; withstands limited exposure & moisture for some years.

D — Poor; either exposure or moisture resistance limited.

Cleaning off	Main Applications	Commercial Examples
Water	Very easy & cheap to use. Non-loaded interior & protected joinery.	Evo-stik Resin W. Freeze/thaw stable in storage. Bostik 8

Solvent	Plastic laminates, fabric & foams in cabin. Temporary sail repair, repair inflatables.	Evode Impact, general-purpose time bond, non-stringing & allows positioning before bonding.
		Bostik 1—general-purpose nitrile type.
		    2762—2-part high-performance nitrile for sails, metals, rubber.
		      3—general-purpose for wood, formica & rubber inflatables.
		    2402—2-part high-performance for rubber inflatables.

	Iron-on wood & plastic veneer trim.	Wood edge—variety of timbers up to 4 in wide. Melaroll—plastic edging up to $\frac{3}{4}$ in wide.
Solvent or rubbing	General-purpose bedding for hatches, port-holes, skin fittings etc. Also fixing fabrics in place in cabin.	Farocaulk Flo-caulk Easiseal BR
Solvent	General high-performance bedding, sealing, caulking.	Farocure Life-caulk Rubbokol
Solvent	*In situ* gaskets for portholes etc. Encapsulating electrical connections.	Farocure silicone Marine silicone rubber

Appendix E

Comparison of Material Properties

(values given are mid-range figures)

Material	Specific Gravity	Tensile Strength p.s.i. (kN/m²)	Compressive Strength p.s.i. (kN/m²)	Modulus of Elasticity p.s.i. (kN/m²)	Coefficient of Thermal Expansion °F (°C)	Melting Point °F (°C)
		$\times 10^3$	$\times 10^3$	$\times 10^6$	$\times 10^{-6}$	
Plastics						
GRP						
Chopped mat 25–30% glass	1.45	13 (90)	18 (124)	1.1 (7.6)	12 to 40 (22 to 72)	400 to 500 (200 to 260)
Woven Roving 40 to 50% glass	1.75	30 (207)	20 (138)	2.1 (15.2)	ditto	heat distortion
Perspex	1.19	9 (62)	16 (110)	0.42 (2.9)	39 (70)	212 (100) softening
Nylon 66	1.14	9 (62)	12 (83)	0.33 (2.3)	56 (100)	510 (265)
Delrin	1.43	10 (69)	18 (124)	0.43 (3.0)	45 (81)	340 (175) softening
P.T.F.E.	2.2	4 (27.6)	1.2 (8.3)	0.07 (0.48)	56 (100)	625 (330) breakdown
Metals						
Mild Steel	7.86	65 (448)	65 (448)	30 (207)	6.7 (12.1)	2760 (1515)
Stainless Steel Type 316	8.02	90 to 150 (620 to 1035)		28 (193)	8.9 (16)	2500 (1370)
Aluminium Sheet	2.68	42 (290)	32 (220)	10 (69)	13.2 (23.8)	1150 (620)
Copper (Annealed)	8.91	32 (220)		17 (117)	9.3 (16.7)	1980 (1080)

Material	Specific Gravity	Tensile Strength p.s.i. (kN/m²)	Compressive Strength p.s.i. (kN/m²)	Modulus of Elasticity p.s.i. (kN/m²)	Coefficient of Thermal Expansion °F (°C)	Melting Point °F (°C)
		$\times 10^3$	$\times 10^3$	$\times 10^6$	$\times 10^{-6}$	
Silicon Bronze	8.53	95 (656)		13 (90)	9.5 (17.1)	1865 (1020)
Phosphor Bronze 10% tin	8.77	122 (842)		16 (110)	10.2 (18.4)	1830 (1000)
Brass 65/35 (Annealed)	8.47	48 (331)		15 (104)	10.5 (18.9)	1710 (930)
Manganese 'Bronze'	8.36	80 (552)		15 (104)	11.2 (20.2)	1645 (730)
Lead	11.35	2.5 (17)		2 (13.8)	16.4 (29.5)	621 (327)
Wood—3 examples; see Appendix A for detailed data. Western Red Cedar	.37	9 (62)	1.9 (13)	0.8 (5.5)	Movement with moisture content	
American Mahogany	.54	12 (83)	6.7 (46)	1.5 (10.4)		
Teak	.64	20 (138)	8 (55)	1.8 (12.4)		
Ferrocement Square welded mesh & high-tensile armature	2.69	1.6 (11) till first crack	10 (6.9)	1.9 (13)	6.7 (12.1)	

Appendix F

Wire and Metal Gauges

(In inches except for Column Two. Odd gauges have been omitted for brevity. Also very thick and very thin gauges.)

Gauge No.	Metric Wire Gauge mm	Imperial Wire S.W.G.	Standard Birmingham B.G. (for sheet)	U.S. Standard (for sheet)	Birmingham B.W.G.	U.S. Steel Wire	American A.W.G.
0		.324	.396	.312	.340	.307	.325
2	0.2	.276	.315	.266	.284	.263	.258
4	0.4	.232	.250	.234	.238	.225	.204
6	0.6	.192	.198	.203	.203	.192	.162
8	0.8	.160	.157	.172	.165	.162	.128
10	1.0	.128	.125	.141	.134	.135	.102
12	1.2	.104	.099	.109	.109	.106	.081
14	1.4	.080	.0785	.078	.083	.080	.064
16	1.6	.064	.0625	.062	.065	.0625	.051
18	1.8	.048	.0495	.050	.049	.0475	.040
20	2.0	.036	.0392	.0375	.035	.035	.032
22	2.2	.028	.0313	.0312	.028	.0286	.0253
24	2.4	.022	.0248	.0250	.022	.0230	.0201
26	2.6	.018	.0196	.0188	.018	.0181	.0159
28	2.8	.0148	.0156	.0156	.014	.0162	.0126

Appendix G

Metric Conversion Factors

To Convert	To	Multiply by
Inches	Centimetres	2.54
Centimetres	Inches	0.394
Feet	Centimetres	30.5
Centimetres	Feet	0.0328
Feet^2	Metres^2	0.0929
Metres^2	Feet^2	10.76
Feet^3	Metres^3 (1000 litres)	0.028
Metres^3	Feet^3	35.32
Imperial Gallons	Litres	4.55
Litres	Imperial Gallons	0.220
Imperial Gallons	U.S. Gallons	1.20
Pounds	Kilograms	0.454
Kilograms	Pounds	2.2
Pounds/foot^3	Kilos/metre^3	*16.02
Kilos/metre^3	Pounds/foot^3	0.0624
Newtons	Kilos weight	0.102
Newtons	Pounds weight	0.225
Pounds/in^2	Kilonewtons/metre^2	6.895
Kilonewtons/metre^2	Pounds/in^2	0.145

$$*\text{Specific gravity} = \frac{Kg/m^3}{1000}$$

INDEX

Acrylic glues, 57
  paints, 136
  plastic, *see* Perspex
Adhesives (*see also* Glues), 49–58, Appx. C, D
  selection table, 50
Admiralty chart dimensions, 108
  pilot dimensions, 91
African mahogany, 15, 16
African 'teak', 15
Afrormosia, 15
Air/water separation, 112, 113
Aluminium, 161–3
  painting, 147
  primer, 137
American mahogany, 15, 16
Anaerobic glues, 57
'Anchorfast' nails, 62
Angle gauge, 31, 32, 39
Annealing metals, 163
Appearance, Design-rules for, 76, 77
Ash, 17

Backing pads, 122, 123, 156, 157, 164
Bedding compounds, *see* Sealants
  on rough surfaces, 31
Beech, 16
Bench hook, 47, 48
Bending metals, 156, 163
Bilge paint, 143
Bits, 39
  high speed, 161
  router, 45, 131
Blocks, 122, 123
Boarding ladder, 125, 126
Body proportions, 65
Bolts, 61, 62
Books, dimensions, 91
  stowage, 91, 92
Boots, stowage, 98
Box joints, 25, 26, 97
BR classification, 52
Brass, 63, 161–3
Bronze, 63, 163
Bulkheads, 25, 26, 30, 33, 34, 78, 79, 157

Bunk bases, 89, 90
  designs, 85–90
  double, 86–7
  ergonomic design, 66, 67
  lee boards, 85, 89, 90
  quarter, 86
  slope, 86

Caps, for fastenings, 133, 134
Carbon fibre, 155
Carpets, 152
Casting metals, 163
Cedar, 14
Ceramic tiles, 152, 153
Chart dimensions, 108–9
  tables, 108, 110
Chisels, 43
Chlorinated rubber paint, 145, 146
Cladding, 150, 151
Clamps, 45
Cleaning adherends, Appx. C
Cleats, 122, 123
Clothes, dimensions of, 98, 100
Cockpit cushions, 129
  design, 79, 80
  ergonomic design, 68
  floor, 80, 158
  table, 125, 126
Condensation, drainage, 79, 80
  insulation, 143, 152, 154
Companionway design, 111, 112
  ergonomic design, 72, 73
  seats, 111, 112
Conversion factors, Appx. G
Cook, supports for, 107, 108
Cork tiles, 152
Covers, 127–9
Cramps, 45
Crawlways, 72
Crockery dimensions, 106
  stowage, 105–7
Curves, fitting to, 31–5
Cushions, 127–9
Cutlery stowage, 107

Cutting ferro, 166
  metals, 161, 162
  plastics, 155, 159, 160
Cyanacrylates, 57

Deal, *see* Pines
Deck, fitting to, 29–31
  paint, 143
Delrin, 160
Design layout, 78–80
  thinking, 75–77
Dimensions, 7
Door cutouts, 135
  jamb, 131
  locker, 93–6
Doorways, 69
Dorade boxes, 115–17
Douglas fir, 13
Drainage, 79, 80
  cockpit seats, 124–5
Drawers, 96–9, 103
Drawings, 75
Drilling ferro, 164
  metals, 161
  plastics, 155, 157, 159, 160
Drills, 39
Drip prevention, 112–14
Drying wood, 18
Dunnage, 18
Durability of glues, 52
  of woods, Appx. A

Edging, 130–2
Elm, 16
Emulsion paint, 142
Enamel paints, 136–9
Engine paint, 143
Epoxy adhesives, 55–7, 133
  paints, 140, 141, 145, 146
Ergonomic design, 66–74
'Everdur', 63
Expansion of ferro, 31
  gaps, 111, 112
  of plastic, 159
  thermal values, Appx. E
  of wood, 10–12
  of wood with other materials, 29–31
Exterior grade ply, 18

Fabrics, 127
Fastenings, 59–64
  beautifying, 132–4

materials, 63, 64
Ferrocement, 163–7
  painting, 145, 146, 147
Fibreglass, *see* GRP
Fiddles, chart tables, 109
  design, 90–2
  stove, 105
Files, 46, 162
Fillers, 56, 133
Finger, fingerholes, 73, 74
  catches, 94, 95
  lifts, 111
Fir, 13
Floors, 78, 79, 152
Floor hatch gaps, 111, 112
Fluon, 160
Foam, polystyrene, 152
  sandwich, 157, 158
  stuffing, 89, 127, 128
Formica, 150–2
Fretwork, 134, 135

Galley layout, 104, 105
  sinks, 105
  stowage, 105–8
Galvanised steel fastenings, 63, 64
  painting, 137
Gauge equivalents, Appx. F
Gel coat, 155, 157
Glass, 115
Glues, 49–58, Appx. D
  acrylic, 57
  anaerobic, 57
  cleaning schedule, Appx. C
  cyanacrylate, 57
  durability, 52
  epoxy, 55
  gap-filling, 51
  hot melt, 58
  resorcinol, 54
  safety, 53, 54
  setting action, 50, 51
  solvent base, 57
  solvents, 58
  strength, 51, 52
  urea, 55
  water base, 57
  workability, 52, 53
Grabrail design, 110, 111
  varnishing, 144
Gratings, teak, 125, 126
'Gripfast' nails, 62

GRP, 155–9
  fatigue, 157
  fitting to, 29–31, 156, 157
  painting, 138, 139, 140, 142, 146

Hacksaw blades, 161
Half-cut joints, 20, 21
Hammers, 45
Hammock stowage, 98, 100
Handgrips, 110, 111
Hand proportions, 73, 74
Hanging lockers, 98, 100
Hardwoods, 14–17
Hatches, 112–21
  ergonomic design, 72, 73
Headroom, 69
Hinge bin, 97, 99
Honing, 48, 49
Hot melts, 58
Housepaints, 138, 139
Human body proportions, 65

Inlay, 135
INT classification, 52
Instrument rack, 109
Insulation, 143, 152, 154
Iroko, 10, 15
Iron-on trim, 58, 130–2
  veneer, 150, 153

Joining wood to other materials, 29–31
Joints in wood, 19–26

Kematal, 160
Keruing, 17
Kevlar, 155
Khaya, 15, 16

Laminating, 26–9, 131
  glues for, 29
Lanoline, anhydrous, 64
Larch, 14
Lauan, 16
Layout, galley, 104, 105
  general, 78–80
Lead, wandering, 46
Leeboards, leecloths, 85, 88, 89, 90
Linings, 151, 154
Lockers, design, 92–6
  reaching depth, 71
Lumber, *see* Wood

Mahogany, 15, 16
Makrolon, 117, 159

Marine ply, 18
Material properties, Appx. E
Mattresses, 89, 127
Measuring tools, 39
Melamine varnish, 142
Meranti, 16
Metallic pink primer, 136, 137
Metals, 156, 160–3
Metric conversion factors, Appx. G
  bolts, 61, 62
  dimensions, 7
Mitre joints, 20, 21
Moisture content, wood, 10–12
Monel, 63
Mouldings, 130–2, 150, 151
Movement of wood, 10–12
MR classification, 52
Mugs, dimensions, 106
  stowage, 105–7
Multiple angles, 31, 32

Nails, 62, 63
Neoprene, 113, 114
Net stowage, 98–100
Nylon, 160
  carpet tiles, 152

Oak, 16
Oils, sealers, 142
Oilstone, 48, 49
Osmosis, 140, 143

Paint, 135–41
  brushes, 147, 148
  coverage, 147
  pads, 148, 149
Painting, preparation, 146, 147
  tools and techniques, 146–50
Perloid, 159
Perspex, 113, 115, 117, 121, 159
Piano hinge, 94
Pines, Oregon and Columbian, 13
  pitch, 14
  strip lining, 154
  various, 14
Pipe cot, 87, 88
Planes, planing, 42–5
Plastics, 155–60, Appx. E
  laminate, 150–2
Plexiglass, 159
Plug cutters, 39
Plugging, 133, 134

Plywood, 18, 19
    thicknesses and weight, 19, Appx. B
Polyacetal, 160
Polycarbonate, *see* Makrolon
Polysulphide rubber, 59
Polyurethane paints, 139, 140
    primer, 137
    varnish, 142
Power tools, 35–7, 39, 41–4, 46, 146
Preservative, 12, 13, 145
Primer, priming, 136–8
Properties of materials, Appx. E
P.T.F.E., 160

Ramin, 17
Reactive glues, 54–7
    paints, 139–41
Resorcinol glue, 54
Riveting, 162, 163
Roller painting, 148
Root berths, 87, 88
Rot, wet and dry, 12, 13, 145
Router, 44, 45
    edges, 131
Rubber, chlorinated, 145, 146
    seals, 113, 114

Safety, glues, 53, 54
    GRP, 155
    line heights, 70
    paints, 139, 146
    power tools, 42, 46
Salt, 12
Sanders, 37, 38, 46, 49
Sandpaper, sanding, 37, 137–41, 146, Appx. C
Sapele, 16
Sapwood, 12
Saucepans, 104–6
Saws, 39–42, 161, 162
Saw guides, 47
Scarfs, 22–4
Screws, capping and concealing, 132–4
    machine, 59–61
    self-tapping, 61
    wood, sizes, 60
Screwdrivers, 37, 40, 45
Sealants, 58, 59, Appx. D
    butyl, 58
    polysulphide, 59
    silicone, 59
Sealers, oils, 142
Sealing wood, 12, 144, 145

Seals, 113–15
Seasoning, 12, 18
Seats, companionway, 111, 112
    design, 81, 82
    ergonomic design, 67, 68
Separation, air/water, 112, 113
Seraya, 16
Shakes, 18
Shapes, irregular, 31–5
Sharpening tools, 48, 49
Sheathing wood, with epoxy, 140
    with GRP, 159
Shelves, design, 90, 92
    reaching height, 71
Shockcord, 91, 92
Silicone rubber, 59, 114, 115, 153
Sinks, 105
Skin fittings in ferro, 156, 166, 167
Skylights, 117
Sliding bevel, 31, 32, 39
    doors, 95, 96
    hatches, 119, 120
Softwoods, 13, 14
Soles, 78, 79, 152
Solvent-base glues, 57
Solvents, 58, Appx. C
Spice rack, 108
Spiling, 32, 33
Spray painting, 149
Spruce, 14
Stainless steel, 63, 161, 162
Stanley bits, 39, 59, 60
Steaming, 26, 132
Steel, 29–31, 161–3
    painting, 140, 147
    primer, 137
Steps, *see* Companionway
Storage of wood, 18
Stove, galley, 104, 105
Stowage, boots, 99, 100
    cook, 107, 108
    galleyware, 105–8
    lamp, 101
    nets, 99, 100
    software, 99, 100
    tools, 100–3
Strength, glues, 51, 52
    materials, Appx. E
    wood, 9, 10, Appx. A and E

Tables, 81–4
    ergonomic design, 67, 68

Tanks, 78
　painting, 143
Tape measure, 39
Teak, 14
　treatment, 142
Teflon, 160
Teredo, 15
Thundercrack, 18
Tick stick technique, 33, 34
Tiles, 152, 153
Tillers, ergonomic design, 68
　laminating, 27
Timber, see Wood
Tools, 35–49
　husbandry, 48, 49
　stowage, 101–3
　table of, 36–7
Trash bucket, 107, 108
Trim, 130–2
Tufnol, 160
　sheaves, 122, 123
Tungsten carbide tips, drills, 164
　saws, 42,166

Undercoat, 138
Upholstery, 125–9
Ureas, 55
Utensils rack, 107
Utile, 16

Vacuum cleaner, 46, 47
Varnish, 141, 142
Veneers, 150–4
Ventilators, 115–17
Ventilation, 112–17
Vinyl fabric, 127
　lining, 152, 154
　paint, 142, 143

Wallpaper, 153, 154
Washboards, 120, 121
Warping, 10, 11
Wastage of wood, 17
Waterproofing, 112–15
WBP, ply, 18
　classification, 52
Weatherproof ply, 18, 52
Welding, 162
Wet-and-dry paper, see Sandpaper
Wheel, ship's, ergonomic design, 68
Whitewood, 14
Windows, 113, 115
Wire gauges, Appx. F
Wood, bulk, 17
　buying, 17, 18
　coating, 144, 145
　colour plates, 16–17
　composition, 9
　hardwoods, 14–17
　joinery types, 13–17
　joining to other materials, 29–31
　jointing, 19–26
　moisture and movement, 10–12
　preservative, 145
　primer, 136, 137
　properties, Appx. A
　softwoods, 13, 14
　staining, 145
　standard sizes, 17
　strength, 9, 10, Appx. A
　veneer, 150, 151
　wastage, 17

Yacht paints, 138, 139

Zinc plating, 64